Thinking through Sociality

THINKING THROUGH SOCIALITY
An Anthropological Interrogation of Key Concepts

Edited by

Vered Amit

berghahn
NEW YORK · OXFORD
www.berghahnbooks.com

Published in 2015 by

Berghahn Books

www.berghahnbooks.com

© 2015 Vered Amit

Library of Congress Cataloging-in-Publication Data
Amit, Vered, 1955-
 Thinking through sociality : an anthropological interrogation of key concepts /
edited by Vered Amit.
   pages cm
 Includes bibliographical references.
 ISBN 978-1-78238-585-1 (hardback) – ISBN 978-1-78238-586-8 (ebook)
 1. Ethnology. 2. Social interaction. 3. Anthropology. I. Title.
 GN325.A44 2015
 302–dc23

                                                              2014033522

British Library Cataloguing in Publication Data
A catalogue record for this book is available from the British Library

ISBN 978-1-78238-585-1 (hardback)
ISBN 978-1-78238-586-8 (ebook)

Contents

Acknowledgements

This book is the product of numerous conversations and exchanges between the contributors, which took place over a number of years. I would like to thank all of the contributors for their unwavering commitment to this ongoing dialogue and to the fulfilment of this volume. Over the course of our exchanges over the years, we also benefited from the participation and contributions of a number of other scholars. I would therefore like to thank Philip Moore, Steffan Igor Ayora Diaz, Noel Dyck, Christine Jourdan and Sarah Pink for their insights and encouragement. The development of this book was also greatly enabled by two opportunities to come together as a group in extended face-to-face meetings, the first taking place in October 2009 at the University at Buffalo, the second taking place in October 2011 at Concordia University (Montreal). I would therefore like to acknowledge the support of the Baldy Center for Law and Social Policy in the University at Buffalo Law School, which sponsored our 2009 meeting and to thank Deborah Reed-Danahay for organizing this event. I would also like to thank the Social Sciences and Humanities Research Council of Canada for providing a grant, which enabled us to meet again in 2011. Finally but by no means least, I would like to thank the Concordia Department of Sociology & Anthropology for providing us with a venue for the 2011 meeting.

Vered Amit

Introduction

Thinking through Sociality
The Importance of Mid-level Concepts

Vered Amit with Sally Anderson, Virginia Caputo, John Postill, Deborah Reed-Danahay and Gabriela Vargas-Cetina

PART 1: THE MANDATE OF THE VOLUME
Vered Amit

Moving Away from Meta Concepts

The history of scholarly efforts to conceptualize the social has been replete with successive enthusiasms for certain meta or master concepts. Some of these concepts – for example, culture, society, community – have been part of the lexicon of social theory from the outset for disciplines such as anthropology and sociology. Others – for instance, practice, network or identity – have been more recent introductions. Some were wide-ranging from their earliest use; others began their scholarly career with fairly modest applications, and became sweeping as they grew more popular. Sooner or later, however, the success of concepts such as these has also been the source of greater or lesser dissatisfaction with them. 'Too vague or too general' to be of analytical utility is a genre of complaint that has, at one point or another, been lodged against one and all of these concepts. And with the complaints have often come calls for some kind of theoretical 'reboot', ranging from jettisoning the concept altogether to providing a more precise definition, and to reinventing it by affixing a new descriptive qualifier. So community may get a new conceptual life as 'imagined community', network as 'actor-network' theory and so on.

1

But these premises for conceptual reboots usually do not resolve the sources of dissatisfaction, or at least not for long. After all, jettisoning a concept is not the simple prerogative of the academy, let alone any one discipline within it. Many of these concepts have a discursive life beyond the academy. Indeed, it is the pervasiveness of the use of a concept in popular discourse that may often serve as a catalyst for frustration with it. Thus, as Ulf Hannerz noted, anthropologists became increasingly sceptical and frustrated with 'culture' just at the point when it seemed to be 'everywhere' (Hannerz 1996: 30). And the waning of interest within one discipline is not necessarily echoed in sister disciplines. So when anthropological interest in 'network' markedly faded away during the 1980s and 1990s, this was in marked contrast to its continued salience in disciplines such as sociology and geography (Amit 2007: 55). Finally, concepts usually become ubiquitous for a reason, most often because they signal, even if very loosely and imperfectly, concerns or ideas that have some broader purchase. So key concepts selected for theoretical banishment rarely disappear. They usually linger on, available for eventual resurrection. Hence Robert Redfield once wondered whether 'whatever is thoroughly repudiated by one generation of anthropologists is not likely to reappear in the next generation' (Redfield 1962: 439).

But we cannot afford to be complacent about this kind of conceptual perseverance. What goes around may come around, but not necessarily without incurring some important costs along the way. First, the repeated tendency to reinvent the wheel that Redfield identified over a half century ago means that we can lose important opportunities to build upon earlier debates and reflections. The reappearance of a concept – or a particular iteration of it – is all too often treated as if it was utterly new, with little acknowledgement let alone review of earlier reflections on the term. There is a familiar complaint among some anthropologists that their students or colleagues refuse to review any literature with a publication date of more than five to ten years ago. If to a degree this is a cliché, it is one that still contains an uncomfortable grain of truth.

Secondly, this kind of theoretical faddishness tends to produce the very conditions for dissatisfaction that arise when we try to make concepts do too much. Hence the invocation of network variously as a descriptor for 'our age' (O'Brien 2003: 1), a globalizing type of contemporary society (Castells 2000) and part of a theory that involves a radical 'recasting of the central hopes of social science' (Latour 2005: 40) are far cries from the modest pragmatism with which the term was introduced into anthropology during the 1960 and 1970s as a call to avoid 'presuppositions of closure and equilibrium' (Mitchell 1969: 47) in tracing social links. The development of network into a master narrative has not been a particularly anthropological enterprise, although anthropologists have also contributed to its extension. But for an ethnographically grounded discipline such as anthropology, the very sweep and successive dominance of these kinds of meta-concepts is likely, sooner or later, to prove analytically frustrating. It is therefore not surprising that John Postill (2008) found the paradigmatic dominance of community and network in internet studies constraining rather than helpful for opening up the study of electronically mediated socialities. In expressing his frustration, Postill was not making a statement about the general status or scope of community and network as theoretical concepts so much as noting that their 'paradigmatic dominance blinkers our view of the ongoing adoption of internet technologies by local authorities, companies and residents around the globe' (ibid.: 417).

The aim of this volume is therefore not to champion a few paradigmatic concepts of sociality or a new comprehensive theory of sociality. Our exploration of the history of ideas and the ethnographic grounding of several concepts is intended as one small volley in a broader enterprise of opening up and/or refining the repertoire of analytical questions anthropologists, and their colleagues in sister disciplines, can pose about sociality. We could just as reasonably have chosen any number of other useful concepts; in other works we have, indeed, used other notions. For example, elsewhere I have argued that community can be 'good to think with' (Amit and Rapport 2012). And so too are the concepts that we have included in this volume. They are all 'good to think with' because they are neither too narrowly defined nor too sweeping. They can be used to think through ethnographic situations, but they are not particular to one kind of ethnographic circumstance. They are, in short, of the 'not too hot, not too cold' version of conceptual articulation. This kind of mid-range conceptualization is something that anthropologists, wary of abstractions that soar too far from the ground they are trying to explain, have usually been good at.

Working with Ambiguity
In their introduction to a recent volume on sociality, Nicholas Long and Henrietta Moore (2013) note the extraordinary variety of ways in which the concept of sociality has been employed across a broad swathe of scholarly disciplines, including but also extending far beyond anthropology. Rather than dismissing the term as lacking substance because of this variability, Long and Moore argue that this 'definitional haziness' can be more constructively viewed as 'evidence of human sociality's capacity to take many forms' (ibid.: 2). The strength of this term, for Long and Moore, lies in its open-ended invocation of process, in contrast to the emphasis on bounded and static social entities which is associated with terms such as 'society' or

in a view of the social as a product of social interaction or relations (ibid.). Accordingly, they suggest that sociality should be conceptualized 'as a dynamic relational matrix within which subjects are constantly interacting in ways that are co-productive, and continually plastic and malleable' (ibid.: 4).

Within the terms of this kind of open conceptualization, sociality cannot be a domain of investigation, Christina Toren points out, because it 'pervades literally every aspect of being human. Or put it another way, sociality is not part of what we are, but rather the sum total of human being – its entirety' (Toren 2013: 46). Sociality in other words cannot be separated out as a distinct analytical category; rather, it is the ontological ground for a wide range of domains that can be investigated. 'It follows that a social analysis may take sociality for granted as the fundamental condition of human being, but how sociality evinces itself in personhood and other structuring ideas and practices – kinship, political economy, ritual and so on and so on – remains, always, to be found out' (ibid.: 48).

The chapters in the present volume are oriented towards the kind of mid range of conceptualization identified by Toren. Together, the chapters interrogate several key concepts in terms of their scope and effectiveness in eliciting and framing questions about various instantiations of sociality. As I noted earlier, these are not intended to serve as master concepts; both singly and collectively these are deliberately partial conceptions. This orientation is very much in keeping with Bruce Knauft's contention that contemporary anthropological work increasingly eschews master narratives in favour of pursuing mid-level connections that link 'individual facets of large-scale theories, topics and methods to particular but not entirely local objects of study' (Knauft 2006: 411).

Among the connections that we are pursuing in this volume are earlier scholarly efforts oriented towards related conceptual terrains. If we accept an expansive treatment of sociality as the 'fundamental condition of human being' (Toren 2013: 48), then it stands to reason that whether they were using this term or not, social theorists of other eras would have had a lot to say about this ground. And indeed a primary assumption that has guided the choice and treatment of the concepts highlighted in our volume is that earlier theories can be usefully enlisted in a dialogue with contemporary processual concerns. Put baldly, there is no need to start from scratch in reviewing sets of issues and concerns that have been squarely at the heart of disciplines such as anthropology and sociology from their inception. Thus underpinning our approach in this volume is the premise that all of the concepts on which we are focusing – disjuncture, social field, social space, organization, sociability, network – can be productively dealt with as enmeshed in an ongoing if uneven history of debates and reflections.

But this kind of historical review suggests that the orientation towards mid-level conceptualization that Knauft attributes to contemporary work, in fact, has a much more venerable standing in anthropological analysis. Thus senior members of the Manchester School of social anthropology (lasting roughly from the 1940s to the 1970s), such as Max Gluckman and Clyde Mitchell, cautioned that key terms associated with their work, such as network and equilibrium, were not intended to serve as overarching concepts. Gluckman argued that, as a heuristic device, his concept of equilibrium constituted a method rather than a theory per se, and that it was 'only *one method* ... [O]ur field of study is so complex that there are necessarily many different approaches to analysis, each fruitful in its own way; if I argue the merits of one method, this is not to deny that others have advantages' (Gluckman 1968: 219; original emphasis).

In his overview of the various usages of social networks, Mitchell argued that, while there was no network theory in the sense of a set of 'basic assumptions together with a set of derived propositions which are interlinked and capable of being tested' (Kapferer 1973: 84, quoted in Mitchell 1974: 283), 'there are few theories in social anthropology of this kind at all' (Mitchell 1974: 283). Anthropologists have employed a variety of concepts at different levels of abstraction in order to deal with different kinds of analytical problems. In short, here was an earlier assessment of anthropological analysis that would not be too far adrift from Knauft's depiction of the pragmatism of contemporary Anglo-American anthropology.

One could argue, therefore, that within anthropology, perhaps rather more so than in some sister disciplines, there is and has been a pragmatic orientation towards conceptualization that has often evaluated the effectiveness of concepts in terms of their utility for the investigation of certain issues or research domains. Many concepts are judged in terms of whether or not they are 'good to think with' as a framework for investigation, rather than as a set of general propositions that seek to provide comprehensive explanations. In other words, concepts are good to think with when they open up rather than cap off inquiry. Hence the question is less one of method versus theory than what level of abstraction works most effectively to deal with different kinds of questions or domains.

But if social concepts are treated too narrowly, as singular definitions rather than as terms able to encompass a class of phenomena, then they are not likely to be useful to think with except in the most particular of circumstances. So on the one hand, a term that is too close to a particular empirical ground may not be more generally useful because it cannot be applied to any other instance. On the other hand, if concepts are so broad that they could be said to mean almost anything, they run the risk either of being dismissed as empty – as has repeatedly happened for concepts such as culture – or of not 'indicating [effective] ways into the comparative investigation of what it is to be human' (Toren 2013: 46). Hence the attraction towards mid-range levels of conceptualization is comprehensible, especially for an empirically grounded and comparative discipline such as anthropology.

Yet any concept that moves beyond one case necessarily incorporates a measure of ambiguity. As Kenneth Burke noted, 'Since no two things or acts or situations are exactly alike, you cannot apply the same term to both of them without thereby introducing a certain margin of ambiguity, an ambiguity as great as the difference between the two subjects that are given the identical title' (Burke 1955: xiii). Burke argued that it is in these areas of ambiguity that important transformations can take place and distinctions arise. And these transformations arise from – to use Knauft's terms – the variety of connections that are being linked empirically and hence conceptually. Hence ambiguity is not in and of itself a conceptual deficit but a potentially useful heuristic vehicle. Of course, not all ambiguity is equally effective. Thus Burke argues that rather than avoiding ambiguity, what the analyst needs are 'terms that clearly reveal the strategic spots at which ambiguities necessarily arise' (ibid.).

So the 'right' kind of conceptual ambiguity can provide sufficient flexibility to accommodate complexity and variability, while also serving to train our attention on the critical junctures upon and the resources through which transformations and differentiation can occur. At this point, it may be useful to draw in Rodney Needham's notion of polythetic concepts. A polythetic classification groups organisms or phenomena that share common features but in which no one feature is shared by all constituents of the category, nor is any one feature sufficient to define membership in this category (Needham 1975: 356). In outlining the principles and utilities of polythetic as opposed to monothetic classification, Needham drew on a variety of historical as well as interdisciplinary influences. For L.S. Vygotsky, the formation of classes through a principle of 'chain complex' meant that the 'definitive attribute keeps changing from one link to the next; there is no consistency in the type of bonds, and the variable meaning is carried over from one item in a class to the next' (ibid.: 350). During the same period, Ludwig Wittgenstein invoked the metaphor of a rope to denote this kind of concept: 'the rope consists of fibres, but it does not get its strength from any fibre that runs through it from one end to another, but from the fact that there is a vast number of fibres overlapping' (Wittgenstein 1958: 87, quoted in Needham 1975: 350). These overlapping but sporadic similarities, Wittgenstein referred to as 'family resemblances' (ibid.). Needham argued that these conceptions – 'chain complex', 'family resemblances' – represented a radical shift in classification; one could no longer assume substitutability between members of the same class since 'it was no longer true that what was known of one member of a class was thereby known of the other members' (Needham 1975: 350). This 'conceptual revolution', however, was not new or unique to social anthropology. Indeed, Needham discovered that polythetic concepts had a venerable history in natural sciences such as botany.

If, as Burke noted, ambiguity is inherent to any form of classification, polythetic concepts make this element an explicit constituent feature. They overlap, they cannot rest on a single defining criterion, and borderline cases are essential rather than exceptional. But they can also accommodate a variety of variables and be used for many different purposes. In other words, their ambiguity imparts a measure of flexibility that allows them to be adapted to new information and situations as these arise. These are features that seem well suited to an ongoing discussion about various expressions of a ground as expansive as sociality.

Accordingly, the concepts on which we have chosen to focus our attention in this volume are all polythetic in nature. Each is 'good to think with' across a wide range of social situations and issues. But the circumstances being considered through each of these conceptual frames in turn are not reducible to one or even a small set of features, nor can one situation be substituted for another. Invoking a concept to consider particular expressions or workings of sociality should not be taken as offering a definition of a type of instantiation or matrix of relations. Rather, the concept is useful to the extent that it encourages us to focus our attention on the similarities, transformations and discrepancies arising amongst a diverse range of more or less overlapping situations or issues.

But a notion of family resemblances can also be usefully employed to denote a set of related or overlapping concepts. Thus as Vered Amit points out in this volume a concept like disjuncture can more usefully be viewed as one of a family of related concepts such as dissociation and disengagement. Gabriela Vargas-Cetina considers organization among a set of related concepts that also include such notions as cooperative, corporate and ephemeral associations. But we can also extend the notion of a family of concepts to the broader range of concepts through which manifestations of sociality may be considered. Hence the six concepts explored in this volume could usefully be regarded as part of a family of related concepts.

There are several implications arising from this characterization. First, it means that we should not be surprised to find overlaps between these concepts since they are related efforts to explore the same broad terrain. Second, it means that each of these concepts is not intended, in and of itself, to serve as a master theoretical framework or overriding classification. Indeed, as one among an inventory of related concepts, each of these ideas is necessarily and self-consciously partial. As mid-range abstractions, each concept is good to think with for some issues and situations, but it is not intended to cover all or even most of the ways through which sociality is revealed. Even taken together, the domains covered by the six concepts interrogated in this volume are necessarily selective and partial. But given the reach of issues, relationships and situations that could reasonably be viewed as manifestations of sociality, it is difficult to imagine any plausibly useful set of concepts that could cover this ground comprehensively.

So why then this particular set of concepts? This collection of essays arises out of a longstanding conversation among the contributors to this volume. What was initially intended as one meeting led, over the course of several years, to numerous meetings and exchanges in which on occasion other more intermittent participants also joined us. Our discussions were animated by the view that, as the issues and circumstances being investigated by anthropologists have become ever more diverse, there has been a corresponding need to further develop a conceptual repertoire that can be drawn on to explore expressions of sociality in contemporary situations of mobility, urbanity, transnational connections, individuation, media and capital flows.

If in responding to these situations we did not wish simply to resort to pro forma invocations of overly familiar concepts such as 'community' or 'society', neither did we want unnecessarily to 'reinvent the wheel'. As the chapters in this volume illustrate, there is a rich history of reflection on many of the issues or terms that have also proven useful in more recent analyses. This volume therefore endeavours to interrogate concepts of sociality by combining a review of older, classical theories with more recent theoretical innovations across a wide range of issues, locales, situations and domains.

Our reflections on the concepts that we have chosen to highlight in this volume arose through our respective ethnographic studies. That is to say, they have proven useful as frameworks of analyses for our respective inquiries. But as Long and Moore argue, conceptions of sociality that are too closely tied with efforts to account for particular ethnographic cases run the risk of converting 'an ethnographically interesting gloss, which needs to be accounted for, into an analytic gloss to be taken up within social theory, and in doing so, they cut the very phenomenon they are seeking to describe off from other important sources of insight' (Long and Moore 2013: 8). Hence, while the concepts on which we are focusing have already proven useful in framing examinations of specific empirical cases, their inclusion in this volume is a reflection of their broader analytical effectiveness. These concepts do not, by any means, exhaust the inventory of ideas through which anthro-pologists can think about manifestations of sociality. But each of these con-cepts is good to think with across a wide range of issues, locales, situations and domains and that makes them very useful.

PART II: THE CONCEPTS

Disjuncture
Vered Amit

Rather than just one concept, disjuncture is best apprehended as compris-ing a family of ideas or terms such as disassociation and disengagement that have historically been both omnipresent and undeveloped in social theory. This is because disjuncture has rarely featured as a concept in its own right. More commonly it has served as a foil for converse concepts such as commu-nity, association and engagement. One of the effects of this ordering of ideas has been to treat association and engagement as the norm against which disjuncture acts as an extra-ordinary derogation. In this kind of conceptual ordering, therefore, disjuncture always comes after, as a development affect-ing existing social affiliations or links. This kind of interpretation has run the gamut over a wide range of circumstances including, for example, social boundaries – those ensconcing ethnic groups or localized communities – ritual liminality as well as historical shifts. But when it is rendered as an exceptional development, disjuncture often draws more sociological atten-tion than the status quo it is seen as influencing. Ironically, therefore, while as an abstraction disjuncture may be delineated as a conceptual offshoot of the dominant idea of social association, when it is treated as an unusual or extraordinary development it often appropriates the analytical spotlight. As a result, the more mundane disjunctures that are integral to the generation of everyday social routines, interactions and engagements can be obscured. Equally, the tendency to take social affiliation and collectivity for granted as the expected norm obscures the efforts that it takes to form and sustain social associations.

But there is another more recent genre of work that has sought to shift this conceptual ordering by training a spotlight on the agents and processes that have to be catalysed to extend or fix association and innovation over time and space. In this version, stability or endurance itself has to be ex-plained rather than assumed as the status quo. While productively shifting the ground for the conceptualization of the relationship between continu-ity, on the one hand, and innovation or association, on the other, examples of this approach that I examine in the chapter on disjuncture – namely, Bruno Latour's actor-network theory (Latour 2005) and Karin Barber's discussion of cultural creativity (Barber 2007) – still tend to focus on dramatic or 'noisy' instances. For an inclusion of the small acts of creativity involved in quieter and more humble forms of quotidian disjuncture, I turn to Michel de Certeau's notion of the 'art of the weak' (de Certeau 1984). Often comprised of ordinary, daily practices, this art is tactical in nature, exercised in the absence of power to set the broader strategic conditions in which it is employed. It is about the capacity to discern in the slippages and gaps of institutional arrangements opportunities for winning space, which are then quietly grasped. In the anonymity of obscure daily practice there abound limitations on agency, but also opportunities for creativity.

Given the association of disjuncture with winning space, it is hardly surprising that it can also be actively desired rather than feared or endured. In my own research the desire for disjuncture has featured in the aspirations of a variety of travellers, desiring a break from routines, commitments and obligations. But the desire for respite or distance even from highly valued relationships and involvements is by no means associated only with mobility. It can also feature in the pursuit of local places or activities that offer alternative means of engagement or association. Or it can figure in efforts to effect more permanent transformations in the range or nature of one's social involvements. If these quests for disjuncture do not necessarily transform the world around us, they still count as personal, intimate endeavours that are critical to the way in which people seek to fashion their associations. So fully granting attention to ordinary as much as to extraordinary disjuncture can serve as an important starting point from which to consider the dynamics of sociality.

Social Field
John Postill

As defined in Chapter 2, a social field is an organized, internally differentiated domain of practice or action in which unequally positioned social agents compete and cooperate over the same rewards. Commonly associated with the work of the French sociologist Pierre Bourdieu, the concept of field is, in fact, of diverse ancestry. Any comprehensive account of its history must consider at least three other lineages. This concept deserves inclusion in a volume devoted to sociality for the following four reasons.

First, because it broaches a central problem in social theory since Durkheim and Weber, namely the growing complexity and differentiation of modern societies into specialist domains such as politics, law, journalism or sport (Benson and Neveu 2005). Moreover, in contrast to differentiation theory concepts such as Luhmann's societal 'sub-systems', the notion of field does not make the deterministic assumption that modern fields will always tend towards greater differentiation; in some cases, the opposite is true, for instance, when a field like academia becomes less autonomous from the field of government (Hallin 2005). In addition, human agency and sociality are integral to the concept of field; they are not erased, as occurs in Luhmann's highly abstract systems theory (Gershon 2005).

Second, while notions such as community or network skirt around the question of power, the concept of field is based on a relational account of power. In other words, different agents bring to the field uneven amounts of economic, social and cultural capital, and this makes them relatively dominant or dominated in relation to other field agents.

Third, the concept of field invites us to explore the distinction between social action and social practice, two notions that are often conflated in the literature. In its well-known Bourdieuan variant, a field is an enduring domain of habitual practice. By contrast, in the tradition of the Manchester School of anthropology, fields are often volatile, rapidly changing domains of action, for example, following a leadership crisis in a 1950s rural African setting (Turner 1957). In other words, the concept of field suggests a potentially fruitful ideal-type distinction between sustainable fields of practice (such as art, sociology, charity) and unsustainable fields of action (such as protest, war, disaster relief) as two poles in a practice–action continuum.

Finally, unlike community, network or public sphere, the notion of field is descriptive rather than prescriptive. Field is an inherently neutral term with in-built resistance to the kind of normativity that has rendered emotive notions such as community or nation practically unusable as theoretical concepts (Postill 2008). That is to say, it is a concept that sheds light on the way things are, not the way things ought to be within a specific domain of human life. This allows us to investigate the empirical actualities of a given social process or phenomenon with an open mind, without imposing on it our communitarianism, networked horizontalism or critical rationalism. In short, there are no signs of 'fieldism' on the horizon.

Social Space
Deborah Reed-Danahay

Social space is a concept with a long history in anthropological thought that has renewed potential for understanding many aspects of contemporary life related to displacements, emplacements, boundaries and border zones. It provides a way to think about people and places that does not depend upon assuming fixed or rigid boundaries of groups of people or of the geographic territories in which they dwell, but, rather, leaves open for investigation the content, forms taken and experiences of affiliation. That ideas about social space are intrinsic to sociality is evidenced by the numerous spatial metaphors used to express it, such as those invoking social proximity or distance. The recent 'spatial turn' in the humanities and social sciences has provided new interest in applying ideas about social space to understandings of sociality.

Social space is useful for thinking about the ways in which it is increasingly evident in contemporary social life that you can be close to someone socially but distant in physical space, or close in physical space but distant socially. This is a feature of virtual communication, where people who are quite distant geographically can feel close to those with whom they connect through cyberspace – even when they have never met in person. In another example, immigrants and other travellers can also feel socially close to family members and friends who are far away in geographic space, but at the same time feel socially distant from people with whom they are in close physical proximity in their new surroundings. In everyday life, we are frequently in physical proximity to people with whom we do not associate or feel close to socially, yet we can also feel socially close to people who are not geographically close to us. Whereas these metaphors of social distance or proximity may be most apt at the individual level, there is also a group component to social space: the problem of the existence and visibility of social groups as an ongoing project of group-making. For immigrants, particularly in the realm of political mobilization and civic engagement, becoming visible as a group and being able to have some control over the image and meaning of that group in social space is an important component of inclusion and participation.

Social space is connected to physical and geographic places, but there are also ways in which social space can be understood as a more abstract realm in which social relationships are imagined and enacted. There have been several approaches in anthropological traditions of research that focus on spatiality and cultural constructions of space in their approaches to the study of society. Classic theorists who have written about social space include Durkheim, Simmel, Bachelard, Sorokin, Lévi-Strauss, Evans-Pritchard, Goffman, Barth, Lefebvre and de Certeau. It is a central concept in the work of Pierre Bourdieu, although less recognized as such than his notion of field.

Contemporary theory in anthropology has been concerned less with issues of social morphology that preoccupied anthropologists in the mid-twentieth century and more with those of movement, process and the effects of globalization. The question of how to understand the relationship between territorial or geographic space and social space continues, however, to be a theoretical problem in contemporary work. One approach to social space in sociology and anthropology has been to consider how much the physical environment, geographic space, should (or can) be analytically separated from the more abstract idea of one's position in an imagined social space that has to do with moral values, status, prestige, affinity, identity and so on. There are three overlapping areas of inquiry to which ideas of social space contribute: the relationship between territory and social group; thresholds, boundaries, and borders; and social distance and proximity.

Like social field, social space is a theoretical construct that attempts to capture the spatiality inherent in sociality, and provide tools for understanding social interactions and connections as well as their absence. The most useful way to distinguish between these concepts is to consider how they articulate physical or geographic place and sociality. The term field (see Postill, this volume) is most often used to describe forms of social action or interaction in which geographic space is less important than social action, and given more or less attention depending on the analyst. Social space, in contrast, is a concept for which the question of the relationship between social and physical or geographic space is central. I suggest that the lens of social space provides perspectives on the landscape of possibilities, world-views and values in which fields may emerge with more or less permanency and autonomy. Social space also engages with concepts of spatiality as understood, enacted and perceived by ethnographic research participants.

Sociability
Sally Anderson

Including sociability as a key concept for interrogating sociality is perhaps obvious, not least because of their similar etymological origins. Yet embarking on this collaborative work, I was not convinced that sociability merited inclusion. Why not choose interaction, with its long theoretical history and established seat in behavioural and social theory? Why select instead an undertheorized, intuitive concept with Anglophone undertones of social morality, cocktail-party convention, and leisure, pleasure or posturing, depending upon ones point of view. I was not convinced of the analytical purchase to be gained by interrogating this intuitive sister concept. Although not exactly twins, sociability and sociality are often used interchangeably and without reflection, indicating that the conceptual space between them is muddled.

Speaking for inclusion, on the other hand, was Simmel's strong conviction that sociability is a very particular play-form of sociation, meriting a whole chapter in his book on foundational sociological questions (Simmel 1950). This was oddly in accord with my Danish informants' insistence on distinguishing between ordinary *samvær* (being together or sociality) and *socialt samvær* (being together socially or sociability), and their moral claims that the former was not enough for proper associational life, as if Simmel's ideas had been internalized in Danish notions of proper civil society (Anderson 2008).

My awareness that anthropologists frown on a priori dismissal of empirical distinctions, coupled with the theoretical challenge of exploring sociability as a key concept, have convinced me of its merit. Given that the aim of this volume is not to arrive at a rigid definition of sociality, but to explore a set of related concepts, sociability – with its double edge of conceptual muddle and empirical distinction – is a prime candidate. As I argue in Chapter 4, sociability's value, both as a concept and as abstracted performative form, lies in this labile combination of blurring and distinction. Sociability is not the same as sociality, but the distinction is often unclear. Sociability is more than sociality, but how exactly? What drives our own and others' sense of distinctness, and the sense that sociability is 'more' than sociality? How might these two concepts divide in China, Amazonia or Libya? Where do people draw empirical lines, what ends up on which side of the line, and importantly, who decides? What conceptual, political and social work does the division do? And with what emotional intensity and tone do people engage, both as players and linesmen?

Sociability compels us to consider the necessity of playing to conventions of form – to stabilize a relational genre and be recognized as a legitimate player. It also pushes us to consider the 'as if' reality of any abstracted form thus jointly improvised, and the question of how people make any form of sociation 'real' through joint acts of purification (Anderson 2011). This points to the relative instability of all abstracted social form, and specifically the heightened lability of forms of sociation, which in foregrounding moral and aesthetic acts of relating make evaluating how well participants play to and on conventions of form intrinsic to the situation. This raises questions of where, when and to whom such aesthetics are significant, as well as on what legitimacy and whose authority they are judged.

Finally, sociability affords a particular window on ongoing political interest in monitoring, shaping and controlling the sociality of subjects and citizens. If – as Simmel posited – sociability is a form of sociation in which people feel compelled to act as if associated, the concept opens a whole set of questions regarding the character and understanding of acts and feelings of 'association'. It also allows us to engage with the instrumentality and involuntariness of much sociality. What motives and desired outcomes drive forceful policies and pedagogies promoting and enforcing particular sociable forms, and how are these engaged with and contested? In conclusion, the significance of including sociability is that it allows us to interrogate and move between scales of deeply personal and strongly political concerns with human sociality.

Organizations
Gabriela Vargas-Cetina

Organizing and organizations are direct results of sociality, and most human action relies on them. There is perhaps a utopian tint to the study of local organizations and cooperatives: the idea that people coming together will be stronger, more powerful and will accomplish more than a single individual could on their own. They are key ways in which individuals find the strength, the resources and the resolve to face and to participate in contemporary life. Organizations, however, can also carry the seed of authoritarianism, since in them the rules of the collective become obligatory in spite of the particular wishes or interests of the individual member. They might attempt to dictate individual will and thought, as occurred in Germany during the Nazi Third Reich. There is also the danger that organizations might act as individuals that harm persons and groups, and destroy other organizations.

The nation-state, a specific form of organization, relies in turn on certain organizations as its particular tools, to exert control, collect taxes, create and distribute services, and regulate, as much as possible, conflicts between individuals and between groups. Today's multinational corporations, which are organizations too, have the means and the power to impose their rule and their conditions around the world, and force even nation-states into accepting this new state of affairs. Multinational corporations, however, also have the ability to effect world change in positive ways, if they choose to do so. The ways in which their shareholders and stakeholders may influence their direction in one sense or another might ultimately rest on available forms of sociality and responsibility.

Many anthropologists are currently working in circumstances where the actions of multinational corporations are producing critical effects on people and environments. In different settings, certain common threads have included rapidly shifting local contexts that are responding to international, national and regional pressures; and large political and economic transformations that have become ever more present in local life because of the augmentation of communications technology. In a very real sense, anthropology today has to be what Rabinow (2009) calls the anthropology of the contemporary: the study of the most recent past, the present and the immediate future. In Chapter 5 I look at the ways in which anthropology has approached organizations through several interrelated concepts: organization, corporation, cooperative and association. I close the chapter by looking at ephemeral associations. As recently embodied by the 'disorganized' movements that swept the world between 2010 and 2012, ephemeral associations seem to run against the grain of organizational processes as we used to know them. What now seem disorganized forms of action are changing, if not the world itself, at least our perceptions about the world, about organizations and about the place of locality in an increasingly global, inter-connected social universe. New forms of sociality are also emerging from these movements. Organizations as a key theme in anthropology could not have been absent from a volume such as this.

Networks
Vered Amit and Virginia Caputo

Network is a term whose very familiarity – perhaps overfamiliarity – can detract from the particularity and utility of its application. Indeed, network has a long history, both in scholarly and popular discourses, as a metaphor for social relations. The ubiquity of contemporary invocations of network as a general metaphor for connectedness has in turn contributed to growing dissatisfaction with it as an analytical concept in some scholarly quarters. But this apparent ubiquity has obscured the emergence of far more specific scholarly conceptualizations of the term. In our discussion of this term, we argue that the notion of connectedness associated with network has been marshalled to broach two very different avenues of inquiry, one using network to identify and interrogate systems or organizational forms, and the other seeking to trace the reach and impact of personal social links.

In anthropology, the latter concept of network is best known from its association with the Manchester School of the 1960s and 1970s. For scholars such as J. Clyde Mitchell and A.L. Epstein, the open-ended nature of network made it useful as a heuristic device that complemented rather than replaced other categorical or structural analyses. This open-ended quality derived from the acknowledgement that, since the range of links making up a personal network always extends beyond any one observable interaction, this interaction may well be influenced by relationships with people who are not present as well as with those who are. As a result, one can use the concept of network to trace links that cut across different situations and institutions.

The Manchester School's emphasis on tracing the reach and influence of personal networks, while never altogether disappearing, has been overtaken by other approaches. More recent conceptualizations of network ranging from 'actor-network' theory to 'network society' to the notion of network as a new institutional form vary substantially from each other as well. But, they all share a tendency to treat networks as systems or cultural forms rather than as personal linkages. In moving away from network as a personal assembly of relationships, these conceptualizations tend to displace the individual as the focus of analysis as well as to sidestep the question of agency. As a result, in this rendering, individuals seem more likely to inhabit these kinds of networks than to assemble them.

In looking back on the history of network analysis in anthropology and related disciplines, we are suggesting that a reconsideration of earlier historical applications of the concept may prove to be as useful – if in quite different ways – for understanding social relations as other conceptualizations that have gained in prominence more recently. Rather than dismiss network as a facile metaphor for contemporary connectedness, reviewing some of its earlier applications within anthropology can serve as a useful reminder of two key points. First, as Mitchell noted, there is a difference between the use of network as a metaphor and as an analytical concept (Mitchell 1969: 2). Second, the different conceptualizations of network are not really arguments over how to frame the same field of inquiry so much as suggestions for pursuing rather different sets of questions. The earlier avenue for inquiry, which has been recently eclipsed, encourages an exploration of the ways particular situations may be shaped by social linkages extending well beyond them. It thus allows us to probe the workings of association without overly presuming, a priori, the nature of these links. And it also reminds us to consider the nature, extent and intentionality of the efforts individuals invest in forming, mobilizing, sustaining or limiting these social links. This poses a set of questions, a focus on agency and an open-ended approach to social relations that seem just as relevant and perhaps even more pertinent to contemporary circumstances of mobility, globalization and mediated communication as they were to the urban, migrant contexts being probed by the Manchester School some forty years ago. It therefore bears reminding ourselves of the connotations and utility of an earlier concept of network for contemporary anthropological enquiry before the term is entirely effaced by contemporary commercial banalities or overshadowed by an altogether different scholarly orientation.

REFERENCES

Amit, V. 2007. 'Globalization through "Weak Ties": A Study of Transnational Networks among Mobile Professionals', in V. Amit (ed.), *Going First Class? New Approaches to Privileged Travel and Movement*. Oxford: Berghahn, pp.53–71.

Amit, V., and N. Rapport. 2012. *Community, Cosmopolitanism and the Problem of Human Commonality*. London: Pluto Press.

Anderson, S. 2008. *Civil Sociality: Children, Sport, and Cultural Policy in Denmark*. Charlotte, NC: Information Age Press.

—— 2011. 'Going through the Motions of Ritual: Exploring the As If Quality of Religious Sociality in Faith-based Schools', in S.B. Ridgley (ed.), *The Study of Children in Religions: A Methods Handbook*. New York: New York University Press, pp.139–156.

Barber, K. 2007. 'Improvisation and the Art of Making Things Stick', in E. Hallam and T. Ingold (eds), *Creativity and Cultural Improvisation*. Oxford: Berg, pp.25–41.

Benson, R., and E. Neveu. 2005. 'Introduction: Field Theory as a Work in Progress', in R. Benson and E. Neveu (eds), *Bourdieu and the Journalistic Field*. Cambridge: Polity Press, pp.1–25.

Burke, K. 1955. *A Grammar of Motives*. New York: George Braziller.

Castells, M. 2000. 'Materials for an Exploratory Theory of the Network Society', *British Journal of Sociology* 51(1): 5–24.

de Certeau, M. 1984. *The Practice of Everyday Life*, trans. S. Rendall. Berkeley: University of California Press.

Gershon, I. 2005. 'Seeing Like a System: Luhmann for Anthropologists', *Anthropological Theory* 5(2): 99–116.

Gluckman, M. 1968. 'The Utility of the Equilibrium Model in the Study of Social Change', *American Anthropologist* 70: 219–237.

Hallin, D.C. 2005. 'Field Theory, Differentiation Theory and Comparative Media Research', in R. Benson and E. Neveu (eds), *Bourdieu and the Journalistic Field*. Cambridge: Polity, pp.224–243.

Hannerz, U. 1996. *Transnational Connections: Culture, People, Places*. London: Routledge.

Kapferer, B. 1973. 'Social Network and Conjugal Role in Urban Zambia: Toward a Reformulation of the Bott Hypothesis', in J. Boissevain and J.C. Mitchell (eds), *Network Analysis: Studies in Human Interaction*. The Hague: Mouton, pp.83–110.

Knauft, B.M. 2006. 'Anthropology in the Middle', *Anthropological Theory* 6: 407–430.

Latour, B. 2005. *Reassembling the Social: An Introduction to Actor-network Theory*. Oxford: Oxford University Press.

Long, N.J., and H.L. Moore. 2013. 'Introduction', in N.J. Long and H.L. Moore (eds), *Sociality: New Directions*. Oxford: Berghahn, pp.1–24.

Mitchell, J.C. 1969. 'The Concept and Use of Social Networks', in J.C. Mitchell (ed.), *Social Networks in Urban Situations: Analyses of Personal Relationships in Central African Towns*. Manchester: Manchester University Press, pp.1–50.

—— 1974. 'Social Networks', *Annual Review of Anthropology* 3: 279–299.

Needham, R. 1975. 'Polythetic Classification: Convergence and Consequences', *Man* 10: 349–369.

O'Brien, R. 2003. 'The Global Network Knowledge Gap', *Global Networks* 3(1): 1–7.

Postill, J. 2008. 'Localizing the Internet beyond Communities and Networks', *New Media and Society* 10: 413–431.

Rabinow, P. 2009. *Marking Time: On the Anthropology of the Contemporary*. Princeton: Princeton University Press.

Redfield, R. 1962. *Human Nature and the Study of Society*. Chicago: University of Chicago Press.

Simmel, G. 1950. 'Sociability: An Example of Pure, or Formal, Sociology', in *The Sociology of George Simmel*, trans. and ed. K.H. Wolff. Glencoe, IL: Free Press, pp.41–57.

Toren, C. 2013. 'Imagining the World that Warrants Our Imagination: The Revelation of Ontogeny', in N.J. Long and H.L. Moore (eds), *Sociality: New Directions*. Oxford: Berghahn, pp.43–59.

Turner, V. 1957. *Schism and Continuity in an African Society: A Study of Ndembu Village Life*. Manchester: Manchester University Press.

Wittgenstein, L. 1958. *The Blue and Brown Books*. Oxford: Blackwell.

Disjuncture
The Creativity of, and Breaks in, Everyday Associations and Routines

Vered Amit

The analysis in this chapter takes as its starting point the premise that sociality is as much a matter of disjuncture as of engagement and association. Indeed, our various social involvements and interactions are regularly punctuated and enabled by the intervals between them. Over the course of our lives, as we move across time and space, we are repeatedly engaging and disengaging. To move towards one activity, we usually need to break from another; different activities may well involve interactions with different interlocutors; at various points in our life course, we may assume distinct roles and statuses; to assume one role or status, we often need to disengage from other positions and responsibilities; to be in one place, we need to move from another location and so on. Spatial and temporal mobility is necessarily always about both moving *from* and *to*, about departure as well as arrival and the necessary gap between them.

Most of these disjunctures are such familiar and seemingly predictable features of our regular routines that we don't think of them as breaks but as signposts marking out ongoing schedules. We might, for example, think of ourselves as still having a home even when we leave it to participate in activities elsewhere. We assume that the structure, its other inhabitants and neighbours, are still available to be reassembled on our return. But the very fact of our constant movements in and out of a variety of situations and interactions means that a whole host of smaller and larger sources of mediation are always imminent in any activity, carrying with them the capacity to ramify and hence magnify daily disjunctures.

It is at the level of this higher magnification – that is, when disjuncture has involved exceptional rather than routine breaches; for example when the home I expected to return to is either no longer available at all, or in the same form – that it is more likely to be treated as requiring consideration. This orientation towards taking account of disjuncture in its exceptional rather than routine forms has also tended to inform a good deal of scholarly work. Thus, until recently, disjuncture came into focus in theorizations of sociality only when it involved major cleavages or transformations, and even then more usually as derogation from a previous state of aggregation rather than as a process worthy of attention in its own right. As the very etymology of related terms such as disjunction, disassociation and disengagement suggests, the significance of this family of concepts is often signalled vis-à-vis more familiar notions of community or continuity than as overt and independent ideas in their own right. That is to say, their shared prefix, dis-, can be taken as signalling a departure or derogation from previous conditions of juncture, association or engagement. So it is not surprising to find Zygmunt Bauman declaring that, 'After the era of "great engagement", the times of "great disengagement" have arrived' (Bauman 2001: 41). Nor is it surprising to find this assessment in a book by Bauman entitled *Community*. Hence, community and disjuncture are often theorized as intrinsically paired concepts dealing with complementary processes of social mobilization and demobilization. And the pairing of these concepts conveys an intrinsic connotation of temporality, a 'before' and 'after' encoded in the very structure of these terms: the deconstruction of an existing state of affairs.

In this chapter I will argue that the starting assumptions that underpin this kind of conceptual ordering can hamper our interrogation of key analytical questions about the nature of social reproduction and change. To illustrate these limitations, I start my overview of this genus of concepts by reviewing some venerable treatments of disjuncture as the interruption, or in some cases the reaffirmation, of existing frameworks for collective mobilization. Disjunctures can thus feature as the punctuation points marking out continuities as well as signalling smaller and larger transitions. I then move on to consider more recent theoretical contributions that propose treating disjuncture as a starting point for analysis of social interaction rather than as a digression from the norm. Finally, I turn to my own and related research to illustrate the ways in which disjuncture may feature as an object of desire in personal projects, as much to be pursued and as difficult to achieve as fixity.

STASIS AND DISJUNCTURE

Historical Transformations

The interrogation of extraordinary disjuncture featured as a major impetus to the early formation of classical social theory. At the end of the nineteenth and the beginning of the twentieth century, scholars like Emile Durkheim, Ferdinand Tönnies and Georg Simmel sought to account for the major social transformations that were reshaping the European contexts of their day. Within these pioneering analyses, disjuncture featured in two major forms. First, it was invoked in terms of the historical discontinuities inherent to processes of modernization: the structures and orientations emerging in the 'modern' world made it very different from its pre-modern past. But secondly, it featured in the very nature of the emerging modes of social organization associated with modernity. Thus, these theorists viewed modernization as eroding the particular form of collective solidarity and conformity that could be enforced and drawn on in small, face-to-face and homogeneous communities, and encouraging instead the atomized individualism and instrumental relationships characterizing more anonymous, specialized and exchange-oriented industrial metropolises (Simmel 1950; Tönnies 1955; Durkheim 1984). Not only was the *fin de siècle* viewed as marking a historical change in the nature of social relations, but disjuncture was itself also viewed as an aspect of modernity, featured in the multiplication of social affiliations that could be held by any one individual, the increasing compartmentalization of these involvements and a concomitant increase in self-consciousness.

According to Tönnies (1955: 272), increasing urbanization is associated with a 'disconnection' in the link between the organizing principles of 'time' and 'space'. In the *Gemeinschaft* (community) form of association that characterizes the village and the town, neighbourhood relations are grafted onto older and ongoing kinship relations. Hence time, in the form of the ongoing intergenerational connections that tie individuals within a family through their descent from common ancestors, becomes coupled with the principle of space in which social relations and ties are formed through connection to the 'physical, real soil, the permanent location, the visible land' (ibid.). But these links become decoupled in the shift towards *Gesellschaft* (association), and 'from this disconnection results the city' (ibid.). This shift is also associated with a:

> dissolution of all those ties which bind the individual through his natural will and are apart from his rational will. For these ties restrict his personal freedom of movement, the salableness of his property, the change of his attitudes and

their adaptation to the findings of science. They are restrictions on the self-determined rational will and on the Gesellschaft in so far as trade and commerce tend to make property and property rights as mobile and divisible as possible and requires unscrupulous, irreligious, easy-going people. (ibid.: 274)

In contrast, Emile Durkheim was critical of Tönnies's presumption that the division of labour in modern societies did not allow the formation of collective solidarity. The specialization associated with industrial capitalism did not, Durkheim contended, necessarily produce fragmentation and incoherence (Durkheim 1984: xxxiv). 'Rather there emerged a new type of social solidarity in the world of modernity once the relatively simple societies of the past had given way to the complex world of an elaborate division of labour' (Coser 1984: xvi). Nevertheless, Durkheim did regard modern economic life as pathologically riddled by class struggles and commercial crises (ibid.: xx). This hostility and struggle was a concomitant of the moral and regulatory vacuum created between the dissolution of the ancient professional groupings of the pre-industrial order and the still 'fragmentary and incomplete attempts [that] have been made to reconstitute them on a different basis' (Durkheim 1984: xxxv).

For Georg Simmel, in pre-modern societies, people were affiliated to only a small number of social circles which were 'firmly closed' and allowed their 'individual members only a narrow field for the development of unique qualities and free, self-responsible movements' (Simmel 1950: 416). As Lewis Coser has noted, Simmel viewed the modern world as involving a very different principle of association because individuals are members of many different and specialized circles: 'Human personality is transformed when membership in a single circle is replaced by a social position at the intersection of a great number of such circles. The personality is now highly segmented through participation in many circles' (Coser 1965: 19). The multiplicity of these involvements heightened self-consciousness, augmented the differences between individuals and liberated them to explore a variety of social situations (ibid.: 20). But if metropolitan citizens were freer than their small-town counterparts, so too under certain circumstances were they more likely to feel lonely and lost (Simmel 1950: 418). Amongst the brief and superficial contacts between urbanites, individuals struggled for notice, striving to attract attention by standing out in some distinctive way (ibid.: 421).

In spite of the differences between their theoretical formulations, these *fin de siècle* theorists shared a tendency to regard with some ambivalence the historical disjunctures implicated in industrial capitalism and urbanization. Individuals were freed from the restrictions inhering in small-scale collectivities, but at a cost: whether in the form of the enduring loss of collective solidarity, the temporary organizational vacuums created by comprehensive economic restructuring, or the loneliness, anonymity and indifference associated with metropolitan scale.

This kind of ambivalence also characterized the efforts of sociologists based at the University of Chicago to account for the early-twentieth-century urban environment around them. The notion of modernity as discontinuity was hardly a stretch for a group of scholars based at a young institution, situated in a city that was dramatically expanding as an industrial centre, and attracting large numbers of immigrants both from other countries as well as other regions of the United States. Like their European predecessors, the Chicago School under the leadership of Robert Park emphasized not only historical disjuncture but also the disconnections that were viewed as inherently characterizing modes of urban association. The multiplicity of possible associations and the relative anonymity of city dwellers allowed individuals to pursue specialized interests that might not be supportable in smaller settlements: 'In the city there were enough people to sustain a variety of styles of life, and enough freedom for many groups not to have to be excessively bothered with the disapproval of others' (Hannerz 1980: 25). The city therefore not only permitted the multiplication of social groups, according to Park, it also featured a high degree of social separation between them, thus establishing a 'mosaic of little worlds which touch but do not interpenetrate' (Park 1952: 47). For Louis Wirth, another famous member of this group of sociologists, the urbanite moving through this heterogeneous world came 'to accept instability and insecurity as normal, an experience which adds to his cosmopolitanism and sophistication' (Hannerz 1980: 63).

In all of these readings, history is seen as moving from the stability and conformity of small-scale communities to the relative unpredictability and individuation associated with urban, industrial capitalism. A century later, the basic thrust of this trajectory – that is, the movement from relative stasis to disjuncture – has been echoed in a new round of *fin de siècle* theorizations. Thus at the end of the twentieth century and the beginning of the twenty-first, we find scholars arguing that the global restructuring of political, social and economic relations entailed in contemporary modernity involves a normalization of uncertainty, an increase in mobility, greater individualization and self reflexivity. According to Ulrich Beck, a first 'age of modernity' based on the nation-state has been replaced by a post-national 'second age of modernity' (Beck 2000a) in which 'people are expected to make their own life-plans, to be mobile and to provide for themselves in various ways. The new centre is becoming the precarious centre' (Beck 2000b: 70). Bauman echoes the theme of precariousness in what he calls 'liquid modernity' (Bauman 2000) and 'liquid life' (Bauman 2005):

Surrender to the pressures of globalization tends these days to be claimed in the nature of individual autonomy and freedom of self-assertion; but more freedom does not seem to the victims and collateral casualties of globalization to be a cure for their troubles – they would rather trace them back to the crumbling or the forceful dismantling of the life routines and networks of human bonds and mutual commitments that used to support them and make them feel secure. (ibid.: 38)

For Richard Sennett (1998), the normalization of uncertainty associated with flexible capitalism leaches out from the domains of work, also reconstituting domestic, friendship and neighbourhood relations. Indeed disjuncture seems to be an integral feature of this 'new' form of capitalism, associated with an 'experience of disjointed time', which threatens 'the ability of people to form their characters into sustained narratives' (ibid.: 31).

Similarly, Arjun Appadurai argues that disjunctures are central to the global cultural economy: 'people, machinery, money, images and ideas now follow increasingly non-isomorphic paths: of course, at all periods in human history, there have been some disjunctures between the flow of these things, but the sheer speed, scale and volume of each of these flows is now so great that the disjunctures have become central to the politics of global culture' (Appadurai 1996: 37). These new global realities of disjuncture, deterritorialization and rapid cultural change are viewed as unsettling points of reference, frustrating the search for certainties and displacing habitus with conscious choice, justification and representation (ibid.: 44).

Two cycles of social theories seeking to explain the import of *fin de siècle* social changes have thus tended to treat disjuncture in terms of historical transformations that entail fundamental ruptures in the continuity of social affiliations and interactions, daily routines and life courses. Most importantly, these changes normalize the disjuncture of time, space and social relations as an ongoing feature of everyday life. In other words, these are changes that put into question the very basis of social reproduction, and with it the organization of sociality. But there has been another approach that, in contrast, treats disjuncture, in the form of social boundaries between groups, as the very basis for enabling continuity in social affiliations.

Social Boundaries

Fredrik Barth argued that the continuity of ethnic groupings is dependent on the delineation of social boundaries between them, and not on the 'cultural stuff' that these enclose (Barth 1969: 14–15). Over time, the particular cultural features that are used to define these boundaries might change, as might also the organizational form of the group and the cultural character-istics defining membership. '[Yet] the fact of continuing dichotomization between members and outsiders allows us to specify the nature of conti-nuity, and investigate the changing cultural form and content' (ibid.: 14). These boundaries do not depend on an absence of interaction between eth-nic groups, but on the continued organization of that interaction in terms of discrete categorical distinctions. And that categorical distinction shapes social life by signalling both the standards upon which members agree to be judged, as well as the rules governing inter-ethnic encounters.

Barth's concept of ethnic boundaries was in turn further extended by Anthony Cohen to apply to communities more generally. Cohen placed the emphasis on the symbolic nature of these boundaries, on the meanings and importance attributed to them (Cohen 1985: 12). For Cohen, community was the arena where 'one learns and continues to practice how "to be so-cial"' (ibid.: 15). Sharing a body of symbols does not, however, necessarily mean sharing the same meanings because symbols are sufficiently imprecise and therefore malleable, such that they can be made to fit different circum-stances and interpretations:

> 'the *common*ality' which is found in community need not be a uniformity. It does not clone behaviour or ideas. It is a commonality of *forms* (ways of behav-ing) whose content (meanings) may vary considerably among its members. The triumph of community is to so contain this variety that its inherent discordance does not subvert the apparent coherence which is expressed by its boundaries. (ibid.: 20; original emphasis)

Cohen also argued that the symbolic nature of boundaries could be a re-sponse to pressures that threatened to undermine the structural bases of community. Industrialization and urbanization, new forms of transporta-tion, communication and production could all threaten the integrity and autonomy of the boundaries that demarcate collectivities. But members of communities could respond to these kinds of pressures by reasserting the symbolic bases of apparently weakened structural boundaries. 'In other words, as the *structural* bases of boundary become blurred, so the symbolic bases are strengthened through "flourishes and decorations", "aesthetic frills" and so forth' (ibid.: 44; original emphasis).

If the *fin de siècle* theorists, both of older and more recent vintage, tended to view the historical transformations effected by industrialization and then globalization as inevitably reworking the basis of social affiliation and interaction, for Cohen the capacity to creatively reassert community boundaries could be a form of resistance to these structural shifts. One approach views the disjunctures penetrating everyday life as the product of the dislocations of structural changes, while the other views disjuncture as the basis for resistance to this restructuring. It is the insistence by members of the distinctiveness of their community vis-à-vis other groupings that enables the continuity of their affiliations, even while the signification of and meanings attached to these identifications can change over time and between individuals.

Liminality

The notion that certain kinds of disjuncture can actually mitigate or contain, rather than magnify, the effects of social changes also appeared in an early-twentieth-century theoretical formulation by Arnold van Gennep (1960). But in this case, rather than the symbolism signifying the distinctions between collectivities, van Gennep was focusing on the rituals demarcating disjunctures between different phases of the life course. Van Gennep argued that rites of passage comprise three stages: separation; limen or margin; and the social reincorporation of the initiate now holding a new status. While the concept of liminality particularly attracted the attention of later scholars such as Victor Turner, for van Gennep, the liminal assumed its significance not as an autonomous concept but as a sub-category of a broader set of ceremonies. 'Our interest lies not in the particular rites but in their essential significance and their relative positions within ceremonial wholes – that is, their order' (ibid.: 191). And van Gennep viewed these rituals as serving an essentially conservative mission, mitigating the potential disruption of these fundamental alternations of the life course. 'Such changes of condition do not occur without disturbing the life of society and the individual, and it is the function of rites of passage to reduce their harmful effects' (ibid.: 13).

However in Turner's treatment of the ritual process, the focus was on liminality as a state requiring attention in its own right, particularly in terms of its capacity to throw up alternative paradigms of social relations (Turner 1969: 96). In this version, liminality was less a transitional threshold in a predictable sequence of socially recognized stages than part of an ongoing oscillation between structure and anti-structure (ibid.: 97). Structure was the domain of conservation, whereas anti-structure was the domain of creativity: 'man is both a structural and an anti-structural entity, who *grows* through anti-structure and *conserves* through structure' (Turner 1974: 298; original emphasis).

Whereas van Gennep emphasized the stabilizing capacity of rites of passage, in their book on pilgrimage, Victor and Edith Turner (1978: 2–3) were especially interested in the transformative capacity of liminality as a sphere beyond convention in which new possibilities and formulations of what 'may be', and not only what is 'going to be', can come to the fore with potentially even revolutionary consequences:

> For liminality cannot be confined to the processual form of the traditional rites of passage in which he [van Gennep] first identified it. Nor can it be dismissed as an undesirable (and certainly uncomfortable) movement of variable duration between successive conservatively secure states of being, cognition, or status-role incumbency. Liminality is now seen to apply to all phases of decisive cultural change, in which previous orderings of thought and behavior are subject to revision and criticism, when hitherto unprecedented modes of ordering relations between ideas and people become possible and desirable. (ibid.: 2)

The models of liminality offered by van Gennep and Turner are therefore quite distinct. But if van Gennep was concerned with delineating the processes facilitating continuities of social order in spite of cyclical transitions, and Turner was instead concerned with identifying the kinds of transitions that might be capable of catalysing profound discontinuities, they appear to have implicitly shared some important assumptions about the interaction between social transformation and social embeddedness. They both presumed that temporary transitions between states of being have the potential to ramify more broadly. And they both seemed to relate this potential for destabilization to the relative autonomy of these forms of transitions: the more tightly integrated within ceremonial, institutional or social orders the more restrained their effects; the more thoroughly liminal, the greater the potential for broader social disruptions or change.

Disjuncture Comes After

The theoretical formulations I have detailed above are not usually grouped together. And they are clearly dealing with a variety of processes and issues: historical transformation, community formation, transitions between states of being. But they do share some key elements. First, they are all posing questions about the nature of the continuities and breaches engaged in processes of social reproduction. Secondly, they all implicitly or explicitly assume that the starting point for their divergent interrogations entails relatively stable situations: disjunctures come *after*. In other words, these disjunctures are

viewed as developing in, and acting upon, situations involving already existing collectivities, structures, relations, daily routines and practices. Thirdly,
while of different orders and effects, all of these disjunctures are *extra*ordinary. They may be viewed as signalling the ruptures of ineluctable and comprehensive political and economic changes and the resulting normalization
of increasing individuation, specialization and anonymity. Or, they may be
viewed as offering an experience that can elicit transcendent solidarities and
creativities. In contrast, they can also be viewed as defining a heightened
consciousness that mediates or contains the effect of change, and hence enables the continuous integrity of social collectivities. But in all these cases,
the disjuncture serves as an agent marking the limits, in time, space or form,
of social affiliations or interactions. It thus stands apart from the links it
signifies.

But by interpreting disjuncture as processes working *upon* existing forms
of sociality, this conceptual order tends to place more onus on explaining
this rupture/dissociation/disengagement than the status quo it is viewed as
influencing. Ironically, therefore, the more that disjuncture is treated as exceptional rather than mundane, the more it takes centre stage as the focus
of theoretical interrogation. But what if we turned this conceptual order on
its head and viewed disjuncture as the starting rather than the end point of
analysis?

DISJUNCTURE AS AN ANALYTICAL STARTING POINT

In his introduction to actor-network theory (ANT), Bruno Latour (2005)
is concerned to distinguish between 'sociologists of associations' – that is,
those employing some variant of ANT – and what he calls 'sociologists
of the social' –that is, those relying on more conventional conceptualizations of social structure. One of the major distinctions he outlines between
these two schools of thought is their respective ordering of background and
foreground.

> For sociologists of the social, the rule is order while decay, change or creation
> are the exceptions. For the sociologists of associations, the rule is performance
> and what has to be explained, the troubling exceptions, are any type of stability
> over the longer term and on a larger scale. It is as if, in the two schools, back-
> ground and foreground were reversed.
>
> The consequences of this inversion are enormous. If inertia, durability,
> range, solidity, commitment, loyalty, adhesion, etc. have to be accounted for,
> this cannot be done without looking for vehicles, tools, instruments, and ma-

terials able to provide such stability – see the third and fourth uncertainties. Whereas, for the sociologists of the social, the great virtue of appeals to society is that they offer this long lasting stability on a plate and for free, our school views stability as exactly what has to be explained by appealing to costly and demanding *means*. (ibid.: 35; original emphasis)

The starting premises of ANT are unsettling because it seems, at first glance, to throw open so much for questioning and investigation. Concepts such as society, social context, institutions, aggregations and formations that serve as starting grounds for most sociological analyses are what ANT claims to be trying to explain, or more correctly to trace. And to trace associations, one must include both human and non-human actors; indeed, *'any thing* that does modify a state of affairs by making a difference is an actor – or, if it has no figuration yet, an actant' (ibid.: 71; original emphasis). Latour is not claiming that the world around us is chaotic and up for grabs; instead, he is arguing that stability needs to be accounted for, rather than being taken for granted. To explain stability by reference only to an a priori conception of society is to risk positing a tautological explanation in which the 'durability, solidity and inertia of society' is somehow explained by society itself (ibid.: 67). So, for Latour, all means that serve to create associations and to extend them further in time and space need to be included in the analysis.

ANT is a bold enterprise, seeking nothing less than the 'recasting of the central hopes of social science' (ibid.: 40). But we don't have to be as ambitious to consider that this approach has useful implications for the premises with which we initiate investigations of sociality. If we interrogate sociality by an over reliance on stable social ties as our analytical starting point, then we risk pre-empting the investigation by treating the ground it is seeking to explain as already, for all intents and purposes, settled. Yet at the same time, it is clear that Latour's focus on group formation is selective rather than total. Indeed, Latour proposes listening to the controversies surrounding the effort to form groups, the 'uproar' created by the numerous contending voices seeking to claim the existence of and define the boundaries of some groups while denying the validity of other forms of affiliation (ibid.: 32–33). If the existence of a group comes to be seen as unproblematic and to be taken for granted, it no longer generates the kind of controversy that drives ANT analysis (ibid.: 33).

Group formations leave many more traces in their wake than already established connections which, by definition, might remain mute and invisible. If a given ensemble simply lies there, then it is invisible and nothing can be said about it. The ensemble generates no trace and thus produces no information whatsoever; if it is visible, then it is being performed and will then generate new and interesting data. (ibid.: 31)

So controversies over group formation are visible because other kinds of existing affiliations and aggregations are invisible – that is, they are sufficiently well established that they do not need to be fought for, or to use Latour's phrasing, 'performed'.

Karin Barber's focus is on cultural creativity and improvisation rather than group formation. But like Latour's distinction between 'sociologists of the social' and 'sociologists of associations', Barber argues that contemporary efforts to explain innovation have drawn on two long-standing models, one which regards inertia, stability and repletion as the norm, the other adopting a starting assumption that, 'everything that happens is new, unrepeatable and not wholly predictable from what went before' (Barber 2007: 25). The former model regards change as extraordinary, and therefore requiring explanation, while the latter paradigm treats continuity as a social creation that needs to be accounted for (ibid.: 26). But this kind of binary distinction falls down in the effort to explain innovation, which, Barber argues, challenges us to regard the emergent event in relation to efforts to fix things: 'People's ceaseless innovative and re-creative activity is often directed precisely towards making a mark that transcends space and time. Improvisation and the art of making things stick cannot be separated: we find them everywhere fused and intertwined' (ibid.: 25).

If Barber is therefore unlikely to accept that it is necessary to choose one or the other ordering of foreground and background that Latour uses to distinguish ANT from more conventional sociology, the starting point and orientation of their respective analyses nonetheless features a good deal of overlap. Both analyses embark from the disjunctures or dislocations associated with creative action, whether the effort to mobilize new groups or the effort directed at innovating new expressive forms. And both analyses are directed at working out the performative modalities or 'agents' that people employ to fix or stabilize these novelties. Both are concerned with tracing these kinds of innovations from the ground up, so the task of working out if they are meant or made to last involves tracing whether and how these new forms or aggregations can be extended over both space and time – that is, can they be made to extend beyond the efforts of particular individuals at a specific point and place in time? So for both, questions surrounding disjuncture and perdurance are aspects of the same project of creation.

There are two key advantages to the overlapping approaches offered by Latour and Barber to which I want to draw attention. First, by not starting off from the stable and already conjoined as a given, they train our attention on the effort that it can take to fix things. From this perspective, the workings of innovation do not only broach the question of novelty; as much or even more, they also implicate the considerable efforts and variety of means that would need to be employed to make that novelty more than an ephemeral or entirely idiosyncratic moment. Secondly, they allow for the possibility that disjuncture – in the form of an aspiration for the formation of new modes of association, activity, expression and so on – may be desired rather than only reluctantly accepted, or even feared. Applied to the ground of sociality, this perspective reminds us that people may actively and consciously seek to shift the basis of their social interactions and relationships by establishing new ties, modalities of social interaction and/or engagement. It also entrains us to probe into whether or not these new ties or encounters are meant to stick, and if so, what kinds of efforts have to be mobilized to sustain new forms of association.

But as useful as these reminders are, there are also ways in which these treatments of disjuncture draw us back to the emphasis on the extraordinary with which we started. The disjunctures with which both Latour and Barber are concerned are explicitly noisy and dramatic, performances that are calculated to attract attention. I have already noted Latour's emphasis on the importance of 'controversy' and its associated 'uproar' as spotlighting means for group formation that are hidden from view in more unquestioned, taken for granted aggregations. In turn, Barber notes:

> One of the startling facts about human cultures is their sheer excess, the inordinate expenditures of energy, skill and attention on the creation of form. Many cultural forms, far from being in any obvious sense 'naturally' fitted for self-reproduction and self-propulsion through time and space, seem to be created to advertise the high human cost of their production and reproduction. (Barber 2007: 36)

Yet the forms of disjuncture in social relationships that punctuate everyday routines do so, more often than not, in quiet ways that usually do not attract attention beyond the particular individuals they involve: the attenuating effects that time and space may exert over the strength of particular personal network links; regularly navigating the boundaries between associates and roles that may separate spheres of work, home, street and recreation; 'getting away' for a holiday break, changing residence and so on. To the extent that the understated and familiar nature of these breaks do not ordinarily elicit the kinds of uproar that might make them a subject for broader and more public debate, they may have some of the invisibility that Latour attributes to established associations. So why should we make them a focus of analytical inquiry?

GRASPING OPPORTUNITY

The innovations with which Latour and Barber are concerned are deliberate, self-conscious attempts to effect a disjuncture, in the shape of a new form of association or expression, and then to extend it – that is, to make it stick. But much of everyday practice may not be a matter of seeking to make such transformations happen, but of making the most of circumstances as they arise. These kinds of responses are therefore far more akin to what Michel de Certeau describes as the 'art of the weak' than of Latour's notion of an 'uproar'. In delineating the art of the weak, de Certeau distinguishes between strategies and tactics:

> I call a 'strategy' the calculus of force-relationships which becomes possible when a subject of will and power (a proprietor, an enterprise, a city, a scientific institution) can be isolated from an 'environment'. A strategy assumes a place that can be circumscribed as *proper* (*propre*) and thus serve as the basis for generating relations with an exterior distinct from it (competitors, adversaries, 'clienteles', 'targets', or 'objects' of research). Political, economic, and scientific rationality has been constructed on this strategic model. (de Certeau 1984: xix; original emphasis)

In contrast, tactics cannot determine their own place but must operate within a set of imposed conditions. The action involved in tactics:

> cannot count on a 'proper' (a spatial or institutional localization), nor thus on a borderline distinguishing the other as a visible totality. The place of a tactic belongs to the other. A tactic insinuates itself into the other's place, fragmentarily, without taking it over in its entirety, without being able to keep it at a distance. It has at its disposal no base where it can capitalize on its advantages, prepare its expansions, and secure independence with respect to circumstances. The 'proper' is a victory of space over time. On the contrary, because it does not have a place, a tactic depends on time – it is always on the watch for opportunities that must be seized 'on the wing'. Whatever it wins, it does not keep. It must constantly manipulate events in order to turn them into 'opportunities'. (ibid.)

This is the 'art of the weak' (ibid.: 37) because 'a tactic is determined by the *absence of power* just as a strategy is organized by the postulation of power' (ibid.: 38; original emphasis). Often comprised of mundane practices such as walking, reading, shopping or cooking, tactics are positioned in the realm of the interstitial, the 'cracks, glints, slippages, brainstorms within the established grids of a given system' (de Certeau 1980: 6), and they involve the art of 'grasping' opportunities as they occur, not creating them (ibid.: 40). But as Pasteur famously observed, 'chance favours only prepared minds' (cited in Van Andel 1994: 635); or as de Certeau would put it, opportunity draws on memory. New circumstances recall invisible inscriptions of past encounters and, '[t]his system of responsible alter-ation organizes, moment by moment, the delicate touch whereby an intervention into a set of circumstances is achieved' (de Certeau 1980: 41).

In one sense, de Certeau's conception of tactics seems to narrow the room for the exercise of agency for most people, particularly in his insistence that in this kind of art, opportunities are grasped rather than made. But there is another sense in which his reading of the power of improvisation and serendipity both overlaps with some of the emphases made by Karin Barber, but also extends it further into the broader domain of social life. Memory is also a critical feature of Barber's notion of improvisation. Innovation, Barber suggests, relies on an expectation that one's audience will recognize the genre in which it is occurring, and with it the conventions that are being broken. Like de Certeau's notion of the alter-ation of memory, Barber (2007: 32) argues that recognition of genre is thus at one and the same time retrospective and prospective. But the improvisations with which de Certeau is concerned are successful because they are exercised *sotto voce*. Biding one's time for the right opening is not a depiction of passivity but of a genre-like discernment of opportunity. In other words, knowing how to recognize and take advantage of opportunity requires a similar mobilization of retrospective and prospective memory. Some examples: a worker who is stuck in a dead-end job bumps into an acquaintance he barely knows, and who tells him of a new company that will soon be hiring;[1] changing jobs provides the possibility of employment with better prospects but it also provides him the possibility of getting away, without confrontation, from an annoying colleague. A woman with a demanding job and two young children uses the long, daily train commute between work and home as a respite to read or listen to music. A chance visit to a coffee shop provides a new patron with an opportunity for a more sociable 'home away from home' than his previous haunt.[2]

The cost but also the advantage of this 'under the radar' form of day-to-day creativity is its particularity. Because it does not seek to challenge the strategic distribution of power within which it is being exercised, the improvisations it entails are highly particular, and are therefore not likely to, and indeed may not be intended, to extend beyond that particular intersection of people, time and place. On the other hand, there may be far more opportunity for exercising this kind of quiet daily agency than for the kind of more visible, ambitious and possibly therefore more contentious performances with which Barber and Latour are concerned.

Barber's essay is part of a larger volume on creativity and cultural improvisation. In their introduction to that volume, Tim Ingold and Elizabeth Hallam present it as a challenge 'to the idea that the capacity for creative improvisation is exercised by individuals against the conventions of culture and society. Improvisation and creativity, we contend, are intrinsic to the very processes of social and cultural life' (Ingold and Hallam 2007: 19). This stance is certainly reconcilable with de Certeau's conceptualization of the 'art of the weak'. But de Certeau's notion of the grasped opportunity is also useful for reminding us of three additional properties that are associated with improvisation. First, it reminds us that amidst the predictable routines of daily life, serendipities also occur, which can provide people with openings for changing, in smaller or larger ways, aspects of their lives. Second, it proposes that there are slippages and gaps – disjunctures in other words – even in the most thoroughly severe and unyielding set of institutional arrangements. Finally, it suggests that the very obscurity and anonymity of the lives of many ordinary people may provide them with the possibility, when the right opportunity arises, to take advantage of these slippages and gaps. Disjuncture may provide an opening for creative responses that provide those exercising them with some room for manoeuvre within frameworks over which they can exercise little direct influence.

These elements all feature in Mattison Mines's account of how Kalyani, an Iyangar Brahman woman was helped by three of her closest kin to deal with the ruptures occasioned by the illness and subsequent death of her husband, Narayan (Mines 2006). But Kalyani's marriage, which had not been a happy one, had featured a series of earlier tensions and breaches. When she and Narayan first lived with his parents, Kalyani had suffered serious abuse from her parents-in-law, who had sometimes locked her in a room for days. Eventually, under pressure from Kalyani's sister (Nalani) and brother-in-law (Krishnan), Narayan grudgingly agreed to move out of his parents' house and moved to Chennai, where his affines resided. When Narayan was diagnosed with a brain tumour, he, Kalyani and their children were invited to move into a complex of four flats in Chennai owned by Krishnan. Krishnan and Nalani, as well as Nalani's (and Kalyani's) parents also lived in the complex, which Krishnan had inherited from his father. Initially after her move to Chennai, Kalyani was able to work in a private school, but she was forced to resign from this position when her husband became ill. In her search for a job that would allow her some flexibility, Kalyani happened upon a part-time job as a copywriter for a small advertising firm. Because the firm didn't have much work, it afforded Kalyani both the flexibility she needed to look after her ailing husband, as well as the opportunity to learn this new trade. Eventually, when she was able to handle more work, Kalyani was able to avail herself of these skills and take up an opportunity to move to a larger firm.

Mines explains that, for an Iyangar woman, widowhood 'is far more than a crisis of bereavement. The death of her husband unmoors a woman from social relations, transforming her and denying her positions of merit and value in her marriage house, among her kin and in the greater society' (ibid.: 22). Kalyani thus faced the limitations of what she called social 'stereotypes' or 'taboos' about how a widow should behave. Lakshmi, her mother, thought that Kalyani 'should be strong enough to ignore old foolish customs', and when Narayan died she pressured Kalyani to return to work and not to be cowed by the prospect of gossip (ibid.: 36). In her interview with Mines, Kalyani however explained that:

> I still don't attend weddings. I don't go to the temple. I don't visit friends or relatives because for a year or so we are not supposed to, I believe. So I would rather not find out. I would rather not go there and ... face a snub. I don't feel it's necessary. Why should I? I have had enough hassles in life. So, why go there and wonder if they've turned away or maybe [I've] imagined [the] slight ... ah ... maybe they don't mean to hurt but they do hurt you all the same. So there are a lot of things I still can't do or rather that I don't want to do. (ibid.: 40–41)

In spite of her reluctance to go as far in flouting convention as her more radical mother urged, Kalyani still defied several of the expectations of conservative neighbours and kin. Far from coming down in the world, she was pursuing a career that she enjoyed and that offered the possibility of professional success. She was also learning to drive a car. A few months after Kalyani's interview with Mines, she attended the wedding of her nephew, Varsha, and began again to wear jasmine flowers and fashionable saris. Nalani, who had encouraged and supported her sister, used the occasion of her own son's wedding to involve Kalyani in an 'auspicious function' in which widows do not normally participate, thus announcing to 'kin and friends that they and the bride's family had rejected the notion that Kalyani was made inauspicious by her widowhood' (ibid.: 47). Mines notes that these actions and the narratives of the three women, as well as the support provided by Krishnan, featured a 'reworking and repositioning of a widow's place in society' (ibid.). But Mines also observes that Kalyani, her mother Lakshmi, her sister Nalani and her brother in law Krishnan, were striving at this reworking carefully, quietly seizing small openings when possible, rather than proclaiming loud or public defiance to established convention:

> They believe that simply to reject the old ways would cause them great difficulty with others and in all likelihood would in the future also cause trouble for their children. They choose to be thoughtful in their actions, therefore. They pick mindfully calculated paths that move them towards the society that they imagine. They keep their intentions to themselves and strive without much public comment. As little by little they move towards the achievement of some of their goals, they are modest before others, and they try to show regard for others. They believe that modesty and keeping their own counsel enables them to avoid multiplying their difficulties. They seek to avoid envy. It is their style. (ibid.: 47)

SEEKING A BREAK

In this closing section, I want to further explore a possibility that, as I noted earlier, is suggested in both Barber's and Latour's work, namely that disjuncture may in some circumstances be actively desired rather than feared. In taking up this possibility, I want to turn to several examples from my own work that are associated more with the kind of personal and everyday 'modest' goals that are cited by Mines in his account of Kalyani's family than the more extraordinary and comprehensive ruptures highlighted in *fin de siècle* theorization. But this is not to say that these kinds of goals are unaffected by large-scale structural shifts. Indeed, much of my own research has concerned various forms of contemporary cross-border mobility that have been critically enabled and shaped by wide-ranging institutional, technological, political and economic developments.[3] But while the desires for disjuncture I am exploring work with and in terms of these developments, they are still personal rather than systemic. They are 'grasped opportunities' that are made possible by but which are not always entirely consonant with the institutional interests or rationales sponsoring these openings.

Among contemporary forms of mobility, the desirability of disjuncture is perhaps most closely associated with tourism, a global industry that over the course of the last 150 years has been transformed from the select pastime of an elite few into a mass industry facilitating 'breaks' of longer or shorter duration for millions of travellers. Hence Valene Smith accordingly defined a tourist as a 'temporarily leisured person who voluntarily visits a place away from home for the purpose of experiencing a change' (Smith 1989: 1).

The association of leisure with the desire for an ambulant form of change has, however, been overtaken by increasing acknowledgement that there are various forms of mobility that are not as singularly recreational, but which can also be animated by similar desires. In particular, the emergence of a category of 'lifestyle migration' has also been associated with the desire for 'escape'. Hence Michaela Benson and Karen O'Reilly have defined lifestyle migrants as:

> relatively affluent individuals of all ages, moving either part-time or full-time to places that, for various reasons, signify, for the migrant, a better quality of life. Ethnographic accounts especially have revealed a narrative of escape permeating migrants' accounts of the decision to migrate, further emphasised by their negative presentations of life before migration. Migration is thus often described using language like 'getting out of the trap', 'making a fresh start', 'a new beginning'. (Benson and O'Reilly 2009: 609)

In several of my own studies of mobility, a sense of escape has also featured, but often in tones that are more reminiscent of the kind of change that Valene Smith associates with tourism – that is, as an exciting if only temporary 'break' from stale and predictable routines. But if Smith associated tourism both with leisure as well as travel, the travellers with whom I have been concerned have combined their mobility with ongoing work or educational involvements.[4]

I interviewed Keith, a hydroelectric-engineering consultant as part of a study of travelling professionals who specialized in international work. What, I asked Keith, had kept drawing him back to a life of frequent assignments outside Canada where he was based? He replied:

> Well, there aren't the same opportunities here. I mean, it's partly the excitement, because if you're working on a job here in Quebec or in Canada, you're part of a large team, and it will be 9 to 5 work and there won't be any excitement to it, there won't be any intensity. And I think to a large extent, that's part of it, plus the lure of going to different places and seeing new parts of the world. And then my next job is in Mongolia, which I've never been to but I'm excited about the idea of going there.

Michael, a Canadian environmental consultant whose work also involved frequent travel, explained that any sense of glamour that might be associated with this kind of occupational mobility quickly faded.

> Michael: Fourteen hour days, seven days a week, having to be in meetings and the meetings go late, and you're dealing with cranky people, and you're dealing with language barriers and cultural barriers, and having to try and understand what the heck the other guy is trying to get across without you getting mad and him getting mad. It's pretty stressful.

V.A.: So what attracts you about this kind of work?

MICHAEL: I don't know. I'm a true type A. I'm on the go constantly. I *love* to travel. I *love* working in other cultures. I don't like ruts. I will get to a certain point working here where [I wonder] what's the next fix. It's like the entrepreneur, the thrill isn't in the acquisition so much as it is in the chase, in getting there. And I guess for me, it's the journey, it's getting from here to there and then getting immersed in these different projects.

Michael and Keith's ability to take up this kind of itinerant consulting was not a function simply of their respective predilections. It occurred within the context of a growing privatization of international development work, which is increasingly being allocated by both multilateral and national agencies to private companies looking to extend their operations across national borders. Michael already had two years experience working abroad for an international volunteer agency when, on returning to Canada, he learned, through an old associate, of a position with an engineering and consulting firm that operated internationally. They were looking for people with experience in the environmental area, but it was several years more before he was finally able to secure international assignments. Keith had started his career in the hydroelectric sector in his native Australia, but moved to Montreal when a Canadian consulting group recruited him.[5] Almost immediately he was sent on international assignments. Unlike Michael, he hadn't intended to get involved in 'the international field', but 'once I was working in it, I was very happy doing that'.

It is expensive for a corporation to send a consultant abroad to work on an international project. When a specialist, however well trained, has not had experience working internationally, there is always a risk that they will not be able to adapt well to the circumstances of working abroad. So corporations tend to seek out people who want to work abroad and who have demonstrated their capacity to do so effectively. In time, Keith and Michael came to exemplify both these criteria, so for a while at least their personal desires and capacities accorded reasonably well with their employers' international activities and priorities. But the companies they worked for didn't create Keith's and Michael's attraction to the 'excitement' and intensity of a peripatetic international career. Their work concerned a succession of projects involving different colleagues and locales. If arduous and stressful at times, the novelty and intensity of the constant succession of sites and interlocutors appealed to them as much more exciting than the predictability of sedentary '9 to 5' domestic occupational routines, the very predictability on which some of their co-workers relied. Not every associate who had the opportunity to work internationally either took it up or, if they did, necessarily enjoyed and pursued it over the long term. Michael's and Keith's opportunities to pursue international work might have been provided by firms competing in transnational corporate fields, but the enjoyment which drove them to pursue this kind of occupational travel over the long run was not created by these employers.

A similar trope of restlessness occurred in Martine's explanation of why she had decided to undertake a university exchange in Australia in the course of her post-secondary studies in Montreal.[6]

> I needed to get away, to go as far as possible. I hadn't been travelling – apart to go see my mom in the States – for four years since Tunisia, well since CEGEP [Collège d'enseignement général et professionnel] [when] I went for three weeks to Italy as my last class. My last three credits in CEGEP was three weeks in Italy. So it's been really three years since I had been anywhere and I was getting antsy. I *needed* to leave. I loved Italy and just travelling around like that, but what I really love is to go and live somewhere, just change scenery and move somewhere.

Donald had enjoyed his studies in an Ontario university, but 'it was kind of, I dunno, boring me in a lot of ways', so he opted to take up an opportunity for a university exchange in Britain:

> You know, you're there for four years at university, and you're sort of, I wouldn't say stuck there, because I'm actually having a really good time in Toronto, but its just, it's an opportunity, I think, it's – I mean, a lot of people do it, they say, you know, third year is the year that a lot of kids go travelling. And since you're there, I mean, I don't know if I'm gonna get another opportunity to spend a year living somewhere else unless my job takes me there, and I don't know what I really want to do. So, you know what I mean, it seems like I have an infinity of school and commitments that maybe I won't get a chance to run away from. So, that sorta motivated me to do it.

Martine and Donald's university exchanges occurred within the context of an increasing emphasis on student mobility within the post-secondary sector in many countries. As a result, many universities in Canada have encouraged their students to acquire some form of 'international experience' in the course of their studies, and provide opportunities for this kind of travel in the form of academic exchanges, internships, volunteer programmes and so on. Martine and Donald appeared less swayed by the promotional rhetoric extolling the career advantages of these programmes than for the opportunity to 'get away' without interrupting their studies. And they grasped the opportunity to travel when it appeared in the course of their studies.

I subsequently interviewed Mark in the course of a study of inherited dual citizenship among young Canadian adults.[7] Mark actually possessed three citizenships. His Canadian citizenship had been acquired through his birth in Montreal. But Mark also inherited an additional citizenship from his mother, who had migrated to Canada from Western Europe, and yet another from his father, who had emigrated from the United States. During his childhood and adolescence, Mark's travels had largely been shaped by visits to family members living abroad. But in his twenties, he began to pursue openings for extended sojourns abroad that were facilitated by his multiple citizenships, and were associated with educational and career prospects. At different phases of his post-secondary education, he undertook periods of study respectively in Paris, London and New York. He also availed himself of opportunities for short stints of work in the United States and Europe, but eventually pursued a professional career in Canada that frequently involved international travel. While Mark was not altogether sure of his future career trajectory or mobility at the time of our conversation, he was fairly confident that it would not involve a return to settle in Montreal where he had grown up, and which he still visited regularly. Because both of his parents had at one time emigrated to pursue their own respective careers in Canada, Mark felt that:

> I always had this impression that in life you're supposed to go somewhere. You start somewhere and you move somewhere else, and so I have lots of friends in Montreal who love Montreal and want to stay here and, uh, I think it's a great city, but I can't imagine that. For me, the life course is: start somewhere, go somewhere else, and that's what you do.

There were costs, Mark acknowledged, associated with these frequent moves, including the attenuation of friendships, but these were 'completely outweighed by the, you know, being able to take advantage of an opportunity'. And some of these ruptures in relationships would probably, Mark thought, have happened anyway.

> I've lost touch with high-school friends and stuff like that, which is true, um, but to me, that, I don't really see that as a huge loss because in the sense that I think my high-school friends who were staying in Montreal had a very different outlook and were looking for different things in life, so we probably would have drifted apart anyways.

So, the desire to experience 'a change', which Valene Smith identified with tourism, appears as part of a much broader array of travel circuits. And in some of these circuits, it is the possibility of combining this desire with ongoing work and educational commitments that is especially appealing. The desire for a change is thus not necessarily restricted to or resolved by a two-week holiday, nor is it necessarily associated with or only assuaged through travel. For example, Ray Oldenburg's notion of the 'third place', from the German *bierstube* to the Italian *taberna* or the American frontier country store, owes much to the notion that people are attracted to 'neutral' places that have the warmth of a home away from home without its obligations, that people need some distance from people whose company they otherwise enjoy:

> The individual may have many friends, a rich variety among them, and opportunity to engage many of them daily only if people do not get uncomfortably tangled in one another's lives. Friends can be numerous and often met only if they may easily join and depart one another's company. This otherwise obvious fact of social life is often obscured by the seeming contradiction that surrounds it – we need a good deal of immunity from those whose company we like best. Or, as the sociologist Richard Sennett put it, 'people can be sociable only when they have some protection from each other'. (Oldenburg 1997: 22)

So here is a notion of sociability in which the capacity to leave, to break away, even if only briefly, is as fundamental as the capacity to gather, converse, socialize.

But as the example of Mark's move away from Montreal indicates, this capacity to break away may also be desirable when it is more comprehensive and enduring. There are surely times when people may actively wish to ensure more thorough ruptures in their attachments and involvements. What I am trying to stress is that, over and above either comprehensive ruptures in social organization or more permanent severances in social relationships, there is much to be gained from paying close attention to quotidian disjunctures, the comings and goings that are as much a part of everyday relationships and routines as commitment and engagement. The particular modalities through which these disjunctures occur are shaped and enabled by historical transformations and power relationships that most of us contend with but cannot do much to determine. But if we must 'seize on the wing the possibilities that offer themselves at any given moment' (de Certeau 1984: 37) rather than determine a priori the shape and form of these opportunities, our efforts to do so are no less creative for it. This is, as de Certeau has noted, an 'art', not dumb submission to disciplinary regimes. And our day-to-day efforts to seize these opportunities are personal, intimate endeavours that matter to each of us, even if they don't manage – and are perhaps not even intended – to transform the world around us.

ACKNOWLEDGEMENTS

Parts of this chapter previously appeared either in 'The Limits of Liminality: Capacities for Change and Transition among Student Travellers', in N. Rapport (ed.), *Human Nature as Capacity: Transcending Discourse and Classification* (Oxford: Berghahn Books, 2010, pp.54–71), or in 'Disjuncture as "Good to Think With"', in V. Amit and N. Rapport, *Community, Cosmopolitanism and the Problem of Human Commonality* (London: Pluto Press, 2012, pp.28–43).

NOTES

1. This example draws on Mark Granovetter's notion of 'weak ties'. In conducting a random sample of 'professional, technical and managerial job changers living in a Boston suburb', Granovetter discovered that quite often the most useful contacts in the search for a job were quite marginal – or 'weak' – links within an individual's network (Granovetter 1973: 1371).
2. Here I am drawing on a variant of Ray Oldenburg's notion of 'third places', 'places where individuals may come and go as they please, in which none are required to play host, and in which all feel at home and comfortable' (Oldenburg 1997: 22).
3. This was part of a project entitled 'Itinerant Consultancy: An Anthropological Study of Transnational Travel, Work and Social Location among Mobile Professionals', which was made possible by a standard research grant from the Social Sciences and Humanities Research Council of Canada. In depth, semi-structured interviews were conducted with thirty-eight professionals whose work necessitated frequent travel. Most of these interviews were conducted between 2002 and 2004.
4. To protect their confidentiality, in what follows I have used pseudonyms rather than the actual names of the people who were interviewed for this project.
5. See Amit (2010) for a more detailed discussion of Keith's occupational trajectory.
6. This study was part of a larger study of student mobility on which I collaborated with Noel Dyck (Simon Fraser University), which was entitled: 'Coming of Age in an Era of Globalization: Achieving Cultural Distinction through Student Travel Abroad'. The project examined three different programmes enabling extended stays abroad by Canadian students and young adults: work abroad, academic exchanges and athletic scholarships. Ethnographic fieldwork was carried out at various sites in Canada as well as in Britain, the United States and Australia. Interviews were conducted with ninety-nine young travellers as well as with forty-three government, university and NGO officials who were involved in developing, administering or promoting these opportunities for student and youth mobility. Fieldwork and interviews were conducted between 2005 and 2008. The research project was made possible by a standard

research grant from the Social Sciences and Humanities Research Council of Canada, and benefited greatly from the work of three graduate research assistants, Heather Barnick, Kathleen Rice and Meghan Gilgunn. Pseudonyms have been used in place of actual names in order to protect the confidentiality of people who participated in this project.

7. This study, entitled 'Coming of Age as Dual Nationals: An Anthropological Study of Belonging and Mobility among Young Canadians', was supported by a standard research grant from the Social Sciences and Humanities Research Council of Canada. The research involved interviews with young Canadians who inherited either EU and/or US citizenship. Wherever possible, interviews explored the inter-generational meaning and uses of multiple citizenship among members of the families through which this status was transmitted, including siblings and parents. This project greatly benefitted from the efforts of Mona Magalhaes, whose assistance made it possible to carry out interviews with fifty-one dual nationals or their family members between 2010 and 2012.

REFERENCES

Amit, V. 2010. 'Serendipities, Uncertainties and Improvisations in Movement and Migration', in P. Collins and A. Gallinat (eds), *The Ethnographic Self as Resource: Writing Memory and Experience into Ethnography*. Oxford: Berghahn Books, pp.200–214.

Appadurai, A. 1996. *Modernity at Large: Cultural Dimensions of Globalization*. Minneapolis: University of Minnesota Press.

Barber, K. 2007. 'Improvisation and the Art of Making Things Stick', in E. Hallam and T. Ingold (eds), *Creativity and Cultural Improvisation*. Oxford: Berg, pp.25–41.

Barth, F. 1969. 'Introduction', in F. Barth (ed.), *Ethnic Groups and Boundaries: The Social Organization of Culture Difference*. Boston: Little Brown, pp.9–38.

Bauman, Z. 2000. *Liquid Modernity*. Cambridge: Polity.

—— 2001. *Community: Seeking Safety in an Insecure World*. Cambridge: Polity.

—— 2005. *Liquid Life*. Cambridge: Polity.

Beck, U. 2000a. 'The Cosmopolitan Perspective: Sociology of the Second Age of Modernity', *British Journal of Sociology* 51(1): 79–105.

—— 2000b. *The Brave New World of Work*, trans. P. Camiller. Cambridge: Polity.

Benson, M., and K. O'Reilly. 2009. 'Migration and the Search for a Better Way of Life: A Critical Exploration of Lifestyle Migration', *Sociological Review* 57(4): 608–625.

Cohen, A.P. 1985. *The Symbolic Construction of Community*. London: Tavistock.

Coser, L.A. 1965. 'Introduction', in L.A. Coser (ed.), *Georg Simmel*. Englewood Cliffs, NJ: Prentice-Hall, pp.1–26.

—— 1984. 'Introduction', in E. Durkheim, *The Division of Labor in Society*, trans. W.D. Halls. New York: Free Press, pp.ix–xxiv.

de Certeau, M. 1980. 'On the Oppositional Practices of Everyday Life', trans. F. Jameson and C. Lovitt. *Social Text* 3: 3–43.

—— 1984. *The Practice of Everyday Life*, trans. S. Rendall. Berkeley: University of California Press.

Durkheim, E. 1984. *The Division of Labor in Society*, trans. W.D. Halls. New York: Free Press.

Granovetter, M.S. 1973. 'The Strength of Weak Ties', *American Journal of Sociology* 78(6): 1360–1380.

Hannerz, U. 1980. *Exploring the City: Inquiries Toward an Urban Anthropology*. New York: Columbia University Press.

Ingold, T., and E. Hallam. 2007. 'Creativity and Cultural Improvisation: An Introduction', in E. Hallam and T. Ingold (eds), *Creativity and Cultural Improvisation*. Oxford: Berg, pp.1–24.

Latour, B. 2005. *Reassembling the Social: An Introduction to Actor-Network-Theory*. Oxford: Oxford University Press.

Mines, M. 2006. 'In the Aftermath of Death: Presenting Self, Individuality and Family in an Iyangar Family in Chennai, 1994', in V. Amit and N. Dyck (eds), *Claiming Individuality: The Cultural Politics of Distinction*. London: Pluto Press, pp.22–50.

Oldenburg, R. 1997. *The Great Good Place*. New York: Marlowe.

Park, R.E. 1952. *Human Communities*. Glencoe, IL: Free Press.

Sennett, R. 1998. *The Corrosion of Character: The Personal Consequences of Work in the New Capitalism*. New York: Norton.

Simmel, G. 1950. *The Sociology of Georg Simmel*, trans. and ed. K.H. Wolff. New York: Free Press.

Smith, V.L. 1989. 'Introduction', in V.L. Smith (ed.), *Hosts and Guests: The Anthropology of Tourism*, 2nd edn. Philadelphia: University of Pennyslvania Press, pp.1–17.

Tönnies, F. 1955. *Community and Association (Gemeinschaft und Gesellschaft)*, trans. C.P. Loomis. London: Routledge and Kegan Paul.

Turner, V. 1969. *The Ritual Process: Structure and Anti-structure*. Ithaca, NY: Cornell University Press.

—— 1974. *Dramas, Fields, and Metaphors: Symbolic Action in Human Society*. Ithaca, NY: Cornell University Press.

Turner, V., and E. Turner. 1978. *Image and Pilgrimage in Christian Culture*. New York: Columbia University Press.

Van Andel, P. 1994. 'Anatomy of the Unsought Finding, Serendipity: Origin, History, Domains, Traditions, Appearances, Patterns and Programmability', *British Journal for the Philosophy of Science* 45(2): 631–648.

van Gennep, A. 1969 [1908]. *The Rites of Passage*, trans. M.B. Vizedom and G.L. Caffee. Chicago: University of Chicago Press.

2

Fields
Dynamic Configurations of Practices,
Games and Socialities

John Postill

A social field is an organized domain of practice or action in which unequally positioned social agents compete and cooperate over the same public rewards (see Turner 1974; Martin 2003). One notable advantage of 'field'
as a conceptual tool is that it is a neutral term, lacking the normative idealism of other sociality concepts such as public sphere, community and network (Postill 2008). For example, the concept of public sphere is often used
by scholars both as a 'rhetorical token' (Benson 2007: 3) and as a cherished
ideal that guides research away from what is and towards what ought to be.
A further difficulty with public sphere is that its advocates, starting with
Habermas, have failed to explore how public spheres are internally differentiated (ibid.: 4). As Calhoun has argued, 'whatever its qualities, any public
sphere is necessarily a socially organised field, with characteristic lines of
division, relationships of force, and other constitutive features' (Calhoun
1992: 38).

Although today we associate the concept of field with the sociologist
Pierre Bourdieu, this notion has a far longer pedigree, originating in physics
and Gestalt psychology. Martin (2003) distinguishes three main field-theoretical traditions in the social sciences: Lewin's social-psychological theory,
Bourdieu's stratification/domination approach, and DiMaggio and Powell's
inter-organizational theory, to which we could add a fourth tradition, namely
that of Turner and other members of the Manchester School of anthropology (see below). Over the decades, scholars from numerous disciplinary

and national backgrounds have developed a sophisticated field-theoretical vocabulary (such as sub-field, capital, habitus, *nomos*, *hexis*, position, disposition, stakes) and applied it to a vast range of research questions. Yet unlike, say, the fashion-driven diffusion of Derrida's philosophy to certain quarters of American academia in the 1970s (Lamont 1987), Bourdieu's field theory has inspired a 'progressive research program' in key subfields of sociology in the US – and indeed elsewhere – for many years, a sustained process that shows no signs of abating (Sallaz and Zavisca 2007).

At the same time, field theory has come under heavy criticism on both sides of the Atlantic. One oft-rehearsed criticism, today almost a social-science truism, is that field theory stresses socio-cultural reproduction at the expense of change. Particularly problematic, say the critics, is Bourdieu's notion of habitus, which stresses continuity and underestimates the ability of field agents to reflect upon and change the conditions of their existence (Jenkins 2002; Butler 1999; Gledhill 2000; Born 2010). Another perceived weakness of field theory is its focus on individual field agents and their 'strategies', while neglecting field institutions and organizations (Martin 2003; Sallaz 2006; Born 2010). Bourdieu is also taken to task for overlooking social action that takes place outside the field. Since an agent's friends and partners outside the field may be immune to the field's effects, it is argued that other methods will be required to understand their relationship to the agent (Couldry 2003; Martin 2003: 44). Moreover, while concurring with Benson and Neveu (2005) that the concept of field offers media theorists a more powerful tool than Castells's 'media space' or Habermas's public sphere, Couldry (2003) argues that field theory leaves unanswered numerous questions about the limits, overlaps and interrelations of fields, especially with regards to Bourdieu's 'field of power' (see also Panofsky 2011). Other scholars point at over-reliance on the metaphor of fields as games (Martin 2003), an analogy that may apply to sports like tennis or chess but can be misleading in other contexts (Warde 2004). Matters are made worse, adds one commentator, by the lack of integration in Bourdieu's oeuvre between his practice and field theories (ibid.). Still others question the idea of the field as an invisible, metaphysical force not grounded in materiality or actual interactions (but see de Nooy 2004), and insist on the need to include non-human agents (or 'actants') in any field account:

> The strategies of scientists are ... not determined by the scientists' position in the field; rather, their position is a result of their scientific actions. Latour follows Bourdieu insofar as he conceptualizes actors as strategically advancing their position in a field, but he moves the means into the scientific routines and strips them of their structural properties. (Guggenheim and Potthast 2012: 160)

Hidden inside these criticisms are two problematic assumptions. First, there is the assumption that field theory is the virtual monopoly of Bourdieu and his sociological heirs, when we have just seen that there are at least three other field traditions to consider. Second, there is the tacit understanding that the concept of field is inextricably tied to two other Bourdieusian keywords, namely habitus and capital, yet experience tells us that, like other forms of discourse (Spitulnik 1996), theoretical concepts are inherently 'detachable' from their contexts of origin.

In this chapter I address some of these criticisms, but my intention is not to provide yet another appraisal of the strengths and weaknesses of Bourdieu's field theory. Instead, my aim is to examine the potential not of field theory but rather of the concept of field itself to shed light on obscure aspects of human sociality in tandem with other concepts, including non-field concepts. The chapter is organized as follows. First, I reintroduce the Manchester School's concept of field after decades of virtual oblivion, and contrast it with Bourdieu's own field concept. I then take up two of the criticisms just mentioned – namely the view that field theory cannot account for change, and the metaphor of the field as a game – and use them to explore the idea that the concept of field can in fact be an invaluable tool in the study of dynamic, heterogeneous domains of practice and sociality. I conclude with a reflection on the limitations and potentialities of this plural approach to the concept of field and with suggestions for future research.

TWO FIELD TRADITIONS

In anthropology, the first sustained usage and elaboration of the concept of field can be traced to the Manchester School of anthropology (1940s to 1960s). Led by Max Gluckman, the Manchester scholars conducted fieldwork in Central and Southern Africa during the latter days of the British Empire, where they set out to study urbanized localities under conditions of rapid social and political change. This was a time in which 'tribal', linguistic and other 'community' groupings were in flux, and new kinds of affiliations were being constantly made and remade around novel occupational and recreational practices. Faced with such fluid actualities on the ground, Gluckman and his followers moved away from the structural-functionalist paradigm then predominant in British social anthropology and towards historical-processual accounts informed by new concepts such as 'field', 'network', 'social drama', 'trouble case', 'situation' and 'arena' (Swartz, Turner and Tuden 1966; Turner 1974; Evens and Handelman 2006).

Theoretically, the Freudian and Marxian emphasis was on conflicts aris-ing within Lewin-inspired 'fields' of social relations. Methodologically, the stress lay on situational analysis and the extended-case method: new theo-retical insights had to emerge from the painstaking collection and analysis of field data, not from any prior theoretical convictions. Gluckman encour-aged his students to concentrate on 'trouble cases', such as customary litiga-tion, for it was by following these conflicts as they unfolded across various social situations that hidden structural relations would be revealed (Evens and Handelman 2006). The result was a series of now classic ethnographies published in the 1950s (e.g. Mitchell 1956; Turner 1957; Epstein 1958).

Two key concepts to emerge from these post-war efforts were still being developed in the 1960s, namely network and field. On the one hand, Mitch-ell, Epstein and others followed the lead of Barnes (1954) and Bott (1955, 1957), and enthusiastically adopted social network analysis. The hope was that this new method would prove as useful to anthropologists working in urban areas as the genealogical method had been to the study of kinship in rural areas (Sanjek 1996). Their investigations crystallized in the edited vol-ume *Social Networks in Urban Situations* (Mitchell 1969). On the other hand, Turner and his associates – some of them in the United States, to which he had emigrated – continued to work on the concept of social field, and par-ticularly on its cognate, the political field. Their collaboration culminated in the volume *Political Anthropology* (Swartz, Turner and Tuden 1966). The starting point was Gluckman's Zululand research, where he found not the 'tightly integrated systems' of structural-functionalism but rather 'social fields with many dimensions, with parts that may be loosely integrated, or virtually independent from one another' (ibid.: 3; see also Epstein 1958).

By the 1970s, the Manchester School had disbanded and anthropolo-gists' interest in both concepts – field and network – had waned. One no-table exception is Victor Turner's essay 'Hidalgo: History as Social Drama' (Turner 1974), in which he uses both field and network to reconstruct a failed uprising in colonial Mexico. Turner understands this historical episode as a 'social drama' that unfolded across a rapidly shifting political field made up of the people, institutions and resources mobilized to assist or thwart the rebellion. A social drama, for Turner, is a political conflict that originates within a social group but can spread across a wider inter-group field unless appropriate 'redressive action' is taken (ibid.: 128–132).

Defining 'political field' as 'the totality of relationships between actors oriented to the same prizes and values' (ibid.: 127), and in line with Gluck-man's emphasis on conflict, Turner argues that a political field is constituted not by practice but by action, specifically 'purposive, goal-directed group ac-tion, and though it contains both conflict and coalition, collaborative action is often made to serve the purposes of contentious action' (ibid.: 128). Such contentious action is fought out in 'arenas', which he defined as 'bounded spatial unit[s] in which precise, visible antagonists, individual or corporate, contend with one another for prizes and/or honour' (ibid.: 132–133). Arenas are 'explicit frames' in which 'nothing is left merely implied', and major decisions are taken in public view (ibid.: 134).

It is hard to imagine a starker contrast between this conceptualization of the field and our present-day understanding of this notion, largely derived from the work of the French sociologist Pierre Bourdieu (1930–2002). Bourdieu came to develop his concept of field (*champ*) late in his career. This concept is most fully elaborated in his 1992 monograph *Les Règles de l'art*, translated as *The Rules of Art* (Bourdieu 1996; see also Bourdieu and Wacquant 1992). In this book, Bourdieu reconstructs the genesis and structuring of the modern field of art in nineteenth-century France. This field was constituted against the backdrop of the failed revolution of 1848 and the rise of a new bourgeoisie with 'vulgar' tastes. Flaubert, Baudelaire and other leading lights had great contempt for this 'regime of upstarts', and particularly for the new breed of writer-journalists at its service (Bourdieu 1996: 54, 58). These innovators created the cult of 'art for art's sake' and declared their independence from the status quo (ibid.: 59–60). Art for art's sake became the field's *nomos*, its 'fundamental law', but it was only when the field's practices became embedded in agents' minds that they could fully grasp the rejection of external rewards, including money (ibid.: 61). The field of art's relative autonomy from the fields of power and commerce had to be arduously fought for and won. The idea of the pure gaze, of a pure aesthetic divorced from morality and sentimentality, had to be invented and defended at all costs (ibid.: 110–111). This was no easy task. Thus, Flaubert, who was seen by his contemporaries as a 'scholar poet', raised the humble novel to new heights through an 'immense labour of research' and literary innovation (ibid.: 99).

Bourdieu's notion of network differs markedly from that used in social-network analysis (SNA). He does not study Flaubert's oeuvre to marvel at his creative genius. Instead, his aim is to use this literary work as a guide to the concealed 'network' of emergent objective relations and positions binding together artists and other field agents. Bourdieu is critical of SNA for what he regards as its naive commitment to interaction as the basis of human life, developing his field theory in opposition to it. By concentrating on people's visible interactions and ties, he argues, SNA practitioners fail to grasp the invisible network of objective relations binding human agents within a common cultural space (such as France) and its fields of practice. For Bourdieu, SNA conflates structure with interaction, exaggerating the importance of 'social capital' – that is, the capital that accrues from social connections – whilst neglecting cultural and symbolic capital (Knox, Savage and Harvey 2006). For example, two Parisian architects who have never met may nonetheless possess similar amounts of symbolic capital (prestige, renown and so on) and occupy neighbouring positions within their field. In Bourdieu's field theory, it is agents' relative positions and amounts of field-specific capital that matter, not with whom they interact (see also de Nooy 2003).

A key notion in Bourdieu's field theory is habitus. A person's habitus is more than merely a bundle of habits. Habitus is the product of socialization in a given cultural milieu, the product of long years 'reading' our social worlds with our minds and bodies (Gledhill 2000: 140). It is a 'matrix of dispositions' linked to a person's position both within a culture's overall social space and within particular fields. Habitus organizes our perceptions of ourselves and other agents (Johnson 1993: 2–5; Martin 2003: 31). A competent scholar, for example, has a 'sense' of what to do to accumulate further symbolic capital within the academic field, even when they can never be fully aware of their actions, such as when writing an article or giving a keynote address. As Bourdieu observes, 'lucidity is always partial' (Bourdieu 1993: 72).

Although (social) field is a spatial metaphor, it is important not to conflate this term with social space, as often happens in the social-science literature. Bourdieu uses the notion of social space to articulate the complex relationship between the physical world and sociality, as well as to investigate questions of group formation and social distance (see Reed-Danahay, this volume).

For Bourdieu, fields are those slowly changing, established domains of cultural life in which practitioners acquire a 'feel for the game' over many years – for example, the fields of art, sociology, or boxing. Take his account of Flaubert's famous Madame Bovary trial, where the novelist stood accused of publishing immoral materials (Bourdieu 1996: 52). At the time of the trial, the Parisian salons, says Bourdieu, became sites for mobilization in support of Flaubert. Bourdieu mentions in passing this episode to illustrate the importance of the salons as points of articulation between the fields of art, commerce and government, distinguished more by who they excluded than by who they included (ibid.: 51–53). Yet he does not consider the trial to be a political process (or 'trouble case') worthy of detailed analysis in its own right, as Turner and other Manchester scholars might have done. Bourdieu focuses on the cumulative changes that take place within an established field (Swartz 1997: 129; Couldry 2003), not on potentially volatile, unpredictable processes such as trials that often migrate across fields. The Parisian salons, brasseries and courthouses provide Bourdieu with a relatively fixed spatial matrix of objective relations – a socio-physical backdrop to a slowly changing field of practice (Bourdieu 1996: 40–43).

This contrast between the Bourdieuan and Manchester approaches should not make us lose sight of the areas of broad agreement. First, both Turner and Bourdieu employ the metaphor of game to refer to the field whilst rejecting rational-actor models of human agency. Second, despite popular misconceptions of Bourdieu as a theorist who neglects social change at the expense of social reproduction (see below), both Bourdieu and Turner study social fields diachronically and resist the structural-functionalist idea of fields as self-regulating entities. Third, both scholars place conflict at the heart of their field theories, but whilst Turner tracks group-driven conflicts that spill over established fields, Bourdieu is more interested in the field trajectories of individual agents within a given field.

I now turn to the actual and potential uses of a conceptualization of field that draws inspiration from both Bourdieu and the Manchester scholars, while remaining open to other theoretical influences and attentive to the specificities of any given research setting. As a working proposition, I adopt a plural approach to fields as dynamic configurations of practices, games and socialities.

KICKING THE HABITUS

As we have seen, one criticism often levelled at Bourdieu's field theory is its alleged emphasis on reproduction and inability to account for social change (Butler 1999; Gledhill 2000; Jenkins 2002; Mesny 2002; Lau 2004). Bourdieu's pivotal notion of habitus has born the brunt of the attacks for its seeming determinism and downplaying of human agency (Haluza-De-Lay 2008). Thus Born points out that Bourdieu 'repeatedly stresses the enduring, unreflective, "unconscious" nature of habitus and its inscription in gesture and deportment – in bodily hexis' (Born 2010: 18). This dependence on habitus comes at a cost, adds Born, for the resulting field accounts invariably exaggerate the importance of habit and iterative agency at the expense of creative improvisation and change. Missing from these analyses is an explanation of 'how [the] schemas [of the habitus] can be challenged, reconsidered and reformulated' (Emirbayer and Mische 1998: 983, quoted in Born 2010: 12).

Bourdieu's response to his critics is that they overestimate agents' ability to change their social worlds. While individuals do indeed construct their own world-views, this activity is conducted 'under structural constraints' (Bourdieu 1990: 130). A crisis in the field can give rise to numerous opinions, but these may still leave the field's ideological premises untouched. To effect lasting change, the field's dominated agents must change its 'doxa', that is, the tacit knowledge that each field generation takes for granted (Gledhill 2000: 140). A habitus is 'neither compelled by the field (as in structuralism), nor freely chosen by actors (as in rational choice theories or phenomenology)' (Haluza-DeLay 2008: 210). This point is perhaps best demonstrated via Bourdieu's notion of hysteresis, which refers to the lack of fit between habitus and structure during times of change (Reed-Danahay 2005: 130). For example, the mismatch between middle-class students' career expectations, internalized in their childhoods, and the realities of the job market exploded in France in 1968 and in Spain in 2011, giving birth to new protest movements. This lack of fit is poignantly captured by the Spanish slogan 'You won't own a house in your fucking life' (*No vas a tener casa en la puta vida*). In Bourdieu's theory, these crises can only be explained by considering the dialectic 'between the subjective hopes of the habitus and the objective chances of the social structure or field' (Gartman 2007: 391).

I have no intention, however, to join the endless debates on the (de) merits of habitus as a sociological concept. Instead, in this section I wish to argue that no concept is indispensable when putting a theory to work, not even habitus when addressing a question from a field-theoretical perspective. A brief example will demonstrate this point. In a recent article, the sociologist Monika Krause (2011) mobilizes a set of field-theoretical concepts (field, capital, stakes, autonomy, boundaries) to rethink the history of US journalism from 1890 to 2000. Krause begins by asking how 'journalistic ideals of public service' may have arisen in the US, and 'to what extent journalists live up to such ideals' (ibid.: 89). She then suggests that modern journalism displays a highly distinctive practice that makes it unique, namely reporting (or 'active news-gathering'). 'This practice became common in the 1860s and 1870s with the emergence of journalism as a field with its own stakes, relatively independent from political advantage or literary merit. The power of field-specific capital to organize practices in the media has varied since then' (ibid.: 90).

Following Bourdieu, Krause regards field-specific capital, which she defines as 'the value attributed to art as art, journalism as journalism', as 'a stake that orients actors'. When field agents denounce others for not living up to these ideals, they are co-constituting the journalistic field. However, these denunciations cannot be taken 'at face value'; comparative research is needed to understand the import of these competitive stances as well as the shifting tension between intra- and extra-field forms of capital over time (ibid.: 92).

The remainder of Krause's piece is a field-inflected history of American journalism that tracks the chequered career of the field's core practice of reporting. Thus during the 'golden age of reporting' (1945 to 1970) there was an 'ethic of public service' and a strong orientation towards original reporting. By contrast, the era from 1970 to the present has seen fundamental changes in media regulation and ownership, and a steep decline in this practice. Managers now put profit making before field-specific values, and the boundary between journalism and PR has once again become fuzzy – as it was in the interwar years (ibid.: 100).

There are two remarkable features about this article. First, although Krause relies almost entirely on Bourdieu's field theory for her analysis of the empirical materials, she makes no mention of habitus. Second, she places the notion of 'practices' at the centre of the analysis, even though in Bourdieu's own oeuvre field and practice have had a strained relationship:

> Bourdieu worked extensively on the concept of practice in the first half of his career, resulting in significant theoretical formalization in *Outline of a Theory of Practice* (1977 [1972]) and *Logic of Practice* (1990 [1980]). He never subsequently disclaims his attachment to the theory of practice developed in those works. Yet, apart from constant reiteration of the epistemological position which contrasts practical sense with scholastic reason, he allows most other aspects of the theory of practice to fall into desuetude. Its place was taken by the concept of field, the primary analytic tool for his major empirical studies in the 1980s. Only in *Distinction*, which constitutes a crossroads in Bourdieu's conceptual progress, are the two concepts dealt with in tandem. The resulting meeting was far from satisfactory. (Warde 2004: 3)

What are we to make, then, of Krause's replacement of habitus with practices? In what ways, if any, does it undermine or bolster her account? First, I must draw attention once again to the question of plurality: in Krause's account there is no single 'practical sense' or professional 'habitus' spread across the field of journalism. Rather, she highlights the centrality of reporting as the defining practice of a precariously autonomous journalistic field, but this is by no means the field's sole practice. Indeed, it is partly through supporting or undermining different practices that agents compete and cooperate over the field's future. In other words, Krause is tacitly adopting a plural model of the field as, among other things, a dynamic universe of contested practices.

By 'kicking the habitus', Krause is opening up her work to more nuanced, differentiated field accounts of actual field practices, while connecting to a growing interdisciplinary literature on media-related practices found both within and across discrete domains of social life (Bräuchler and Postill 2010). Her 'thin descriptions' of the key practice of reporting (and its alternatives) raise intriguing questions for further ethnographic and ethnohistorical research, including into the possible 'anchoring' of other practices in reporting at different historical periods (Couldry 2004), the current overlap between journalistic and PR practices, a phenomenon that poses significant ontological challenges for practice theory (see Christensen and Røpke 2010), or reporting as a sub-practice within a broader, and changing, journalistic 'meta-practice' (Peterson 2010).

'GAMES' AGENTS PLAY

As noted earlier, some commentators have criticized Bourdieu's reliance on the analogy of games, and particularly sports, to explain field dynamics:

> Several other metaphors were used earlier – market, force field and military field. However, as time passed, Bourdieu became ever more likely to use the analogy of the game to explain the dynamic processes occurring in fields. Many of his demonstrations are based upon the analysis of actual sports ... But sports ... have very particular characteristics making it potentially highly misleading to think of the whole world in such terms. (Warde 2004: 15)

Taking the example of tennis, Warde (ibid.: 19) goes on to argue that Bourdieu's sports analogy may be applicable to a few specific domains of social life, but 'is flawed if applied universally'. Although tennis exhibits 'all the properties of a field', such as competitiveness, strategy, counter-strategy, autonomy, agreed rules, and institutionalization, it is still non-field-like in a number of other respects. For instance, some people may play tennis for social or familial reasons and may not be greatly interested in winning or in sharing the game's *illusio*. Extending the analogy to social practices in general, not all 'reasonable practical conduct' is strategic, and some actions may be merely pleasant and only marginally strategic (ibid.: 21).

The problem with Warde's argument is his literal reading of the notion of 'games'. Of course fields such as sociology, art or plumbing are not games in the narrow sense of the term, namely 'a contest with rules, the result being determined by skill, strength, or chance'. Yet they can still be usefully described as games so long as we understand the term more broadly, as in the following: 'scheme, proceeding, etc, practised like a game ⇒ *the game of politics*'.[1] Here the phrase to note is 'like a game'. While it is obvious that politics is not a game comparable to tennis, chess or Monopoly, this domain of practice nevertheless resembles a game. Prior argues that 'the field is also a space of competition, the analogy being a game of chess where players enter the game and position themselves according to the powers and moves available to them'. But unlike a game of chess with its well-defined rules, powerful field 'players' will also struggle over the definition of what counts as 'the stakes in the field' (Prior 2008: 305).

By the same token, less powerful players may be left out of such struggles. For example, during ethnographic research on the building industry in Perth, Western Australia, Moore found that subcontracting tradesmen ('subbies') refer to their specialist field as 'the building game' (Moore 2013: 59). This is a game that subbies are not well placed to alter in any fundamental way:

> The building game cannot be controlled by a subbie. A subbie knows only the facts of agreements he has negotiated and must guess what others are charging, earning or paying. So while subbies talk a lot to each other when they have the opportunity, listening closely for any clue about the building game, they studiously work not to reveal much about their own private business. (ibid.: 64)

As Victor Turner argued in his earlier mentioned Hidalgo essay, in a (revolutionary) field one side may be playing chess while the other side is playing 'for keeps' (Turner 1974: 141). The sociological implications are significant:

> The understanding of fields as the result of alignments between actors oriented to related prizes clarifies the status of rules: they are neither unalterable constraints that channel our action or make 'illegal' action unthinkable nor mere descriptions of central tendency. When patterns of conduct are recognized by actors as forms of regularity, conformity or nonconformity to the pattern, whatever advantages or disadvantages may also follow, has semiotic import ... Like a poet breaking meter for emphasis, players break the rules precisely because they are rules. (Martin 2003: 32)

Research by Crossley (2002) on the global anti-corporate protests of the early 2000s and my own recent fieldwork on Spain's *indignados* movement suggest that the game analogy is indeed apt. Crossley proposes that the anti-corporate movement is best understood as a protest field (or as a sector of a protest field). Following Bourdieu, he defines fields as 'sui generis social spaces ... organised around the common participation of ... "players" in a historically and culturally specific social "game"' (ibid.: 674). Notice how this author is careful here to hedge his use of the terms players and game with inverted commas. 'Players' may disagree about numerous things, but they nonetheless 'interact in both direct and indirect ways, co-constituting a shared sui generis social space of contention' (ibid.: 674). As a consequence, a 'recognizable and durable "game"' emerges in which participants 'collectively generate and share in a common lived-time trajectory' (ibid.: 675).

Extending Crossley's work on social movements, Ibrahim argues, *pace* Born (2010), that habitus 'is generative and has a reflexive capacity' (Ibrahim 2011: 319). Thus British anti-capitalist activists take part in 'game-like scenario[s]' where they compete and sometimes clash with one another 'as they all try to gain advantages within a given field' (ibid.: 319).

The protest field does not consist solely of activists and other citizens. Crossley includes in the field various 'mediating agencies' such as the news media and the police 'who become involved in "the game"': 'On the one hand, their actions crush, discourage, incite, encourage or amplify support and participation ... On the other, as McAdam (1982) has shown, policing tactics and strategies often interact in a dialogical fashion with protest activity; each move or innovation on one side calling for corresponding moves and innovations on the other' (Crossley 2002: 677).

We are very far removed here from the received wisdom of field theory as a theory that stresses social reproduction and cannot account for dynamism or change. In my own research into social media and activism in Barcelona, carried out in 2010/11, I observed first-hand precisely such dialogical processes at work both within and across sectors of the 'movement-field' (Juris 2008), such as activists, celebrities, politicians, the police, in what came to be known as the *indignados* or the 15M movement. I also participated in a number of social 'games' instigated by the movement's unofficial leaders. For example, a crucial element of the strategy during the build-up to the 15 May protests was to make the campaign a regular occurrence on Twitter's officially 'trending' topics. Knowing that Twitter's trending algorithm favours novelty over volume (Cullum 2010), they succeeded by frequently changing the campaign keywords and encouraging followers to re-tweet the newly agreed hashtag (keyword) so that it would 'trend', thereby reaching a much wider audience. We could call this new game 'working the algorithm'.

To take the analogy of fields as games one step further, highly participatory protest fields such as Spain's *indignados* or the global Occupy movement can be likened to real-time strategy computer games. Gee (2005) argues that the notion of 'communities of practice' (Wenger 1998) is of little use to understanding new forms of digital sociality that do not entail group membership or a sense of belonging. Instead of communities of practice, he proposes the notion of 'affinity spaces'. These are spaces in which people from a variety of backgrounds come together to pursue a common endeavour or goal. Gee's epitome of an affinity space is the strategy game *Age of Mythology*, a plural world in which the common endeavour of playing and transforming the game takes precedence over questions of racial, class or gender identity, a world with various routes to participation, informal leadership and status in which newbies and masters share the same space, and different kinds of knowledge (tacit, intensive, extensive and so on) are fostered and valued. This portrait bears a striking resemblance to new protest movements such as Occupy or 15M, both shaped by the 'hacker', participatory ideals and practices of the open source/free software movement.

FIELD SOCIALITIES

Many research fields are dominated by two or three paradigmatic concepts that serve to focus minds, but which may also impose powerful agendas and slow the fields' advancement (Hobart 1990). In the case of internet studies, the two key sociality concepts are arguably 'community' and 'network' (Postill 2008). One way to loosen the hold of such hegemonic notions, I would suggest, is to broaden our conceptual lexicon. In *Localizing the Internet* (Postill 2011), based on fieldwork in the Malaysian suburb of Subang Jaya, I seek to extend the vocabulary of internet studies in two main directions: first, by borrowing or coining field-theoretical notions such as 'field of residential affairs', 'internet field', 'social field', 'social drama', 'field law', 'arena' and 'action-set'; second, by conceiving of sociality as being inherently plural and context dependent (Amit and Rapport 2002; Jean-Klein 2003), rather than in the overly general terms often found in the existing internet literatures, such as 'community sociality' versus 'network sociality' (Wittel 2001; see below).

My field approach is inspired both by Bourdieu and by the Manchester tradition. In his 1958 monograph *Politics in an Urban African Community*, the Manchester School anthropologist A.L. Epstein, a student of Gluckman, discusses the emergence of a political and administrative system in a mining town located in the Copperbelt region of Northern Rhodesia (today Zambia). Turning away from structural-functionalism and towards historical-processual explanations, Epstein set his study against the canvas of the huge processes of migration and urbanization under way in 1950s Africa. Northern Rhodesia was at the time a profoundly divided society, the main chasm running between Europeans and Africans. In turn, both populations were internally divided along lines such as class, ethnicity, occupation and gender. Yet at the same time there was a high degree of interdependence across these divides, numerous 'bonds of co-operation' linking together Africans and Europeans within 'a single field of social relations' (Epstein 1958: xii).

In Copperbelt towns, a relatively stable socio-political framework was provided by the mine, the municipal council and the district office (ibid.: xiv). District commissioners had no say in the running of the mine township, which was a power unto itself (ibid.: 21). Africans saw commissioners as 'remote Olympian beings who resided in the Government Offices' away from the mines (ibid.: 22). In the interstices of this framework, Epstein found 'a continuous flux in which new groups and associations are constantly springing up' (ibid.: xiv). Many of these social formations were ephemeral, but they nonetheless left traces on the field of social relations.

The emerging urban system consisted of 'many different sets of social relations or spheres of social interaction', and was riddled with 'ambiguity and inconsistency', not least around contested notions of 'tribalism' (ibid.: xvii). Epstein stresses the unevenness of social change across what I call 'the field of residential affairs': that field of practice in which local authorities, residents, firms and other social agents compete and cooperate over residential matters. 'The factors making for social change and development operate over the whole of this field, and are present in every sphere; but they do not impinge upon these spheres with the same weight, or at the same time' (ibid.: xvii).

In *Localizing the Internet*, I synthesize this Manchester approach with the equally historical and processual field model developed by Bourdieu (see above). Rather than positing the existence of a 'local community' being impacted upon by global networks, my focus is on Subang Jaya's field of residential affairs. Transplanting Epstein's observations from a post-war African mining town to an early-twenty-first-century South-East Asian suburb is not as far-fetched as it may seem at first. Although the historical and cultural circumstances are of course vastly different, there are some striking parallels between Epstein's and my own study. Like Epstein, during fieldwork I found myself in the midst of emergent processes of the 'production of locality' (Appadurai 1996), finding both the makings of a politico-administrative framework (in my case, centred on the Subang Jaya municipal council, founded in 1997), as well as a more fluid realm in which various residential associations and initiatives were being constantly formed and transformed, many of them as ephemeral as those described by Epstein for the Copperbelt.

Moreover, I found that processes of change were unevenly spread across the field of residential affairs, with some regions of the field changing more rapidly than others. For example, the fight against crime is an ecumenical issue that has brought together people and agencies from across the governmental divide in Subang Jaya. Crime prevention initiatives led by residents have received governmental support, mass-media coverage and undergone considerable technological development, including new mobile technologies. By contrast, a campaign to reinstate local elections in Malaysia that sought to mobilize Subang Jaya residents was short-lived and made no impact on the field of residential affairs.

One of the book's aims is to track the emergence of new forms of residential sociality in Subang Jaya in and around the field of residential affairs. My argument is that social fields do not necessarily exhibit a homogenous 'field sociality'. This is certainly the case with Subang Jaya's field of residential affairs, where a plurality of socialities has evolved over time. The perils of reducing sociality to totalizing categories are apparent in Andreas Wittel's (2001) discussion of the new media industry in London. Wittel distinguishes two broad kinds of sociality: community versus network sociality. Community sociality is the pre-modern, sluggish sociality of physically localized collectivities. By contrast, network sociality is fast-paced and based on fleeting, instrumental encounters (such as speed dating) with a large set of 'contacts'. Young urban professionals working in the new media industries epitomise this latter form of sociality, which Wittel (following Wellman and Castells) regards as the defining sociality of our era.

The trouble with Wittel's notion of network sociality is that it glosses over significant differences in how people interact with one another within the same field of practice, for example the new media industry in London. Surely the quality of a social interaction within a speed-dating session differs markedly from that in the office canteen or in a board meeting? How do media industry workers in London navigate these different 'field stations' while pursuing their goals (advancing their careers, socializing, mating and so on)? These questions cannot be answered unless we develop a more nuanced understanding of sociality.

In *Localizing the Internet* I unpack the notion of sociality ethnographically, suggesting that it cannot be reduced to a community/network binary. Instead I argue that researchers need to approach this question with an open mind, with the expectation that sociality may take on plural forms even within a single universe of practice. The three distinct forms of field sociality that I discuss are committee sociality, patrol sociality and (web forum) thread sociality. I discuss their specificities in terms of their type of interaction, mode of discourse and field articulations. It is only through these fine-grained distinctions derived from empirical research on the ground, I suggest, that we can begin to theorize the elusive relationship between internet practices and the emergence of new forms of sociality.

For example, I define residents' committee sociality in Subang Jaya as the co-present, synchronous sociality of monthly meetings devoted to discussing local issues (cf. Jean-Klein 2003). Meetings are held at night in air-conditioned rooms, and attendance is restricted to committee members and their guests. The bodily orientation is primarily face-to-face – although this will depend on interlocutors' seating positions relative to one another (Pink 2008). Food and drinks are usually provided and consumed in the

room during the break. These 'ephemeral items ... live on in the form of
the social relations that they produce, and which are in turn responsible for
reproducing the comestibles' (Gell 1986: 112). The discourse is oral, poly-
logical and gesturally rich, but it is also mediated by texts, most of them
shared over the internet (for example, the agenda, e-mails, letters, web sites).
A committee meeting is therefore both a 'literacy event' (Street 2000) and
an internet-related practice. Albeit a largely sedentary activity, attendants
undertake a metaphorical journey whose itinerary is the agenda.

In contrast to the gesturally rich committee meetings, the sociality of
web forums relies on emoticons and avatars to compensate for the reduced
bodily cues of online communication (*pace* Hine 2000: 14–27). Their asyn-
chronicity allows busy suburbanites to participate on web forums at their
own leisure, something that is not possible in the co-present meetings which
take place 'in real time'. Another notable difference is the relative tidiness of
forum exchanges. Despite being web based, this form of sociality is both linear and sequential. While it is true that forum thread participants in Subang
Jaya (and elsewhere) frequently post hyperlinks to other sites, thread users
are still constrained in their agency by the site's linear architecture: thread
postings are discrete, securely bounded communicative acts lacking in the
overlaps typical of face-to-face communication. This is an important point
to stress given the common perception that the web is an inherently multidi-
rectional, hypertextual environment where users are free to create their own
paths as they go along (Castells 2001).

How do these two forms of sociality articulate with the suburb's field
of residential affairs? As we might expect, they do so in different ways.
While residents' committee sociality sits right on the main fault line running through the field (namely the divide between governmental and citizens' field sectors), the suburb's main web forum is resolutely independent.
As a result, committee meetings are awkward occasions in which residents,
councillors and politicians are often at loggerheads over unresolved local
issues, whereas web forum threads are regular sites of 'third place' cordiality
(Oldenburg 1989). However, under certain field conditions (such as a local
political scandal) the online mood can change very swiftly from conviviality to indignation, sometimes leading to episodes of collective mobilization
against the authorities. At such times, the online forum may swiftly mutate
into an arena, a 'bounded spatial unit in which precise, visible antagonists,
individual or corporate, contend with one another for prizes and/or honour'
(Turner 1974: 132–133). As we said earlier, arenas are 'explicit frames' in
which 'nothing is left merely implied', and major decisions are taken in public view (ibid.: 134). In a clear reference to Goffman's dramaturgical model,
Turner adds that, in an arena: 'Action is definite, people outspoken; the

chips are down. Intrigue may be backstage, but the stage it is back of is the open arena' (ibid.: 134). Keen to distance himself from game theory and other rational-actor approaches popular among political anthropologists at the time, Turner emphasizes that an arena is neither a market nor a forum, although they can both become one 'under appropriate field conditions' (ibid.: 134). Such conditions were met in Subang Jaya on a number of occasions during the period covered by my research, resulting in the rapid yet ephemeral expansion of the field. As arenas change, so do the geographical boundaries and socio-technical activities of the political field, expanding and contracting as the social drama unfolds.

In sum, by drawing inspiration and terminology both from the field traditions of the Manchester School and Bourdieu, the concept of field (and its cognates) allowed me to analyse internet-mediated relations between Subang Jaya's local authorities and residents by treating them not as discrete entities but rather relationally, as two sectors of the porous, conflict-prone realm that I call the field of residential affairs. This concept also allowed me to discard totalizing notions such as 'community sociality' in favour of a plural understanding of field-related socialities.

CONCLUSION

In their edited volume *State Formation: Anthropological Perspectives*, Krohn-Hansen and Nustad (2005) argue persuasively for the need to disaggregate 'the state' ethnographically. Through a series of case studies, they explore actual states from a range of positions, laying to rest the idea of states as monoliths. Similarly, in this chapter I have argued for the need to disaggregate the concept of field through ethnographic and other empirical techniques. Fields may be generally smaller than states, but they are still internally diverse configurations of people, practices and technologies.

Before I could proceed with this argument, however, I had to carry out some ground clearing. First, I showed that field theory is not the preserve of Bourdieu and his heirs – other field traditions can be brought into the picture as well, including that of the Manchester School of anthropology. Second, I suggested that concepts should not be imprisoned behind the walls of any single theoretical edifice or shackled to any other concepts. Thus there is no reason to assume that the concept of field can only be used in relation to Bourdieu's capital and habitus, an assumption commonly made in the field-theoretical literature (e.g. Houston 2002). Instead, I explored the analytical potential of field through a number of empirical studies, including my own fieldwork in Malaysia and Spain. The outcome was a new way of thinking about fields as dynamic configurations of practices, games and socialities rather than the conservative domains of habitual practice that we normally take them to be.

Future efforts to pluralize the concept of field would benefit from adding a vertical dimension to the horizontal dimension of field elements (games, practices, socialities and so forth) analysed here. For example, I mentioned the *indignados*'s game of 'playing the algorithm' on Twitter as a form of activist agenda-setting, but had little to say about the 'great game' of the protest-field as a whole. In all fields of endeavour, even in protest movements that espouse the ideal of horizontality, some players will have access to the field's meta-level (where struggles over the very nature of the field take place), while others will operate exclusively at the ground level, playing games that do not challenge the existing arrangements.

Another question meriting further investigation is whether we should distinguish between fields of practice (anthropology, art, rock climbing) and fields of action (protests, war, disaster relief), with Bourdieu's field lexicon perhaps being more suited to the former and Turner's to the latter type of social formation. While there is no doubt that an anthropologist can be aptly described in field terms as a practitioner within the field of anthropology, it is far less clear that the same can be said of a protester with regards to the 'field' formed around an ephemeral protest. How durable must a field be to generate its own specialist practitioners? When does a participant become a practitioner? Are all field practitioners field agents, but not vice versa? When does an ensemble of practices and/or actions become a field?

ACKNOWLEDGEMENTS

Parts of this chapter have been adapted from my book *Localizing the Internet: An Anthropological Account* (Oxford: Berghahn, 2010).

NOTES

1. Definitions taken from the *Collins English Dictionary* (2012). Retrieved on 12 August 2014 from: www.collinsdictionary.com/dictionary/english/games.

REFERENCES

Amit, V., and N. Rapport. 2002. *The Trouble with Community: Anthropological Reflections on Movement, Identity and Collectivity*. London: Pluto Press.

Appadurai, A. 1996. *Modernity at Large: Cultural Dimensions of Globalization*. Minneapolis: University of Minnesota Press.

Barnes, J.A. 1954. 'Class and Committees in a Norwegian Island Parish', *Human Relations* 7: 39–58.

Benson, R. 2007. 'After Habermas: The Revival of a Macro-sociology of Media', unpublished paper presented at the American Sociological Association Annual Conference, New York, 11 August.

Benson, R., and E. Neveu. 2005. 'Introduction: Field Theory as a Work in Progress', in R. Benson and E. Neveu (eds), *Bourdieu and the Journalistic Field*. Cambridge: Polity Press, pp.1–25.

Born, G. 2010. 'The Social and the Aesthetic: For a Post-Bourdieuian Theory of Cultural Production', *Cultural Sociology* 4(2): 1–38.

Bott, E. 1955. 'Urban Families: Conjugal Roles and Social Network', *Human Relations* 8(4): 345–384.

—— 1957. *Family and Social Networks*. London: Tavistock.

Bourdieu, P. 1990. *In Other Words: Essays towards a Reflexive Sociology*. Stanford: Stanford University Press.

—— 1993. *The Field of Cultural Production*. Cambridge: Polity Press.

—— 1996. *The Rules of Art: Genesis and Structure of the Literary Field*. Cambridge: Polity Press.

Bourdieu, P., and L.J. Wacquant. 1992. *An Invitation to Reflexive Sociology*. Chicago: University of Chicago Press.

Bräuchler, B., and J. Postill (eds). 2010. *Theorising Media and Practice*. Oxford: Berghahn.

Butler, J. 1999. 'Performativity's Social Magic', in R. Shusterman (ed.), *Bourdieu: A Critical Reader*. Oxford: Blackwell, pp. 113–128.

Calhoun, C. 1992. 'Introduction: Habermas and the Public Sphere', in C. Calhoun (ed.), *Habermas and the Public Sphere*. Cambridge, MA: MIT Press, pp.1–50.

Castells, M. 2001. *The Internet Galaxy*. Oxford: Oxford University Press.

Christensen, T., and I. Røpke. 2010. 'Can Practice Theory Inspire Studies of ICTs in Everyday Life?' in B. Bräuchler and J. Postill (eds), *Theorising Media and Practice*. Oxford: Berghahn, pp.233–256.

Couldry, N. 2003. 'Media Meta-capital: Extending the Range of Bourdieu's Field Theory', *Theory and Society* 32(5/6): 653–677.

—— 2004. 'Theorising Media as Practice', *Social Semiotics* 14(2): 115–132.

—— 2007. 'Bourdieu and the Media: The Promise and Limits of Field Theory (Review of Benson and Neveu, 2005)', *Theory and Society* 36(2): 209–213.

Crossley, N. 2002. 'Global Anti-corporate Struggle: A Preliminary Analysis', *British Journal of Sociology* 53(4): 667–691.

Cullum, B. 2010. 'What Makes a Twitter Hashtag Successful? *Movements.org*, 17 December. Retrieved on 12 August 2014 from: https://archive.today/sWPMv

de Nooy, W. 2003. 'Fields and Networks: Correspondence Analysis and Social Network Analysis in the Framework of Field Theory', *Poetics* 31: 305–327.

Emirbayer, M., and A. Mische. 1998. 'What Is Agency?' *American Journal of Sociology* 103(4): 962–1023.

Epstein, A.L. 1958. *Politics in an Urban African Community*. Manchester: Manchester University Press.

Evens, T.M.S., and D. Handelman (eds). 2006. *The Manchester School: Practice and Ethnographic Praxis in Anthropology*. Oxford: Berghahn.

Gartman, D. 2007. 'The Strength of Weak Programs in Cultural Sociology: A Critique of Alexander's Critique of Bourdieu', *Theory and Society* 36: 381–413.

Gee, J. 2005. 'Semiotic Social Spaces and Affinity Spaces', in D. Barton and K. Tusting (eds), *Beyond Communities of Practice*. Cambridge: Cambridge University Press, pp.214–232.

Gell, A. 1986. 'Newcomers to the Worlds of Goods: Consumption among the Muria Gonds', in A. Appadurai (ed.), *The Social Life of Things: Commodities in Cultural Perspective*. Cambridge: Cambridge University Press, pp.110–138.

Georgakakis, D., and J. Weisbein. 2010. 'From Above and From Below: A Political Sociology of European Actors', *Comparative European Politics* 8(1): 93–109.

Gledhill, J. 2000. *Power and its Disguises: Anthropological Perspectives on Politics*. London: Pluto.

Go, J. 2008. 'Global Fields and Imperial Forms: Field Theory and the US and British Empires', *Sociological Theory* 26(3): 201–229.

Guggenheim, M., and J. Potthast. 2012. 'Symmetrical Twins: On the Relationship between Actor-Network Theory and the Sociology of Critical Capacities', *European Journal of Social Theory* 15: 157–178.

Haluza-DeLay, R. 2008. 'A Theory of Practice for Social Movements: Environmentalism and Ecological Habitus', *Mobilization* 13(2): 205–218.

Hine, C. 2000. *Virtual Ethnography*. London: Sage.

Hobart, M. 1990. 'Who Do You Think You Are? The Authorized Balinese', in R. Fardon (ed.), *Localizing Strategies: The Regionalization of Ethnographic Accounts*. Edinburgh: Scottish Academic Press, pp.303–338.

Houston, S. 2002. 'Reflecting on Habitus, Field and Capital: Towards a Culturally Sensitive Social Work', *Journal of Social Work* 2: 149–167.

Ibrahim, Y. 2011. 'Political Distinction in the British Anti-Capitalist Movement', *Sociology*, 45(2): 318–334.

Jean-Klein, I. 2003. 'Into Committees, out of the House? Familiar Forms in the Organization of Palestinian Committee Activism during the First Intifada', *American Ethnologist* 30(4): 556–577.

Jenkins, R. 2002. *Pierre Bourdieu*, 2nd edn. London: Routledge.

Johnson, R. 1993. 'Pierre Bourdieu on Art, Literature and Culture', in P. Bourdieu, *The Field of Cultural Production*. Cambridge: Polity, pp.1–25.

Juris, J.S. 2008. *Networking Futures: The Movements against Corporate Globalization*. Durham, NC: Duke University Press.

Knox, H., M. Savage and P. Harvey. 2006. 'Social Networks and the Study of Relations: Networks as Method, Metaphor and Form', *Economy and Society* 35(1): 113–140.

Krause, M. 2011. 'Reporting and the Transformations of the Journalistic Field: US News Media, 1890–2000', *Media, Culture and Society* 33(1): 89–104.

Krohn-Hansen, C., and K. Nustad (eds). 2005. *State Formation: Anthropological Perspectives*. London: Pluto.

Lamont, M. 1987. 'How to Become a Dominant French Philosopher: The Case of Jacques Derrida', *American Journal of Sociology* 93: 584–622.

Lau, R.K.W. 2004. 'Habitus and the Practical Logic of Practice', *Sociology* 38(2): 369–387.

McAdam, D. 1982. *Political Process and the Development of Black Insurgency*. Chicago: University of Chicago Press.

Martin, J.L. 2003. 'What Is Field Theory?' *American Journal of Sociology* 109: 1–49.

Mesny, A. 2002. 'A View on Bourdieu's Legacy: Sens Pratique v. Hysteresis', *Canadian Journal of Sociology* 27(1): 59–67.

Mitchell, J.C. 1956. *The Kalela Dance: Aspects of Social Relationships among Urban Africans in Northern Rhodesia*. Manchester: Manchester University Press.

—— (ed.). 1969. *Social Networks in Urban Situations*. Manchester: Manchester University Press.

Moore, P. 2013. '"On the Tools": The Physical Work of Building and Renovating Houses in Perth, Western Australia', in S. Pink, D. Tutt and A. Dainty (eds), *Ethnographic Research in the Construction Industry*. New York: Routledge, pp.58–72.

Oldenburg, R. 1989. *The Great Good Place: Cafes, Coffee Shops, Community Centers, Beauty Parlors, General Stores, Bars, Hangouts, and How They Get You Through the Day*. New York: Paragon House.

Panofsky, A. 2011. 'Field Analysis and Interdisciplinary Science: Scientific Capital Exchange in Behavior Genetics', *Minerva* 49(3): 295–316.

Peterson, M.A. 2010. '"But It Is My Habit to Read the *Times*": Metaculture and Practice in the Reading of Indian Newspapers', in B. Bräuchler and J. Postill (eds), *Theorising Media and Practice*. Oxford: Berghahn, pp.127–145.

Pink, S. 2008 'Re-thinking Contemporary Activism: From Community to Emplaced Sociality', *Ethnos* 73(2): 163–188.

Postill, J. 2008. 'Localizing the Internet beyond Communities and Networks', *New Media and Society* 10: 413–431.

—— 2011. *Localizing the Internet: An Anthropological Account*. Oxford: Berghahn.

Prior, N. 2008. 'Putting a Glitch in the Field: Bourdieu, Actor Network Theory and Contemporary Music', *Cultural Sociology* 2(3): 301–319.

Reed-Danahay, D. 2005. *Locating Bourdieu*. Bloomington: Indiana University Press.

Sallaz, J.J. 2006. 'The Making of the Global Gambling Industry: An Application and Extension of Field Theory', *Theory and Society* 35(3): 265–297.

Sallaz, J.J., and J. Zavisca. 2007. 'Bourdieu in American Sociology, 1980–2004', *Annual Review of Sociology* 33: 21–41.

Sanjek, R. 1996. 'Network Analysis', in A. Barnard and J. Spencer (eds), *Encyclopedia of Social and Cultural Anthropology*. London: Routledge, pp.396–397.

Spitulnik, D. 1996. 'The Social Circulation of Media Discourse and the Mediation of Communities', *Journal of Linguistic Anthropology* 6(2): 161–187.

Street, B. 2000. 'Literacy Events and Literacy Practices', in M. Martin-Jones and K. Jones (eds), *Multilingual Literacies: Comparative Perspectives on Research and Practice*. Amsterdam: John Benjamin, pp.17–29.

Swartz, D. 1997. *Culture and Power: The Sociology of Pierre Bourdieu*. Chicago: University of Chicago Press.

Swartz, D., V. Turner and A. Tuden (eds). 1966. *Political Anthropology*. Chicago: Aldine.

Thomson, P. 2005. 'Bringing Bourdieu to Policy Sociology: Codification, Misrecognition and Exchange Value in the UK Context', *Journal of Education Policy* 20(6): 741–758.

Turner, V. 1957. *Schism and Continuity in an African Society: A Study of Ndembu Village Life*. Manchester: Manchester University Press.

—— 1974. *Dramas, Fields and Metaphors: Symbolic Action in Human Society*. Ithaca, NY: Cornell University Press.

Warde, A. 2004 'Practice and Field: Revising Bourdieusian Concepts', CRIC Discussion Paper no. 65. Manchester: Centre for Research on Innovation and Competition, University of Manchester. Retrieved on 12 August 2014 from: http://www.cric.ac.uk/cric/pdfs/dp65.pdf

Wenger, E. 1998. *Communities of Practice: Learning, Meaning, and Identity*. New York: Cambridge University Press.

Wittel, A. 2001. 'Toward a Network Sociality', *Theory, Culture and Society* 18(6): 51–76.

3

Social Space
Distance, Proximity and Thresholds of Affinity

Deborah Reed-Danahay

The phrase social space appears frequently in recent scholarship, signalling in part the influence of the so-called 'spatial turn' in the social sciences and humanities.[1] It is not always so obvious, however, what is meant by this term when it is used. Moreover, the historical legacy of ideas about social space in the anthropological and sociological literature is not always recognized in contemporary deployments of this phrase. Social space can be characterized as something localized and fairly specific – to refer, for instance, to an urban market (Ilcan 1999) or a physical education class (Hunter 2004). It has also been used more broadly, as in the social space of postmodernism (Rouse 1991), the social space of ethnic identity (Smith 1992) and transnational social spaces (Pries 2001; Faist and Özveron 2004). As noted by Marchetti (2011: 17), current thinking about social space interrogates the relationship between physical and social space. The ideas of 'non-place' (Augé 1995) and of 'excluded space' (Munn 1996) suggest that the ways in which a physical or terrestrial space constitute or deny a social space are complex. At the same time, there can be forms of interaction and social positioning in social spaces that are not directly tied to co-presence in a physical place – a feature of internet communication.[2] Previous anthropological research has illuminated the ways in which perceptions and uses of space and time are socially and culturally constructed. Although space and time are linked closely,[3] I focus primarily on space in this chapter.

There has already been much attention paid to the built or material environment as geographic or physical spaces that are also social spaces (Harvey 1990, 2005; Lefebvre 1991; Low 1996; Fogle 2011), but less work examines the ways in which sociality is imagined in spatial terms. Rather than view social space as a container for sociality,[4] which is the predominant way in which this phrase is used, I suggest that social space be recognized as a loose and perhaps even 'fuzzy' concept that is nevertheless helpful in thinking about the politics, metaphors and uses of ideas about spatial relationships by individuals and groups.

Like social field, social space is a theoretical construct that attempts to capture the spatiality inherent in sociality, and provide tools for understanding social interactions and connections as well as their absence. The most useful way to distinguish between these concepts is to consider how they articulate physical or geographic place and sociality. The term field (see Postill, this volume) is most often used to describe forms of social action or interaction in which geographic space is less important than social action, and given more or less attention depending on the analyst. Social space, in contrast, is a concept for which the question of the relationship between social and physical or geographic space is central. I suggest that the lens of social space provides perspectives on the landscape of possibilities, worldviews and values in which fields may emerge with more or less permanency and autonomy. Social space also engages with concepts of spatiality as understood, enacted and perceived by ethnographic research participants.

In the first part of this chapter, I trace a brief history of ideas about affinity, mobility and inclusion/exclusion that employ metaphors of 'social space' to describe the setting, parameters and boundaries (fluid and more fixed) of sociality. I review discussions of social space in foundational work, as well as in more recent approaches, organized into three overlapping categories of inquiry: territory; thresholds; and social distance and proximity. In the second section, I discuss in more detail the work of Pierre Bourdieu on social space and the relationship between field and space in his work. In the third part, I turn to the relevance of social space for studies of affiliation and belonging among immigrants. I provide a case study with material drawn from ethnographic research I have conducted among Vietnamese Americans to show how a focus on positionings and group visibility in social space contribute to understandings of processes of emplacement for migrants.

TERRITORY, THRESHOLDS AND PROXIMITY

Territory

One approach to social space in sociology and anthropology has been to consider how much the physical environment, or geographic space, should (or can) be analytically separated from the more abstract idea of one's position in an imagined social space that has to do with moral values, status, prestige, affinity, identity and so on. Emile Durkheim and Marcel Mauss were fundamental to the development of ideas about social space that continue to influence anthropological thought today. Durkheim's emphasis on both cognitive and empirical aspects of social life, collective representations and classification (see Durkheim and Mauss 1963; Durkheim 1995) led him to see social space as reflecting social organization.[5] Earlier anthropological research, focusing primarily on village settings and employing structural-functionalist types of analysis, took for granted the overlap between territorial space and social space. This approach is associated with what Jonathan Spencer (1995) criticized as an overemphasis on social morphology and an attempt to classify various forms of social groupings instead of investigating social processes. The paradigmatic view prevalent in social theory during most of the nineteenth and into the early twentieth century was that a social group was associated with a geographical territory, and that this relationship was a central part of social structure and sociality.

In an essay tracing ideas of social space in earlier twentieth-century social anthropology, Hilda Kuper cautioned that we must 'be wary not to equate space, as a feature of the physical (tangible) world, with "social space"' (Kuper 1972: 411). As Kuper noted, Durkheim's ideas about social space were carried forward in different ways by Radcliffe-Brown and Evans-Pritchard. The empirical emphasis was more prevalent in Radcliffe-Brown's work and subsequent re-workings by Gluckman and Turner, among others, with an emphasis on localities and, later, networks, fields, or 'systems on the ground' (ibid.: 412). For Evans-Pritchard, the cognitive aspects of social space were given more emphasis, and his spatial analysis of the Nuer focused on 'ideational elements' of social space (ibid.: 413). Based on her own fieldwork in Swaziland (in south-east Africa), Kuper drew attention to what she calls 'sites' or social spaces in which political events take place. According to Kuper, Kenneth Burke's idea of the scene was similar to the approach she took in her analysis of the relationship between space and political events. She provided as an example the changing location of meetings at the end of colonial rule in Swaziland, moved to different 'sites' in order to express physical and cultural closeness or distance. One of her informants spoke of feeling closer to ancestors in meetings held at a site related to national gatherings and royal rituals of Swazi leaders, and of feeling not connected to ancestors when meeting at a place related to the British rulers. Kuper argued that there is a politics of space related to where events are held, and that this relates to emotions and feelings of social distance or proximity. Her work points to the ways in which social space, in contrast to the idea of field, incorporates both the physical and social elements of distance and proximity.

Two examples from work published in the 1950s illustrate contrasting ways to treat the complex relationships between territorial (physical) and social space. Neither Max Gluckman nor Clifford Geertz used the phrase 'social space' in the articles to which I will turn, but their work dealt with issues of social proximity and distance and the relationship between social and territorial space. In his classic essay 'Peace in the Feud', a reworking of Evans-Pritchard's Nuer material to discuss the ways that social conflicts are paradoxically also the source of social cohesion, Gluckman (1955) examined relationships of proximity and distance in terms of both social space and territorial space. Because of the seasonal mobility and clan exogamy of the Nuer, the 'local community' consisted of not only close relatives who unite in times of feud but also 'enemies', and the vengeance group is scattered territorially. Therefore, the 'social space' of the Nuer clan in terms of social affinities was a very broad territorial unit, expanding beyond the village. Relations of closeness and distance that are social (such as those who are distant and enemies versus those who are close and agnatic kin) did not correspond directly to the territorial boundary of the village and were, moreover, shifting and not static. The wider 'social space' of the Nuer as a unit was in equilibrium, however, according to Gluckman's model, despite the changing positions of individuals within it as their alliances shifted according to the situation at hand. It was the fluidity of social distance and proximity that kept the possibilities of violence in check, restraining the formation of static groups linked directly to bounded territories.

In a somewhat different juxtaposition of what I would call geographic or territorial space and social space, Clifford Geertz (1957) examined urbanization in Java through the lens of a funeral that provoked and displayed social conflicts. Geertz suggested that in traditional Javanese villages, social closeness was connected to geographical closeness, so that there was a coherence of the social and territorial unit. The physical placement of people (geographically close or distant) corresponded to what Geertz referred to as social structure – 'the form that action takes, the actually existing network of social relations' (ibid.: 33). He contrasted this from what he referred to as 'feelings' and 'judgments' about social interaction (which could include ideas of social distance or proximity) related to culture – 'the fabric of meaning in terms of which human beings interpret their experience and guide their action' (ibid.: 33). According to Geertz, a conflict surrounding the funeral of a young boy illustrated social changes occurring in Java 'perhaps most aptly characterized as a shift from a situation in which the primary integrative ties between individuals (or between families) were phrased in terms of geographical proximity to one in which they were phrased in terms of ideological like-mindedness' (ibid.: 36). Here Geertz was making a distinction between social space in terms of positioning in a moral universe, one in which people can be seen as more or less socially close or 'like-minded', and a geographic space in which people may or may not feel socially close even if they live next to one another, as in the case of the city. Although their approaches to social cohesion and conflict varied in many ways, Gluckman and Geertz were both attempting to distinguish between territorial and social space in their work as a way to include more of a focus on process in social analysis. Both were moving beyond a focus on isolated villages to understand either the social space of an ethnic group (the Nuer) or of cities in an emerging nation-state (Indonesia).[6]

Recent approaches to globalization and contemporary life that emphasize flows, scapes and transnationalism continue this thread of work aimed at decoupling assumptions about the correspondence between social and geographic space. There has been attention, especially since the 1990s, to what Pratt (1992) called 'contact zones' – permeable borders of social spaces. Recent scholarship (e.g. Sassen 2000) also questions nation-state boundaries as suitable units for social analysis. Appadurai (1996: 48) introduced the term 'ethnoscapes' to suggest ways in which landscapes of identity involve more than bounded, local places. He uses the term 'locality' to refer to 'actual social forms' like places, sites and neighbourhoods (ibid.: 204, n.1), and argues that locality is 'primarily relational and contextual rather than scalar or spatial' (ibid.: 178). With the term 'ethnoscape', Appadurai intended to 'get away from the idea that group identities necessarily imply that cultures need to be spatially bounded, historically unselfconscious, or ethnically homogeneous forms' (ibid.: 183). Along similar lines, Gupta and Ferguson have noted that the social sciences tend to represent space in terms of distinctive societies divided spatially and occupying '"naturally" discontinuous spaces' (Gupta and Ferguson 1992: 6). They drew attention to the ways in which space comes to be viewed as a place with a particular identity (ibid.: 8), when a demarcated physical space is associated with particular forms of social interaction.[7] Gupta and Ferguson's focus on interstitiality and Appadurai's focus on flows and scapes both remind us that social space cannot be assumed to overlap with bounded physical spaces or territories.

In an overview of recent trends in ethnography, Bruce Knauft has suggested that the new emphases on global flows does not signal an abandonment of a focus on place but, rather, more attention to 'specific networks of identity and geography' (Knauft 2006: 419). As Knauft observed, 'the anthropological study of phenomena that are bigger than a community and smaller than the world – nation-states, religions, ethnic or diasporic groups, NGOs, government institutions, regional mass media, public cultures, and so on – has greatly increased' (ibid.: 418). I argue that an emphasis on networks, with its actor-oriented approach, cannot, however, capture the wider social landscapes in which affiliations occur and the exclusions which are also part of these social spaces. This leads to the question of the boundaries and thresholds of sociality, a topic I explore in the next section.

Thresholds

A related issue to the problem of groups and territory is that of the limits of social space, and to thresholds of communication, feelings and affinities, and social interaction. This is also connected to the temporal aspect of social space. This was a concern in Claude Lévi-Strauss's structuralist approach to social space. Lévi-Strauss's approach, like that of British social anthropology, developed out of the Durkheimian tradition, but took a somewhat different turn. Lévi-Strauss (1963) outlined an approach to social space in traditional societies that linked social space and social time to perceptions of time and space. These perceptions were products of the social phenomena (underlying structures) that, as he phrased it, 'furnished' them. According to Lévi-Strauss, there is a relationship between social structure (as 'surface structure') and 'spatial structure', but these are not identical. In clarifying this point, he wrote:

> A large number of native societies have consciously chosen to project into space a schema of their institutions: thus, for instance, the circular distribution of Sioux camping sites and Ge villages in central Brazil; or the layout of towns, the network of roads, and the location of temples and shrines in ancient Peru. Study of these spatial phenomena permits us to grasp the natives' own conception of their social structure; and, through our examinations of the gaps and contradictions, the real structure, which is often very different from the natives' conception, becomes accessible. (ibid.: 332)

Lévi-Strauss introduced the element of time to that of social space by pointing out that a spatial configuration could be temporary (as in ritual or dance) or more durable, as in village layout. He employed the idea of 'isolates', a concept he borrowed from French demographers who looked at intermarrying groups and the prevalence of cross-cousin marriage, to suggest that cultural isolates can be found in urban as well as smaller-scale societies. We should see social groups as 'cultural units' (like isolates), according to Lévi-Strauss, and as communication structures. The borders of these units were the thresholds to their social space – the limit where rates and forms of communication weaken. In his writing about social space, Lévi-Strauss referred to the physical or geographical aspects of space, but also to underlying mental systems for the classification of space.

The idea of spatial settings as comprised of physical boundaries and communication networks, which may or may not coincide with the values and traditions associated with social space, central to Lévi-Strauss's idea of cultural isolates, was also present in the work of Paul-Henri Chombart de Lauwe (1965). In his research on French urban space in the 1950s and 1960s, Chombart de Lauwe developed ideas related to 'objective' and 'subjective' social space. However, unlike Lévi-Strauss, he was more concerned with the perceptions of social actors and their locations in space. For Chombart de Lauwe, social space had to be examined historically and was, in large part, 'the division of space according to the particular norms of a group' (1965: 24; my translation). As Ann Buttimer explains, Chombart de Lauwe introduced a hierarchy of urban social spaces that captured an ever-widening dimension of the 'orbits of group social activity' (Buttimer 1969: 421), suggesting also that there are 'thresholds in space beyond which certain groups cannot travel without experiencing frustrations, tensions, and feelings of anomie' (ibid.: 421). This corresponds to Lévi-Strauss's emphasis on the weakening of communication at the boundaries of cultural 'isolates' (social spaces).

Thresholds of social belonging or exclusion were a central theme in Barth's collection on ethnic groups and boundaries (Barth 1969), with its actor-oriented attention to the ways that ethnicity is shaped through boundaries that are more or less permeable. For Barth, it was more productive to focus on these borders or thresholds rather than to attempt to characterize the cultural content within what were assumed to be discrete ethnic groups. Barth's volume pointed out that such groups are products of social processes. In his essay on Norwegian and Lapp (or Sami) ethnicity,[8] Eidheim explicitly used the concept of 'social space' (Eidheim 1969: 44) to argue that research should not focus on 'a central fixed point' but rather on social landscapes, in which people have orientations and social aspirations (ibid.: 45). Eidheim was influenced by Erving Goffman, to whose work I will shortly turn, and looked at both public and private spheres of sociality. Drawing upon the idea of a sphere of interaction, which is how he conceptualized social space, Eidheim wrote: 'I have used the term sphere of interaction to conceptualize "public life" and "Lappish secret life" respectively. One might alternatively use the term network and define network as a field of relations in which exchangeable values flow,

thus taking exchange in a wide and behaviouristic sense' (ibid.: 53). Eidheim uses in that passage three concepts related to 'sociality' (network,
field, social space) that are closely related. The social space is the 'sphere
of interaction' in which Sami perform a public and a more private version
of their identity.

A focus on thresholds in sociality is also found in the work of Erving
Goffman, who described 'territories of the self' (Goffman 1971) and 'regions' (Goffman 1959) as a way to explore an individual's social space and
its contours and limits. Rather than take a group as a unit for analysis,
Goffman, like many of the contributors to Barth's volume, started from
the perspective of the social actor. In his performative theory of social
interaction, Goffman defined region as 'any place that is bounded to some
degree by barriers of perception' (ibid.: 106). These regions are connected
to Goffman's use of the stage metaphor, and there are back and front regions, with the former being hidden from the 'audience'. In a later discussion of 'territories of the self' (Goffman 1971), Goffman looked at the
claims made about and boundaries of such territories. In one example, he
distinguished between 'fixed' territory such as a house, and 'situational'
territory such as a park bench (ibid.: 29). This approach to social space is
influenced by ethology, and focuses on personal space from the individual's point of view.[9] Goffman's use of territory was not, therefore, that of a
social group but that of an individual. He did, however, point out that the
higher status person will have access to and dominance over a larger spatial territory, and also exert control across boundaries (ibid.: 41).

In a broad sense, Goffman articulated a way to unpack the positioning
of the individual within a wider social space with an emphasis on face-to-
face interaction. In an essay entitled 'Tightness and Looseness', Goffman
(1963) examined gatherings as social spaces in which individuals can display more or less 'presence' or engagement. He also pointed out that social
situations, or gatherings, can have more or less tightly proscribed obligations about the types of behaviour that can be displayed. What Goffman
referred to as the tightness–looseness continuum will vary cross-culturally
(for instance, social interactions on a public street in France versus those
in Britain) and also within cultures (a theatre versus a public park). Goffman showed that individuals are differently positioned in such gatherings
depending on their degree of engagement and their social status. For the
most part, his interest in social space focused on temporary gatherings,
where physical space and social space come together for a limited period
of time.

A focus on the physical locations of social space can lead to seeing
such spaces as 'containers' for sociality, rather than unpacking the rela-

tionships between space, place, and sociality. In a recent attempt to go beyond 'container' approaches to the social spaces in cities, Corsin Jiménez (2003) made a case for seeing space as the 'capacity of social relationships' rather than in terms of the forms of space (landscape or place), when identity is not linked to specific territories. Based on his research in a mining city in a desert region of Chile, Corsin Jiménez wrote:

> Social relationships are inherently spatial, and space an instrument and dimension of people's sociality. Social life is no longer to be seen as unfolding through space but with space, that is, spatially. Space is no longer 'out there', but a condition or faculty – a capacity – of social relationships. It is what people do, not where they are. (ibid.: 140)

Here the uncoupling of territorial fixity and social space comes from ethnographic research in a city seen by its inhabitants as 'unhealthy, dirty, and potentially dangerous' (ibid.: 144), where place does not have value in and of itself but only through social relationships. A shopping district, in this example, becomes not a setting (or container) for sociality but an aspect of social relationships through which what Corsin Jiménez called 'material elements' (restaurants, parks, shops, cinemas) are linked to social practices such as walks and outings. In this approach, the threshold of a social space has more to do with social practices and relationships than physical location.

Closely connected to understandings of threshold in anthropology is the topic of borders, which has in most recent studies centred primarily on the US–Mexico border, and new border zones in Europe related to developments in the European Union and the changes related to post-socialism. As Sarah Green has written, renewed interest in borders considers the 'historical variability of the form and purpose of borders' (Green 2013: 349). In their useful historical overview of the anthropological literature on boundaries, Donnan and Wilson observed that in structural-functionalist approaches, boundaries were of relevance only in order to help 'define and delimit the "edges" of their subject matter' (Donnan and Wilson 1999: 20). In more recent times, tropes of borders are widespread in scholarly research not for the purposes of closing off social units and investigating social identities either within units or even solely at the borders of units but, rather, in order to understand articulations of power and social practices surrounding the construction and control of borders. Wilson and Donnan's (2012) recent edited collection on borders is testament to the enduring interest in the relationships between territory, geopolitical social units and culture in anthropological research.

Distance and Proximity

The prevalence of spatial metaphors in talk about sociality was noted in an early essay by Pitirim Sorokin, a Russian-American sociologist and critic of Simmel (Wolff 1950: xlvi, n.32). Sorokin identified expressions that 'indicate that there is something which could be styled "social space"' (Sorokin 1927: 3). These common phrases include '"upper and lower classes", "social promotion", "N.N. is a climber", "his social position is very high", "they are very near socially", "right and left party", and "there is a great social distance"' (ibid.: 3).[10] Metaphors of social position that include ideas of being inside or outside, higher or lower, peripheral or central are frequently employed by anthropologists and by the people they study. These verbal expressions signal that there is a consciousness about positions in social space. Spatial imagery is also intimately tied to memory, as noted by Maurice Halbwachs (1980) in his discussion of space and collective memory.

Perceptions and positionings related to distance and proximity in social space (often distinct from geographic space) constitute another broad category for thinking about sociality and social space. Georg Simmel brought social space to the fore in his brief essay 'The Stranger' (Simmel and Wolff 1950: 402–408). Simmel described the stranger as: 'fixed within a particular spatial group, or within a group whose boundaries are similar to spatial boundaries. But his position in this group is determined, essentially, by the fact that he has not belonged to it from the beginning, that he imports qualities into it, which do not and cannot stem from the group itself' (ibid.: 402). Simmel addressed issues of 'nearness' and 'remoteness' that are part of social space more so than physical space, noting that the stranger is near but socially remote. The stranger is different from the foreigner, who lives outside the physical boundaries of space, and is therefore a member of the group and not outside it. As Simmel wrote, this figure is 'near and far at the same time' (ibid.: 407). Simmel was particularly interested in boundaries related to social space, and argued that the perception of being outside space (Simmel and Wolff 1950: 140), analogous to the idea of timelessness, was a feature of 'supra-spatial structures' that have no relationship to any particular space but a link to all space (as in the Catholic Church), or have a 'real and fundamental solidarity with space everywhere' (as in the nation-state). Frank J. Lechner has noted that Simmel 'makes the case that many forms of sociation cannot be understood without taking into account both their spatial context and their use of space' (Lechner 1991: 198). He pointed to Simmel's focus on spatial aspects of social life, particularly mobility and migration, arguing that Simmel was interested in increasing abstraction in our understandings of collectivity, so that 'for many practical purposes we no longer have to be physically present and that concrete social settings matter less and less for transactions' (ibid.: 200).

Building upon Simmel's work on the position of the stranger in social space, Susan Ilcan (1999) focused on what she refers to as the 'micropolitics of differentiation' in north-western Turkey. Gypsies, itinerant merchants, immigrants and tourists are constructed as 'strangers' in this context – objects of 'social and political exclusion' (ibid.: 243). Ilcan used the social space of a market town to explore the encounters between locals and those constituted as strangers. She concluded that 'encounters with strangers are not merely about relations between self and other but about perceptions of space, or direction, settlements, inhabitants, proximity and distance, absence and presence' (ibid.: 254). In this work, Ilcan deployed the bounded market town as a space in which to examine the social positions and positioning related to sociality within it.

Sorokin contributed to ideas of social positioning and positions by emphasizing that social space should not be considered the same as what he termed 'geometrical space', referring to physical space. Sorokin illustrated this point by suggesting that a king and his servant were frequently close in 'geometrical space' but distant in 'social space' given their different statuses (Sorokin 1927: 3). He also noted that those distant in 'geometrical space' could be close in 'social space', using as one example that of generals who hold the same rank in the army but may be stationed far from each other, in different nations. For Sorokin, a person's position in social space is composed of several features, including their family status, citizenship and nationality, religious affiliation, occupational group, political party, economic status, race and so on (ibid.: 5). From this it follows that 'human beings, who are members of the same social groups and who within each of these groups have the same function, are in an identical social position' (ibid.: 6). Sorokin also argued that it is necessary to locate people in both horizontal and vertical space to understand their position. To know, for example, that a person was Roman Catholic, which is a horizontal position, would not be sufficient information to locate them in social space; it would also be important to know their vertical position – that related to social stratification. A bishop and a parishioner hold different vertical positions, and are therefore differently positioned in social space despite their shared horizontal position.

Sorokin concluded that there is always a tension in societies between what he called 'flattening' and 'height' in terms of social stratification and the differentiation of positions this entails. He considered the effects of social mobility, arguing that although a society with low mobility tends to have more social order, the flexibility that comes with more fluid social situations permits a more adaptable and resilient situation, so that 'the

lines of solidarity and antagonism in a mobile society become more flexible and more changeable' (ibid.: 540). In situations of high social mobility
(both horizontal and vertical), Sorokin argued, we need to know a person's
'whole curriculum' (ibid.: 542) in terms of their past and future trajectory in
order to know their position in social space. Sorokin connected this trend
of increasing social mobility with a rise in individualism and new forms of
cosmopolitanism and internationalism (ibid.: 543).

  In more recent work, Pierre Bourdieu and Henri Lefebvre investigated
the ways in which distance and proximity to power could occur in both social and physical space. Each drew attention to the idea that in order to have
a social existence, a group must have a spatial existence, and both saw space
as a social construction (following Lévi-Strauss). Lefebvre viewed physical,
mental and social space as domains that cannot be seen to neatly overlap
(Lefebvre 1991: 11). For Lefebvre (ibid.: 38–39), space in neo-capitalist societies includes social practice (linked to particular societies and economic
structures); representations of space (associated with planners and architects
who create the dominant physical spaces in society); and representational
spaces (space as lived and understood through symbols and images by users
who are primarily those of the dominated classes in society).

BOURDIEU AND SOCIAL SPACE

I will here address the ideas of Bourdieu on social space at some length
because they provide an opening for understandings of how physical and
social space connect in ways that can inform sociality. Few who cite the work
of figures such as David Harvey, Henri Lefebvre or Michel de Certeau have
recognized Bourdieu's potential contributions to the 'spatial turn'. Critical
work on Bourdieu produced by scholars in a wide range of disciplines in the
humanities and social sciences emphasizes his deployment of the term 'field'
(see Postill, this volume) at the expense of attention to social space. This is,
I argue, due in large part to Bourdieu's own use of social space (*espace social*)
and social field (*champ*) in both more general and more specific ways, and
to the fact that distinctions between Bourdieu's understandings of field and
social space are often overlooked by readers.[11] Even though field is a spatial
metaphor, Bourdieu's use of the term does not articulate physical and social
space, as does his concept of social space. The idea of field, which became
more explicit in Bourdieu's work over time, is a framework intended to explain the ways in which power and knowledge coalesce in particular realms
of society (education, literature, journalism) that become understood as relatively autonomous 'fields'. Social space, on the other hand, is a theme which

can be traced throughout Bourdieu's career, and is a more general concept expressing articulations between physical space and sociality. It is used by Bourdieu to study the ways in which groups form and take shape in society, and to explore metaphors of social distance and proximity.

For Bourdieu, physical and social space were closely related. He wrote that 'social space tends to be translated, with more or less distortion, into physical space, in the form of a certain arrangement of agents and properties', and argued, sounding like Durkheim or Lévi-Strauss, that physical space is 'reified social space' (Bourdieu 2000: 134). Bourdieu also argued that the places or localizations that people inhabit are related to their position in social space.

For Bourdieu, the habitus is a position within social space.[12] The concepts of habitus and social space are central to Bourdieu's theory of practice, through which he attempted to unravel the conceptual division between social structure and social practices. For Bourdieu, the habitus is an embodied orientation to the world which includes dispositions, tastes, and points of view. It is part of everyday, common-sense understandings of one's social world and how to behave within it. Therefore, it is not a conscious aspect of identity or action under most circumstances, and it is acquired through informal mechanisms of socialization from early childhood and onwards. Bourdieu referred to common-sense understandings of the world as *doxa*. These taken-for-granted assumptions about social reality vary, however, according to the orientations and dispositions of any particular acquired habitus. The orientations and dispositions of the habitus take on differing amounts of value within social space. Bourdieu referred to these as forms of capital – cultural, symbolic and social.

Bourdieu's theory of habitus refers frequently to spatial positioning, both in physical settings and in social life more generally. He wrote that 'each agent has a practical, bodily knowledge of her present and potential position in the social space, a "sense of one's place" as Goffman puts it' (ibid.: 184). Social space, according to Bourdieu, entails 'the relatively stable site of the co-existence of points of view' (ibid.: 183). In his elaborate diagrams showing connections between 'the space of social positions' and 'the space of life-styles' in *Distinction*, social agents are identified through their type of occupation, consumption tastes, education and residence on a rural-to-urban continuum related to population size (Bourdieu 1984: 128–129). Each diverse and stratified nation, such as France, will contain several different types of habitus related to social positions and social positioning within the social space of the nation. For example, people who work in small family-owned companies will have a different position in social space than executives in large corporations. Bourdieu conceptualized a nation as a social space containing a variety of habituses, each taking a different position and having a different trajectory (moving either towards higher or lower status over time). He also noted that those sharing a particular type of habitus will inhabit differently valued geographical settings, so that the rich will live in more pleasant and favoured neighbourhoods within cities. Bourdieu observed that a group's position in society is connected to their position in geographic space in concrete places. Social space is therefore about both positions in geographic space and in the more abstract arena of social positioning. Here, he seems influenced by Sorokin's earlier work.

The relationship between physical space and social space is such that, as Bourdieu noted, people distant in social space will often be distant in inhabited or physical space. Any particular person (or agent) is characterized by the place where they are situated in physical space more or less permanently (their place of residence, for example) and also by localizations (which can be temporary, such as spatial placements during ceremonies; or more permanent, such as a business address) which is in relation to the localization of other agents. These are forms of appropriations or consumptions of space – and can be displays of power. Bourdieu noted that 'the locus and the place occupied by an agent in appropriated social space are excellent indicators of his or her position in social space' (Bourdieu 1996: 11).

Because the idea of a group and its social visibility must be constructed in order to be recognized as such, according to Bourdieu, we can consider that groups are produced in social space, by means of 'symbolic struggles over the perception of the social world' (Bourdieu 1989: 20). This process entails modes of representation of an individual (the presentation of self) or of collectivity through 'demonstrations whose goal is to exhibit a group, its size, its strength, its cohesiveness, to make it exist visibly' (ibid.: 20). Symbolic power involves systems of naming, classifying and describing the social world or individuals within it, producing a group in social space. For Bourdieu, 'the spokesperson, in speaking of a group, on behalf of a group, surreptitiously posits the existence of the group in question, institutes the group, through the magical operation that is inherent in any act of naming' (Bourdieu 1985: 741).

Bourdieu focused primarily on positionings in social space related to social class in his writings, and his most explicit discussions (in *Distinction*) of social space refer to the space of the nation-state. These limitations and others (see Postill, this volume) of his approach to sociality do not, however, prohibit the application of his insights on spatiality to different populations and different social contexts. In the section below, I focus on the ways in which Bourdieu's ideas of social space can illuminate understandings of the existence and positioning of immigrant groups within social space at different levels of scale.

MIGRATION, AFFINITY AND BELONGING

Social Space and Emplacement

Work on migration has been a particularly salient arena for considerations of social space. The dilemmas of how to view the relationship between bounded territories, fixed places and social spaces defined in terms of spaces of affinity and belonging continue to be troublesome for studies of migrants. Is it all about global flows and transnational movement, or is it also about people trying to 'emplace' themselves in new environments? In an ethnographic study of Mexican migration to and from the United States, Roger Rouse wrote that 'the comforting modern imagery of nation-states and national languages, of coherent communities and consistent subjectivities, of dominant centres and distant margins no longer seems adequate' (Rouse 1991: 8). He criticized perspectives viewing migrants as moving from one coherent and bounded social space to another, and argued that neither the discourse of community associated with modernity nor that of centre/periphery associated with political economy were adequate for understandings of migration. It is the circuit of movement that is essential, he argued, and understandings of the importance of the border zone. According to Rouse, 'the place of the putative community – whether regional or national – is becoming little more than a site in which transnationally organized circuits of capital, labor, and communications intersect with one another and with local ways of life' (ibid.: 16). Rouse suggested that these transnational social spaces occur not just at the local level but more broadly, and that questions of scale were essential ones.

In another approach to migration and spatiality, Anne-Marie Fortier (2000) drew upon Brah's idea of the 'diaspora space' – located between the local and the transnational, and at the intersections of staying put and being displaced – to explore Italian migration to Britain. Fortier (2006) has situated her more recent work on immigration in the 'New Europe' within what she identifies as 'critical migration studies' – a movement that, she suggests, questions imaginings of a 'fluid' and 'hyper mobile' world and seeks to understand 'imaginative geographies' and 'migrant horizons' (ibid.: 314). Fortier has traced the idea of scale to Lefebvre's (1991) work and his distinction between everyday social spaces and more abstract spaces created by movements of capital and policies of the state. Europe, therefore, becomes a 'scalar narrative' (Fortier 2006: 315) about local/national/transnational 'communities' and questions about what should be the targeted scalar unit for national social policies. Among immigrants, Fortier wrote, there is a separation between 'the space of belonging and the place of residence' (ibid.: 316).

The idea of scale has also been developed in studies of migration by Nina Glick Schiller and Ayse Caglar (2009), who suggested that the predominance of an 'ethnic lens', and also a view of cities as 'containers' for the incorporation of migrants, have overshadowed attention to spatial processes. They have focused on the scalar positioning of cities on a global level, and the transnational ties of migrants, to examine the different experiences in and relationships with a city that migrants will have, depending on the scalar position of the city to which they have migrated. In this work, cities are viewed as positioned in a global social space, according to their scale. This approach can, I argue, be brought into dialogue with one focusing more on the positioning of social actors within more local social spaces. Seeing local social spaces as themselves positioned in a global field adds another layer of understanding of the different experiences a migrant group will have depending upon where they settle.

With their emphasis on scale, these authors have drawn important attention to the transnational processes and flows of capital that affect immigrants in the local places to which they migrate. There is still, however, a need to understand not only transnational processes but also modes of emplacement for immigrants. In an essay on refugees and place, Catherine Brun (2001) usefully identified two dominant ways of thinking about social space – neither of which, she argued, adequately captures the experiences of refugees. One views social space as a 'flat, immobilized surface' and considers refugees as having been 'torn loose from their place and thus from their culture and identity.' In this view, all people have a 'natural place in the world.' The other view decouples people and place, and views space as 'constructed from the multiplicity of social relations across all spatial scales' (ibid.: 15). This is the perspective associated with many attempts to focus on global flows, contact zones and transnationalism. Brun adopted the concept of social spatiality to argue that a deterritorialized view of refugees neglects their experiences, and the different attitudes and policy environments in which they are placed. Her work on refugees in Sri Lanka draws attention to the strategies used by refugees who have 'the contradictory experience of being physically present in one location but at the same time living with a feeling of belonging somewhere else' (ibid.: 23), and points to the spatial strategies used by refugees as they find a position in the host setting. Her argument is that even though much contemporary social theory argues that links between territories and people may be social constructs, refugees themselves use such essentialisms in thinking about place. We must not, therefore, overlook this feature of their experience in our own work.

The lens of 'social space' can help illuminate the ways in which immigrants, as newcomers, are positioned and position themselves within the places in which they settle. Through spatial practices, immigrants can exercise social agency as they find ways to 'belong' and become civically engaged in their new host setting.

Vietnamese American Group Making and Positioning in Social Space

One example of the ways in which the 'group-ness' and political clout of an immigrant population is demonstrated in and through social space comes from my fieldwork among former Vietnamese refugees, now Vietnamese Americans, in the Dallas-Arlington-Fort Worth (DFW) region of Texas.[13] I focus here on a controversy over which flag should represent this refugee population at a large, major public university located near the centre of the city of Arlington (with an enrolment close to 25,000). The flag protest galvanized thousands of Vietnamese Americans, from across the state of Texas and beyond, and also drew into its orbit non-Vietnamese politicians. It began with a conflict involving two student organizations and the International Office at the university, but developed into a major protest orchestrated by Vietnamese American anti-communist political activists that engaged the attention of politicians, the mainstream press and the wider public not only of the region but beyond. The reverberations of this protest continue, and DVDs of the event are still sold at the annual Tet (New Year's) festival sponsored by local Vietnamese American civic organizations. This controversy was in many ways about social space at different scales, involving claims about the location or position of Vietnamese Americans within a wider diaspora, within the United States, within a region of Texas and within a large public university.

The flag protest occurred at a moment in the history of Vietnamese settlement in this region at which there was already an established base of organization and a substantial population and 'presence' of this group. Its visibility to non-Vietnamese residents was, however, not yet very strong, despite this growing population that was becoming more engaged in the wider civic sphere. The DFW region has been a major hub for Vietnamese Americans since the 1990s. There are currently approximately 50,000 foreign-born Vietnamese in the region, but estimates place the total number of Vietnamese Americans as closer to at least 80,000 when American-born children and grandchildren of former refugees are included. Vietnamese Americans have inscribed themselves in social space at the local level (as they were also inscribed at the national level through the history of the Vietnam War). This population began to arrive in the United States in large numbers after the fall of Saigon in April 1975, towards the end of the Vietnam War. Many of these first-wave refugees arrived in one of the four refugee camps set up in different regions of the United States, and were then resettled through refugee agencies or individual sponsors to cities and towns. Subsequently, newer waves of refugees, including the so-called 'boat people', arrived, with the slow ebbing of Vietnamese refugee arrival by the mid 2000s.

Arlington is a suburban-type city, with a small downtown centre and dispersed residential settlement, located between the cities of Dallas and Fort Worth. According to the 2010 US census, the population of Arlington is approximately 365,000, and Vietnam-born residents comprise about 3 per cent of the total population. A high percentage of the population in Arlington is foreign born – higher than the national average. Vietnamese Americans have been drawn to the DFW region due to its mild climate, and its strong economic growth and prosperity relative to other regions. They have also, however, been drawn to it because of the growing population of Vietnamese Americans there, especially in Arlington. Although many refugees were settled directly in this region by refugee agencies, many also came later from the former refugee camp in Fort Chafee, Arkansas. In addition, secondary migration from other locations such as the Louisiana coast, California and Canada has also occurred as families joined other relatives who had already settled in the DFW region.

Arlington has two dominant ethnic groups, Anglo and Latino, among whom Vietnamese Americans as a group must make their own presence known in order to achieve political and social visibility in the social space of the city. Over the past decades, Vietnamese Americans have established religious, civic and educational institutions in the DFW region. There is a vast array of Vietnamese-language print and electronic media, and also a radio station targeting Vietnamese Americans of younger generations that use English. Many businesses, stores and restaurants have also been established. Although the population is spread out over several towns and cities, certain places like Arlington have specific shopping districts identified as Vietnamese. Vietnamese restaurants were known to many residents of the city who were not Vietnamese, but the broader presence of civic and religious institutions that they had formed were not visible in the social space of the city. The strip-mall shopping centres, although providing a physical presence, were located in particular areas not frequented by the majority of the population.

The conflict over a flag arose during the spring 2006 International Week at the university, a week devoted to celebrations of international students (of which the university has a large number). Various student organizations linked to different international groups organized booths for an exhibit hall and performances at a fashion show. The initial event that triggered the protest was a message from the staff of the International Office that only the flag recognized by the United Nations, which is the official flag of the current Socialist Republic of Vietnam, could be used to represent Vietnamese students in the exhibit hall and during the 'parade of flags' that kicked off International Week. This is a red flag with a yellow star in the middle. I was sitting in a meeting of the Vietnamese Student Association (VSA), whose members are the children of Vietnamese refugees, when the news reached them; at the time they were in the midst of making plans for their participation in the events of International Week.

The flag became an emotionally charged issue, especially for the members of the VSA. Vietnamese American students, who are either citizens or permanent residents of the United States and whose parents were refugees, identify with the former Republic of South Vietnam and not with the current regime. The Vietnamese diaspora is symbolized through and represented by the so-called 'freedom and heritage' flag, which was the official flag of South Vietnam, a country that no longer exists. This flag is yellow with three red stripes running horizontally across the middle. Vietnamese Americans display both this flag and the American flag at their events. For Vietnamese Americans who arrived in the United States as refugees fleeing persecution from Vietnam after the war, the flag of the current regime signals a Vietnamese government which they oppose. For them, the 'freedom and heritage' flag denotes democracy and human rights; the other represents communism and the suppression of human rights.

International students who are citizens of the Socialist Republic of Vietnam identify with that nation's flag, the only one deemed permissible at the events of International Week. Two different student organizations represented these two groups of 'Vietnamese' youth: the International Student Organization, headed by a president that year who was an international Vietnamese student from Hanoi; and the Vietnamese Student Association (VSA), then headed by a former refugee who had lived in a refugee camp as a child before settling with her family in Arlington. The position of the International Office and their prohibition of the use of the flag of former South Vietnam by the VSA sparked an opportunity for a wider group of anti-communist activists to not only protest over the university's policy but to make the existence of Vietnamese Americans visible in the existing social space of Arlington, and to position themselves within the wider social space of the Vietnamese diaspora.

Vietnamese Americans use the 'freedom and heritage' flag to signal both geographic and social space, and the flag protest was itself carried out through activities involving both geographic and social space. At the various public ceremonies I observed, ranging from awards banquets to summer leadership camps for Vietnamese American youth, to the annual Tet festival, paper or cloth versions of the 'freedom and heritage' flag were always used to both show the location of an event and to help people find it by placing the flags along the way, staking flags with poles into the ground at intersections and attaching flags to lamp posts. The 'freedom and heritage' flag, along with other symbols of South Vietnamese national identity such as anthems, is also very present during public ceremonies organized by Vietnamese American civic associations in the DFW region. Vietnamese Americans make a political statement as a diaspora community vis-à-vis the current regime of Vietnam by displaying copies of the flag in physical space. A more abstract Vietnamese American 'social space' is made tangible and visible through these markers.

When the student leaders of the VSA learned that they could not use the 'freedom and heritage' flag in their exhibit, they contacted local adult leaders of Vietnamese American organizations that identified themselves as anti-communist (the two dominant Vietnamese ethnic organizations in DFW), who immediately began to send messages of protest not only to university officials but also to state legislators and the governor, Rick Perry. The 'freedom and heritage' flag had already been recognized officially by the state of Texas and the city of Arlington as one representing Vietnamese Americans. Vietnamese American leaders also used electronic means of communication to alert fellow political activists across the country and beyond. The political clout of the Vietnamese American population in Arlington had already been established through a recent voting campaign, and support by this population for the referendum to build a new Dallas Cowboys football stadium in Arlington (which has now been constructed). Former Vietnamese refugees have become American citizens in large numbers, and have high voting and naturalization rates. Their leaders were able to galvanize the population to vote for the stadium, and in return they felt that those in power should respond to their protest about the flag. Because Texas is a politically conservative state, the anti-communist stance of the protestors resonated very strongly with many politicians.[14]

There were two major sites of protest, protests that could be seen as more 'soft' and more 'hard'. The first was during the International Week fashion show and the performance there organized by the VSA. As the crowd assembled for this event, the presence of a large group of Vietnamese adults in the audience became increasingly evident. With other attendees, this group poured into the auditorium. Reporters from Vietnamese print and radio media were also present. When the Vietnamese students came on stage, many of the Vietnamese adults began to stand and wave small South Vietnamese flags, and some came close to the stage waving these flags. The group in attendance sat down after doing so and this 'soft' protest ended when the next group of students left the stage. This behaviour was not disruptive, but sent a message to the administration of the university that the flag issue was of concern for a broader group of people beyond it. Although this behaviour was not physically disruptive, it was socially disruptive in that it inserted Vietnamese American visibility into the general social space of the university and its region. It surprised administrators.

A much larger, and 'harder' form of protest occurred soon thereafter, when a parade of protestors marched down the central street that runs through the university in the centre of Arlington. This time, the protest had a more profound and disruptive physical presence as well as a social one. This spectacle, which also included speeches and performances on a stage set up in a car park before and after the march, drew approximately 3,000 participants. With banners proclaiming that the university administration's position on the flag was an insult to their political beliefs and their former refugee status, the marchers shouted chants about freedom and democracy. Several politicians, including city council members, attended and spoke on behalf of the protestors. Taking over the physical 'social space' of the campus for these protest activities established the political legitimacy of their claims. The Vietnamese Americans who participated also positioned themselves in the more abstract sense of social space through these events as not only anti-communist political activists, but also as a new 'group' in the social space of the region who demanded that they be taken seriously and be respected.

Other actions included writing letters to political leaders in Austin (the capital of Texas), and conducting a 'teach-in' concerning the Vietnam War. Several responses by the university eventually resulted from these protests. First of all, the 'hall of flags' that had hung in the College of Engineering for many years in order to honour the many international students who attended the university (and especially the College of Engineering) was dismantled. Because the university did not want to hang the 'freedom and heritage' flag, no flags would fly there permanently. Second, flags became a less important feature in International Week events. Third, the university formed a commission to examine its 'diversity' policies, and solicited a more moderate Vietnamese American and alumni of the university to participate on the committee. Other outcomes, more difficult to tie directly to this particular set of events related to the protest, indicate, however, that the visibility of Vietnamese Americans within the social space of this particular metropolitan region had improved. For example, during the Fourth of July Parade held in Arlington later that summer, the float put together by a Vietnamese American civic organization that had been active in the protest had the special honour of receiving the 'mayor's prize' for best float (see Reed-Danahay 2010). Soon after this, a Vietnamese American man was elected to political office in Tarrant County, in which Arlington is located. He has subsequently been re-elected.

Through activities such as the flag protest, members of the Vietnamese diaspora make their presence in the social space of American society visible to non-Vietnamese, including politicians who recognize the importance of Vietnamese political support.[15] The flag was a materialized symbol of this 'group' and their moral claims in the social space of the United States at several levels of scale (local to national). The example of the flag protest shows efforts at emplacement, at civic participation, within social space. The leaders of the protest were signalling this at several levels: including the specific place of the DFW region of Texas, but also the wider space of the Vietnamese diaspora and its relationship to the current regime of Vietnam. Through their actions, the leaders of the protest occupied physical spaces in ways that also positioned their group within a more abstract form of social space. The flag protest illustrates what Bourdieu was getting at when he mentioned, as quoted above, 'demonstrations whose goal is to exhibit a group, its size, its strength, its cohesiveness, to make it exist visibly'.

The case of the flag protest shows how social space, a concept that explores the relationship between social and geographic space, can help illuminate processes of emplacement and civic engagement for migrant populations. Although the Vietnamese American population in the DFW region was quite large, and there were several institutions and physical places associated with this population (in addition to other forms of material culture such as print media), their visibility in both geographic and social space was minimal to the general public. The controversy over the flag made their presence visible in ways that enhanced their political position as a group. This ethnographic illustration points to the ways in which geographic and social space do and do not overlap, making it an area for investigation and not assumptions. For example, the flag protest shows that ideas of Vietnamese nationalism do not reside solely on Vietnamese legal territory but exist within the social space of diaspora that extends in both time and space beyond the former South Vietnam, and that can affect local places such as a city and university in Texas.

CONCLUSIONS

This chapter has argued that social space is a useful lens though which to understand emerging forms of sociality related to mobility and migration in the contemporary world. Social space incorporates both physical and more abstract spaces in which people and groups interact and position themselves vis-à-vis others in terms of their perceived differences and similarities. Visibility in social space is an essential part of group making, and involves active forms of engagement in the civic sphere, as the example of the flag controversy demonstrates. An enduring theoretical problem in anthropology has been that of how to understand the relationship between territorial or geographic space and social space. I have reviewed here several approaches to understanding how much the physical environment, geographic space, should (or can) be analytically separated from the more abstract idea of one's position in an imagined social space that has to do with moral values, status, prestige, affinity, identity and so on.

The boundaries, borders or thresholds of a social space must be problematized in research, interrogated and not take for granted. Recent approaches caution that it narrows our understandings of sociality to assume that the tribe, village, community or nation is the relevant social space, as did previous generations of anthropologists. Social spaces can be more or less enduring and can have more or less rigid borders, ranging from a 'gathering' (as studied by Goffman) to a city, nation-state or global diaspora. Physical or geographic spaces and places are imbued with social meaning and are thereby social spaces, but there can also be social spaces that are more abstract and less tied to co-presence in physical space. Social spaces are those realms or landscapes in which social affinities and aspirations are expressed. They are constructed and understood via sociality and do not exist independently of social relationships and interactions. Sociality makes social space.

Major questions for studies of sociality surround issues of how people perceive their lives in terms of the social space(s) they inhabit. That is, do they feel part of a cosmopolitan, trans-regional social space (like that of the 'third space' of diaspora),[16] or as part of a local social space only? How do the particular social spaces in which they dwell affect their aspirations and understandings of their positions within them? In what ways can social space be a space of exclusion for certain people or groups?

NOTES

1. The 'spatial turn' in anthropology and related disciplines, especially since the mid-1990s, has been an influential trend. Several key texts that bear mentioning include Soja (1989), Ardener (1993), Pellow (1996), Gupta and Ferguson (1997), Low and Lawrence (2002), Coleman and Collins (2006), Warf and Arias (2009) and Tally (2013).

2. The topic of the internet as a social space is one I cannot address adequately in this chapter. Two examples relevant to my arguments about social space from this vast and rapidly growing literature include Hine (2000) and Slane (2007).

3. The literature is vast on this topic, but I would point to the work of Johannes Fabian (1983) in particular, for its insights on the historical constructions of a link between being distant in space and distant in time. See also Munn (1992).

4. See Rehbein (2007) for a critique of Bourdieu's concept of social space as one of a container. See also Glick Schiller and Caglar (2009) for a critique of the view of cities as containers for immigrant incorporation.

5. Durkheim's contributions to social space have also been noted by Sorokin (1927), and more recently by Anne Buttimer (1969: 418–419). See also Corsin Jiménez (2003), who points to Durkheim's focus on social differentiation and social morphology.

6. Later post-Durkheimian considerations of the relationship between social space and territory in social anthropology that considered spatial categories and practices include Moore (1986), Parkin (1991), and Munn (1996).

7. See also Gupta and Ferguson (1997).

8. Although Eidheim, writing in the 1960s, used the term 'Lapp', I recognize that 'Sami' is now the preferred term to refer to this ethnic group.

9. Proxemics, developed and promoted in anthropology by Edward T. Hall (1966), is another important area of research on social space. Hall's work is also relevant to discussions of spatial practices (cf. de Certeau 1984, 1997; Lefebvre 1991). Although she does not cite Goffman's contributions to this field, Low's more recent attention to the idea of 'embodied space' addresses 'the creation of place through spatial orientations, movement, and language' (Low 2003: 10).

10. See also Silber (1995).

11. See Bourdieu (1987) for an explicit discussion of the differences between the structure of the field and the structure of social space in an analysis of spatiality in Flaubert's novel *Sentimental Education*.

12. See Reed-Danahay (2005, 2009, 2013).

13. This example draws from and occasionally reproduces material published in Reed-Danahay (2008), but involves a significant reworking due to subsequent research and analysis. I conducted fieldwork among Vietnamese Americans between 2005 and 2008 in Arlington, Texas, and in surrounding cities. The label Vietnamese American (without a hyphen) is the term used by this population to describe itself. There are various civic organizations that have been formed by former Vietnamese refugees that refer to themselves as associations of Vietnamese Americans. My research was funded by a generous grant from the Russell Sage Foundation and was done in collaboration with Caroline B. Brettell, who studied the Asian Indian population in the Dallas region of Texas. Our project has resulted in a book (Brettell and Reed-Danahay 2012). See also Reed-Danahay (2008, 2010, 2012a, 2012b).

14. I have observed during subsequent research in Buffalo, New York, that politicians who are Democrats also support the anti-communist activities of the

much-smaller former Vietnamese refugee population there. The politics of freedom and democracy and anti-communism voiced by Vietnamese American activists is one that, apparently, crosses party lines and permits alliances between Vietnamese Americans and local politicians in different social spaces.

15. I have elsewhere written about other public events in which Vietnamese Americans made their presence more visible to the wider public – including participation in a Fourth of July parade (Reed-Danahay 2010) and festivals and commemorations such as the Tet festival and Black April, marking the fall of Saigon (Brettell and Reed-Danahay 2012).

16. See Bhabha (1994) on 'third spaces' of diaspora; see also Hall (1990).

REFERENCES

Appadurai, A. 1996. *Modernity at Large: Cultural Dimensions of Globalization.* Minneapolis: University of Minnesota Press.

Ardener, S. (ed.). 1993. *Women and Space: Ground Rules and Social Maps.* Oxford: Berg.

Augé, M. 1995. *Non-Places: An Introduction to Supermodernity.* Second edition. Trans. J. Howe. London: Verso Books.

Barth, F. (ed.). 1969. *Ethnic Groups and Boundaries: The Social Organization of Cultural Difference.* Boston: Little, Brown.

Bhabha, H.K. 1994. *The Location of Culture.* London: Routledge.

Bourdieu, P. 1984 [1979]. *Distinction: A Social Critique of the Judgment of Taste,* trans. R. Nice. Cambridge, MA: Harvard University Press.

—— 1985. 'Social Space and the Genesis of Groups', *Theory and Society* 14: 723–744.

—— 1987. 'The Invention of the Artist's Life', trans. E.R. Koch, *Yale French Studies* 73: 75–103.

—— 1989. 'Social Space and Symbolic Power', *Sociological Theory* 7(1): 14–25.

—— 1996. 'Physical Space, Social Space, and Habitus', unpublished lecture delivered to the Department of Sociology, University of Oslo, 15 May.

—— 2000 [1997]. *Pascalian Meditations,* trans. R. Nice. Stanford: Stanford University Press.

Brettell, C., and D. Reed-Danahay. 2012. *Civic Engagements: The Citizenship Practices of Indian and Vietnamese Immigrants.* Stanford: Stanford University Press.

Brun, C. 2001. 'Reterritorializing the Relationship between People and Place in Refugee Studies', *Geografiska Annaler* 83B(1): 15–25.

Buttimer, A. 1969. 'Social Space in Interdisciplinary Perspective', *Geographical Review* 59(3): 417–426.

de Certeau, M. 1984. *The Practice of Everyday Life,* trans. S. Rendall. Berkeley: University of California Press.

—— 1997 [1974]. *Culture in the Plural,* trans. T. Conley. Minneapolis: University of Minnesota Press.

Chombart de Lauwe, P.-H. 1965. *Paris: Essais de Sociologie 1952–1964.* Paris: Les Editions Ouvrières.

Coleman, S., and P. Collins (eds). 2006. *Locating the Field: Space, Place and Context in Anthropology*. Oxford: Berg.

Corsin Jiménez, A. 2003. 'On Space as a Capacity', *Journal of the Royal Anthropological Institute* 9: 137–153.

Donnan, H., and T.M. Wilson (eds). 1999. *Borders: Frontiers of Identity, Nation, and State*. Oxford: Berg.

Durkheim, E. 1995 [1912]. *The Elementary Forms of Religious Life*, trans. K.E. Fields. New York: Free Press.

Durkheim, E., and M. Mauss. 1963. *Primitive Classification*, trans. R. Needham. Chicago: University of Chicago Press.

Eidheim, H. 1969. 'Where Ethnic Identity is a Social Stigma', in F. Barth (ed.). *Ethnic Groups and Boundaries*. Boston: Little, Brown, pp. 39–57.

Fabian, J. 1983. *Time and the Other: How Anthropology Makes Its Object*. New York: Columbia University Press.

Faist, T., and E. Özveron (eds). 2004. *Transnational Social Spaces: Agents, Networks, and Institutions*. Aldershot: Ashgate.

Fogle, N. 2011. *The Spatial Logic of Social Struggle: A Bourdieuian Topology*. Lanham, MD: Lexington Books.

Fortier, A. M. 2000. *Migrant Belongings: Memory, Space, Identity*. Oxford: Berg.

—— 2006. 'The Politics of Scaling, Timing and Embodying: Rethinking the "New Europe"', *Mobilities* 1(3): 313–331.

Frisby, D., and M. Featherstone. 2000 [1997]. 'Introduction to the Texts', in G. Simmel, *Simmel on Culture: Selected Writings*, eds. D. Frisby and M. Featherstone. London: Sage, pp.1–28.

Geertz, C. 1957. 'Ritual and Social Change: A Javanese Example', *American Anthropologist* 59(1): 32–54.

Glick Schiller, N., and A. Çaglar. 2009. 'Towards a Comparative Theory of Locality in Migration Studies: Migrant Incorporation and City Scale', *Journal of Ethnic and Migration Studies* 35(2): 177–202.

Gluckman, M. 1955. 'The Peace in the Feud', *Past and Present* 8: 1–14.

Goffman, E. 1959. *The Presentation of Self in Everyday Life*. New York: Doubleday.

—— 1963. *Behavior in Public Places: Notes on the Social Organization of Gathering*. New York: Free Press.

—— 1971. *Relations in Public: Microstudies of the Social Order*. New York: Harper Colophon.

Green, S. 2013. 'Borders and the Relocation of Europe', *Annual Review of Anthropology* 42: 345–361.

Gupta, A., and J. Ferguson. 1992. 'Beyond "Culture": Space, Identity, and the Politics of Difference', *Cultural Anthropology* 7(1): 6–23.

—— (eds). 1997. *Culture, Power, Place*. Durham, NC: Duke University Press.

Halbwachs, M. 1980 [1950]. *On Collective Memory*, trans. F.J. Ditter and V.Y. Ditter. New York: Harper and Row.

Hall, E.T. 1966. *The Hidden Dimension*. Garden City, NY: Doubleday.

Hall, S. 1990. Cultural Identity and Diaspora. In *Identity*, ed. J Rutherford. London: Lawrence and Wishart, pp.222–237.

Harvey, D. 1990. 'Between Space and Time: Reflections on the Geographical Imagination', *Annals of the Association of American Geographers* 80(3): 418–434.

—— 2005. 'The Sociological and Geographical Imaginations', *International Journal of Politics, Culture, and Society* 18(3/4): 211–255.

Hine, C.M. 2000. *Virtual Ethnography*. London: Sage.

Hunter, L. 2004. 'Bourdieu and the Social Space of the PE Class: Reproduction of Doxa through Practice', *Sport, Education, and Society* 9(2): 175–194.

Ilcan, S. 1999. 'Social Spaces and the Micropolitics of Differentiation: An Example from Northwestern Turkey', *Ethnology* 38(3): 243–256.

Knauft, B. 2006. 'Anthropology in the Middle', *Anthropological Theory* 6(4): 407–430.

Kuper, H. 1972. 'The Language of Sites in the Politics of Space', *American Anthropologist* 74: 411–425.

Lechner, F.J. 1991. 'Simmel on Social Space', *Theory, Culture and Society* 8: 195–201.

Lefebvre, H. 1991 [1974]. *The Production of Space*, trans. D. Nicholson-Smith. Malden, MA: Blackwell.

Lévi-Strauss, C. 1963. *Structural Anthropology*, trans. C. Jacobson and B. Shoepf. New York: Basic Books.

Low, S.M. 1996. 'Spatializing Culture: The Social Production and Social Construction of Public Space', *American Ethnologist* 23(4): 861–879.

—— 2003. 'Embodied Space(s): Anthropological Theories of Body, Space, and Culture', *Space and Culture* 6(1): 9–18.

Low, S.M., and D. Lawrence (eds). 2002. *The Anthropology of Space and Place: Locating Culture*. Oxford: Blackwell.

Marchetti, M.C. 2011. 'Space, Mobility, and New Boundaries: The Redefinition of Social Action,' in G. Pellegrino (ed.), *The Politics of Proximity: Mobility and Immobility in Practice*. Farnham, Surrey: Ashgate, pp.17–30.

Moore, H.L. 1986. *Space, Text and Gender: An Anthropological Study of the Marakwet of Kenya*. Cambridge: Cambridge University Press.

Munn, N.D. 1992. 'The Cultural Anthropology of Time: A Critical Essay', *Annual Review of Anthropology* 21: 93–123.

—— 1996. 'Excluded Spaces: The Figure in the Australian Aboriginal Landscape', *Critical Inquiry* 22: 446–465.

Parkin, D. 1991. *Sacred Void: Spatial Images of Work and Ritual among the Giriama of Kenya*. Cambridge: Cambridge University Press.

Pellow, D. (ed.). 1996. *Setting Boundaries: The Anthropology of Spatial and Social Organization*. Westport, CT: Bergin and Garvey.

Pratt, M.L. 1992. *Imperial Eyes: Travel Writing and Transculturation*. New York: Routledge.

Pries, L. (ed.) 2001. *New Transnational Social Spaces: International Migration and Transnational Companies in the Early Twenty-First Century*. Abingdon, Oxon: Routledge.

Reed-Danahay, D. 2005. *Locating Bourdieu*. Bloomington: Indiana University Press.

—— 2008. 'From the "Imagined Community" to "Communities of Practice": Immigrant Belonging among Vietnamese Americans', in D. Reed-Danahay and C.B. Brettell (eds), *Citizenship, Political Engagement, and Belonging: Immigrants in Europe and the United States*. New Brunswick, NJ: Rutgers University Press, pp.78–97.

—— 2009. 'Bourdieu's Ethnography in Béarn and Kabylia: The Peasant Habitus', in J. Goodman and P.A. Silverstein (eds), *Bourdieu in Algeria: Colonial Policies, Theoretical Developments*. Lincoln: University of Nebraska Press, pp.133–163.

—— 2010. 'Citizenship, Immigration, and Embodiment: Vietnamese Americans in North-central Texas', in M. Thapan (ed.), *Contested Spaces: Citizenship and Belonging in Contemporary Times*. New Delhi: Orient Blackswan, pp.101–119.

—— 2012a. 'The Vietnamese American Buddhist Youth Association: A Community of Practice for Learning Civic Skills', *Tsantsa* 17: 76–85.

—— 2012b. 'La Notion de "Communauté" à l'Epreuve des Terrains: Des Espaces Sociaux de la France Rurale à la Diaspora Vietnamienne', in A. Raulin and S.C. Rogers (eds), *Parallaxes Transatlantiques: Vers Une Anthropologie Réciproque*. Paris: Editions du Centre Nationale de la Récherche Scientifique, pp.159–180.

—— 2013. 'Habitus', in R.J. McGee and R.L. Warms (eds), *Theory in Social and Cultural Anthropology: An Encyclopedia*. Thousand Oaks, CA: Sage, pp.374–376.

Rehbein, B. 2007. *Globalization, Culture and Society in Laos*. New York: Routledge.

Rouse, R. 1991. 'Mexican Migration and the Social Space of Postmodernism', *Diaspora* 1(1): 8–23.

Sassen, S. 2000. 'Spatialities and Temporalities of the Global: Elements for a Theorization', *Public Culture* 12(1): 215–232.

Silber, I.F. 1995. 'Space, Fields, Boundaries: The Rise of Spatial Metaphors in Contemporary Sociological Theory', *Social Research* 62(2): 323–355.

Simmel, G. and K. Wolff. 1950. *The Sociology of Georg Simmel*. New York: The Free Press.

Slane, A. 2007. 'Democracy, Social Space, and the Internet', *University of Toronto Law Journal* 57(1): 81–105.

Smith, M.P. 1992. 'Postmodernism, Urban Ethnography, and the New Social Space of Ethnicity', *Theory and Society* 21(4): 493–531.

Soja, E. W. 1989. *Postmodern Geographies: The Reassertion of Space in Critical Social Theory*. London: Verso.

Sorokin, P. 1927. *Social Mobility*. New York: Harper and Brothers.

Spencer, J. 1995. 'Post-colonialism and the Political Imagination', *Journal of the Royal Anthropological Institute* 3: 1–19.

Tally, R.T. 2013. *Spatiality*. Abingdon, Oxon: Routledge.

Warf, B. and S. Arias (eds). 2009. *The Spatial Turn: Interdisciplinary Perspectives*. Abingdon, Oxon: Routledge.

Wilson, T.M., and H. Donnan (eds). 2012. *A Companion to Border Studies*. Malden, MA: Blackwell.

4

Sociability
The Art of Form

Sally Anderson

Across disciplines, generations and eras, the etiquette, courtesies and formalities of human sociality have met with critique. While some bewail the loss of decorum, others rail against the vacuous rigidity and shallow veneer of social conventions that thwart more informal and genuine modes of sociality. Formalized conventions, indexing taste and refinement and couching assessments of social merit and worth, have been critically examined as instruments of class distinction, social reproduction and dominance (Bourdieu 1984). In another vein, scholars claiming that organized sociable activities are the mainstay of democratic society have agonized over the decline of civil society (Putnam 1995).

Such moral, aesthetic and political critiques are instructive of the controversial yet fundamental import of social convention and form in human relationality. All sociality, that very 'condition of being human' (Toren 2012: 69), is inevitably constitutive of and contingent upon conventions and forms that afford some measure of common ground across idiosyncratic asymmetries of knowledge, view, position and language. Such convention and form are compelling because they are precarious. They do not precede interaction, but are improvised as people monitor, (mis)interpret, recognize (perhaps) and acknowledge (or not) each other's actions and words in trying to figure out what to do next (Varenne 2009).

This chapter explores sociability as a potential domain of anthropological investigation. Probing Simmel's insights, it inquires into aesthetic conventions and ludic forms, the import humans attribute these, the domains and relations to which they are relegated, and the ways in which sociability – understood as stylized interaction with particular categories of others – is taken for granted even as it lends itself to endless debate among the moral guardians and explicators of appropriate sociation. The point of the exercise is to set sociability off from sociality to investigate its potential as a heuristic device for interrogating valued forms of human sociation and relation.

SIMMEL'S SOCIABILITY

Georg Simmel (1858–1918) proposes an ideal type of 'pure' sociability as a highly stylized form of sociation.[1] Simmel characterizes sociability as a democratic form through which people engage with each other as if equal, with no immediate instrumental purpose other than the success of the sociable moment. Simmel also portrays sociability as good form, an artful, autonomous play-form of sociation (Simmel 1950: 40–57). This idealized version of egalitarian sociality among autonomous individuals in modern social venues has captured the imagination of many scholars.

Despite Simmel's widely acknowledged seminal article, and the ubiquity of sociable forms and conventions, sociability as such has not received much specific historical, ethnographic or theoretical attention (cf. Baker 1999). Few have looked beyond the civil domains and convivial stances implied in Simmel's work, and even fewer have attempted to work out in any detail what Simmel's notion of sociability as a 'play-form' – conceived of as both play *at* form and *on* form – might entail (Beaurepaire 2011: 375). I follow Simmel's lead in this chapter by interrogating the processes, moments, and venues that afford and frame precarious and compelling plays on form intrinsic to all good form.

SOCIABILITY MATTERS

Reviewing studies of sociability, I found the concept regularly treated as though all are familiar with and agreed upon its meaning and application (e.g. Ericsson 1989). While some authors alternate between sociability and sociality with little reflection, others insert qualifiers like 'civil', 'enjoyable', 'amiable' and even 'sociable' to distinguish 'friendly' sociability from more comprehensive sociality. Yet both sociality and sociability are applied to: generic human and animal behaviour; socializing with non-kin, semi-intimate others (friends, acquaintances, workmates); civil encounters with people beyond one's personal circle and professional network; and gatherings in voluntary associations, societies, circles, lodges and clubs. Such usage relies on intuitive understandings of the concept. A case in point is Flanagan's textbook definition: 'Sociability is the tendency to seek the company of others, to be friendly' (Flanagan 1999: 9). Given the extensive theoretical polemics on record for other everyday concepts such as community, field and space (Amit and Rapport 2002, 2012; Postill, Reed-Danahay, this volume), sociability's missing theoretical heritage is baffling.[2]

Across the behavioural sciences, sociability generally connotes desirable, non-aggressive, other-seeking behaviour (Sibbald et al. 2005). In psychology, sociability indexes children's cognitive and social development into well-adjusted human beings (Thompson and Lamb 1983; Broadhead 2001; Kreijns, Kirschner and Jochems 2002). On a different track, historians treat sociability as a characteristic of social life among particular social classes, during specific periods of economic and political conflict and change. Studies of eighteenth- and nineteenth-century Europe focus on emerging forms of urban, elite association – such as salons, intellectual circles, coffee houses, colonial clubs – their development in relation to changing political and economic systems, and their role in fashioning new national, intellectual and civic publics (Kale 2004; Cowan 2005; Cohen 2009; Lilti 2009). Addressing modernizing processes, these studies are pitched towards moral political discourses of civil etiquette, *fraternité*, community and voluntary association. Studies of non-elites argue against prevailing misconceptions of voluntary sociation among peasants and urban working classes. Baker (1999) shows how allegedly 'individualistic' French peasants cultivate *fraternité* (sociability) in voluntary fire brigades and mutual aid societies.[3] Arguing against conventional depictions of working-class leisure as unstructured 'co-mingling' rich in drink, brawling and bad company, Haine (1996: 151) reveals the etiquette and hospitality of Parisian working-class cafés.

Scholarly work on sociability reveals two key approaches. The first, focusing on evolutionary and ontogenetic development of cooperative behaviour, treats sociability as universally recognizable and measurable behaviour generic to animals and humans. The second, referencing modern concerns with social cohesion and concord, treats sociability in the plural as a wide range of organizational forms, joint activities, venues, hierarchies and norms of social behaviour among particular categories of people living in different places and eras. The difficulty of spanning these two approaches with one rigorous definition of sociability is obvious. In the following, I explore how we might proceed without rigorous definition, and without throwing in our hand to normative speculation and arrogation.

SOCIABILITY AS A DOMAIN OF INVESTIGATION

Anthropologists tend to use sociality and sociability idiosyncratically. What some delineate as everyday sociality (Pink 2008: 172), residential sociality (Postill 2008) or the sociality of older persons (Bomhoff 2011: 3), others address as neighbourly sociability (Birenbaum-Carmeli 1999). Yet others employ conviviality to connote a particular 'sociable' sociality (Overing and Passes 2000). Most anthropologists, however, opt for the term sociality, which, where theorized, is treated as a foundational concept. I discuss this treatment briefly before moving to sociability.

Enfield and Levinson posit human sociality as the 'particularly intense, mentally mediated and highly structured way in which humans interact with one another' (Enfield and Levinson 2006: 1). Sociality underpins human social life as people interact in ways that both draw on and strategically augment common ground (ibid.).[4] Dunbar (1994) focuses his study of sociality more specifically on the patterning, nature and number of relationships among sets of interacting individuals, and how these aspects of sociality affect social bonds and group size. Ingold (1993) on the other hand defines sociality as the constitutive quality of relationships. Arguing against building sociality into individual biograms or the forces of collectivity, he views sociality as the 'generative potential of the relational field in which [persons as nodes] are situated and which is constituted and reconstituted through their activities' (ibid.: 160). For Ingold, sociality is not founded in numbers, types and frequencies, but in 'resonance of movement and feeling, stemming from people's perceptual monitoring and mutually attentive engagement in shared contexts of practical activity' (Ingold 2000: 196). From these fundamental perspectives, sociality is the interactional core of all human life. Although manifest in observable patterns of relationality, we ought to think of sociality as the constitutive potential of always emerging relational fields.

That sociality becomes a rather unwieldy object of study when viewed through these approaches has not deterred anthropologists, myself included (Anderson 2008). In a recent effort to lend direction to the growing number of studies of sociality, Long and Moore offer yet another foundational conceptualization. Human sociality is 'a dynamic relational matrix within which human subjects are constantly interacting in ways that are co-productive, and continually plastic and malleable, and through which they come to know the world they live in and find their purpose and meaning within it' (Long and Moore 2012: 41).[5] This definition builds on approaches to sociality advanced during the 1989 Manchester debate on the theoretical purchase of society (see Ingold 1996). Arguing against the concept, Strathern introduced the idea of relational matrices that embed and constitute the lives of persons, and thus contain the potential for relationships. Toren emphasized the importance of attending to dynamic social processes rather than sets of rules, customs, structures and meaning understood as actor-independent systems (Long and Moore 2013: 4–5). Long and Moore accredit sociality's growing popularity within anthropology to this processual pull. Drawing attention to dynamic social processes rather than rigid preset conceptualizations, it promises to overcome the limitations of more static and bounded objects of enquiry such as society, culture, structure and system (ibid.: 2).

Long and Moore caution against common analytical pitfalls, such as smuggling in normative ideas of proper sociality and genuine social relations that equate sociality with mental connection, sharing, harmonious unity and solidarity within groups, and leave the ambivalence, fear, fragility and termination of real relations unexamined. Another common shortcoming is arbitrarily limiting sociality 'to the formation of very specific types of relation' and neglecting the 'broader relational contexts within which people are embedded' (ibid.). Toren contends that the ultimate analytical pitfall is the very attempt to install sociality as a domain of investigation. In Toren's view, sociality's initial promise as a dynamic term was precisely its lack of 'any *determined* conceptual tethering' to reified abstractions (Toren 2012: 67; original emphasis). As a heuristic device akin to relationship and personhood, sociality implied 'processes that remained to be found out' (ibid.), and made no claim to becoming an analytical category.

Both Toren and Long and Moore underline problems to address in deciding whether and how to engage sociability as a domain of investigation. Should sociability be treated as yet another foundational concept and duly equipped with its own processual conceptualizations and imageries of 'unfolding and generative relational fields' and 'dynamic relational matrices'? I think not. In circumventing catchall, intuitive and reified understandings, foundational conceptualizations are ethnographically cumbersome. Offering little clue of how to observe an 'unfolding relational field' or delineate an interface between 'dynamic relational matrices', they are difficult to apply to concrete cases (cf. Rudie 1994: 31–32).

Yet if sociability is not to be foundational, what then? Many scholars already tether sociability to particular societal domains. Baker (1999: 43) situates sociability in a domain thought to lie between two apparently sociability-free domains: family and state. While installing sociability in this conceptual matrix may make intuitive sense, it is ethnocentric, and worse, it runs the risk of analytical ossification by too easily precluding any search for and account of sociable moments in other conceptual and social domains.

Intuitive understandings of what sociability is and where it belongs pose a
challenge to the conceptual work of carving out a domain of investigation
in which sociability may serve as a heuristic device rather than a normative
ideal or blueprint. To probe the concept's potential to further our understanding of human relationality, I turn to anthropological and sociological
studies of sociability.

A DESIRABLE FORM OF SOCIATION

There is wide-ranging consensus regarding the value of sociability. Confident assumptions about the positive consequences of congenial company
and voluntary sociation undergird both scientific studies and the societal
concerns that drive them. Anthropologists have commonly focused more
critically on the structure, function and meaning embedded in human interaction. As a rule, ethnographic studies of sociability investigate concrete
details of interaction and relational processes among particular kinds of
people (working men, islanders), participating in particular cultural events
(festivals, weddings, wakes), particular social venues (cafés, stores, gyms)
or particular modern institutions (day-care, school, nursing homes). Mul-
ti-sited ethnographies invariably analyse the transformation of social ties,
networks and exchange via processes of mobility, social incorporation and
community making (Weisner 1976). A conviction that conversation lies at
the heart of sociability (Simmel 1950; Habermas 1991) underpins studies
of 'languages of sociability', the slang, gossip, sociable argument, small talk
and communicative embellishments that flourish among various kinds of
peers and would-be peers (Bauman 1972; Dueck 2007; Smith-Hefner 2007).[6]
    Anthropologists join historians and sociologists in situating sociability
in extra-domestic gender, age and class-based venues of modern and modernizing societies. Although seldom framed and theorized in terms of civil
society or civil sociality (Anderson 2008), anthropological studies share the
premise that sociability connotes amiable peer exchange distinguishable
from less peaceable exchanges of open conflict and war, even though sociable conversation may be argumentative or about violence (Schiffrin 1984;
Rapport 1987) and wars may have sociable moments.[7] Studies of sociability
predictably assume some measure of commonality premised on joint action,
joint interest, voluntary gathering, social proximity and approachability. As
such, sociability is often imaged as convivial social exchange among consociates or co-citizens posed as universal, autonomous individuals interacting
in extra-domestic (non-kin-based) civil settings and domains (cf. Seligman
1992).

Focus on sociability highlights moral and aesthetic qualities of sociation, politically valid forms of association, and forms and processes of social
exchange deemed beneficial to individuals, communities and polities. Sociability allegedly enhances human growth and social well-being by generating
a sense of cooperation, commonality and belonging. Viewing sociability as
re-creative social exchange, scholars proffer sociable venues as singularly
constructive sites for training open, non-aggressive styles of interaction and
relationality. The claim is that casual, often merry social intercourse among
non-kin fosters (democratic) society or community by levelling instrumental
distinctions and structural divisions based on occupation, age, class, religion and ethnicity (Simmel 1950; Oldenburg 1999).

Such positive assumptions serve as implicit foils for anthropological
analyses of what really goes on or what also is at stake in sociable encounters. Studying social drinking among farm workers in the cafés and bars of
Andalusia, Dreissen (1983) finds exacting principles of reciprocity and male
performativity underlying casual jocularity. He contrasts the easy-going, jo-
vial ambience of cafés with the strict reciprocal protocol guiding a relentless
tracking and circulation of drinks, cigarettes, snacks and talk. Male identity is also at stake in displays of hearty backslapping, animated clapping
(to bring on drinks) and the forceful banging of dominoes. Protocols and
performative aesthetics serve as prototypes against which the stinginess of
too little expenditure or the gracelessness of too vigorous backslapping is
exposed and assessed (ibid.: 128–129).

Urban sociologist Ray Oldenburg (1999) champions sociability in his
call to revitalize American civil society. He includes cafés, bars, book-
stores, beauty parlours and other local hangouts in his stock of sociable
'third places' stationed between the first and second places of home and
work. Oldenburg lauds the positive personal and societal effects of informal social life found in these 'happy gathering places' where everyone is
welcome in 'blissful congregation' (ibid.: ix, x, 14). Critical of the decline
of 'great good places' in American cities, purportedly brought on by post-
war urban and suburban sprawl, Oldenburg claims that they serve communities by hosting voluntary, informal association among decent people.
Distinguishing third places from other public spaces, he extols their merits
as havens of inclusive, status-levelling neutral ground, where individuals
may encounter and join the relaxing conversation of regulars (Ducheneaut, Moore and Nickell 2007). Employing Simmel's concepts and criteria,
Oldenburg touts the 'pure' sociability of third places as democratic interaction, as 'spiritual tonic', and a state of being in which people, stripped of
instrumental roles and purposes, are 'more fully themselves' (Oldenburg
1999: 24–25).

Notwithstanding the clichéd tenor of Oldenburg's work and its bias towards extra-domestic encounters (ibid.: 70), studies of technology-mediated sociability draw on his depiction of socially neutral terrain to assess social exchange in virtual 'third places', such as the world of *World of Warcraft* and other popular massive multiplayer online games (Steinkeuler 2005). As with much ideal-type analysis, this exercise typically results in dualistic evaluation. While some scholars attribute the popularity of online games to the (intentionally programmed) sociability they afford, others argue that online games are a 'life-denying simulacrum' contributing to the demise of social capital because their programmed sociability is 'an empty farce' (Rheingold 1993; Nie 2001; Brown and Bell 2006; Ducheneaut, Moore and Nickell 2007).

Looking across studies, the value-laden concept of sociability refers to forms of sociation requiring: specific venues and attitudes; etiquettes of civility and exchange; a feel for performative aesthetics; and sets of ordinary people in states of 'open' self-subtracted being (cf. Bersani 2009). This level of specificity suggests there is something to gain by installing sociability as a domain of anthropological inquiry. We might begin by investigating how and why the tenuous good form of graceful, *gemütlich*, exacting, yet cathartic sociability, undertheorized as it is, effortlessly musters moral appraisal, political unease and scholarly tracking.

VALUED EXOSOCIALITY

Many studies locate sociability beyond the presumably endosocial, kin-based and 'asocial' household unit (Friedman 1997; Rapport 2007: 381). This follows modernist social and political thinking that posits the involuntary sociation of work and home as less legitimate and virtuous than the open mixing of voluntary sociation. Situating sociability in venues of mixed company, Oldenburg (1999: 72–74) contends that inclusive, open association, and not affiliation deriving from family or employment, is central to the formation of community.[8]

Whereas participating in society and community proper appears to require shedding all involuntary affiliations, an open cosmopolitan stance requires a further shedding of 'one's own' kind of people, people similar to oneself. A nineteenth-century conversation between Eckermann and Goethe calls attention to social adroitness as a badge of refinement. When Eckermann admits to carrying his personal likes and dislikes 'into society', seeking out those 'conforming to his nature', and having 'nothing to do with the others', Goethe reproaches him:

> This natural tendency of yours is indeed not of a sociable kind; yet what would all our education be if we were not willing to overcome our natural tendencies ... I have ... attained the ability to converse with all people ... You ought to do likewise. There's no help for it, you must go into society. (Elias 2000: 28)

Goethe reprovingly contrasts Eckermann's parochial middle-class preference for familiar company with his own cultivated inclination to embrace the society of all.[9]

We find similar deliberations on 'open' and 'closed' interaction and relationality in a recent volume on cosmopolitan sociability (Darieva, Glick Schiller and Gruner-Domic 2012). In their introduction Glick Schiller et al. argue against equating cosmopolitanism with geographical mobility or universalist morality and tolerance. In their view, 'rooted' cosmopolitanism involves concrete social practices, that is, those everyday 'sociabilities in which a shared sense of common sensibilities does not override but coexists with ongoing diversity of perspective and practice' (Glick Schiller, Darieva and Gruner-Domic 2012: 3). They define cosmopolitan sociability as:

> consisting of forms of competence and communication skills that are based on the human capacity to create social relations of inclusiveness and openness to the world. As such cosmopolitan sociability is an ability to find aspects of the shared human experience including aspirations for a better world within or despite what would seem to be divides of culture or belief. (ibid.: 4–5)

Shifting focus from moralistic attitudes to communicative capacities, Glick Schiller et al. invest cosmopolitanism with human propensities for shared experience and inclusion rather than cultivated proclivities for social versatility and virtuous tolerance.

The notion of rooted cosmopolitanism – highlighting the simultaneity of in-group and out-group consociation – raises questions of how to delineate exosociality and endosociality. The French farmers of Baker's (1999) study have only to leave their farms to take part in village fire brigades to be represented as participating in an appropriately exosocial domain of *fraternité*. The religious actors of the studies found in Darieva, Glick Schiller and Gruner-Domic (2012), as active participants in religious communities and NGOs, and members of transnational religious and diasporic networks, are already exosocial in this civil sense.[10] To become appropriately exosocial in the cosmopolitan sense, they must step beyond their 'own' networks to consociate with 'others' of different cultural, religious, linguistic, as well as national, historical or local affiliation.

These studies reveal that sociability rests on a much more specific conceptual ground than sociality. Whereas sociality indexes 'the entire field of all social relations' (Glick Schiller, Darieva and Gruner-Domic 2012: 16), or a 'dynamic relational matrix' (Long and Moore 2013: 4), sociability indexes peaceable, exosocial sociation and relationality open to moral, aesthetic and political assessment. The contrived notion of rooted cosmopolitanism, in acknowledging the simultaneity of endosocial and exosocial relations and affiliations, and multiple senses of commonality and difference, drives questions of how boundaries of difference and commonality are imagined and achieved (Glick Schiller, Darieva and Gruner-Domic 2012: 16). The value commonly placed on exosociality compels us to investigate notions of 'own' and 'other' on which both 'society' and 'mixed company' are construed.

Although Glick Schiller et al. relocate exosociality in human nature, they do not dislodge sociability from its 'natural' habitat in a conceptual domain swept free of the involuntary sociation and utilitarian goals of family, work and state.[11] Tethering sociability to a specific 'exosocial' domain and forms of sociation risks excluding the quotidian relational expediencies and concerns of experiencing human beings. Whereas many studies address 'open' civil sociation and relatedness that purportedly bring consociates and co-citizens together across cultural and structural divides, few investigate the less positive sides of openness and mixing. Pursuing sociability as an object of anthropological inquiry obliges us to move beyond civil society frameworks to explore problems posed by living in close proximity, not just with reference to political stability and moral rectitude, but also with reference to the experiences of individuals wrestling with how to forge desired relations in and across spheres of social exchange. The following studies exemplify the tenuous and ambiguous processes of peer sociability in settings characterized by close daily proximity, institutional restraint and patterns of generalized exchange.

PERSONAL RELATIONSHIPS AND GENERALIZED SOCIABILITY

Birenbaum-Carmeli (1999) studied neighbourly sociability among middle-class Israeli women living in a residential area offering many opportunities for social contact. Examining ongoing relationships between sets of neighbours, she found their exchanges limited to particular times and spaces. Even when plying intensive, prolonged relationships, neighbours kept their distance. They seldom joined each other's social circles, and were careful not to become a burden or reveal too personal information. The study revealed that even close relationships between neighbours were ambiguous and ultimately dispensable. Yet despite the tenuous nature of these relations, residents held 'neighbouring' in high regard, generally investing much time and energy in this form of sociation. Even when harbouring grudges, neighbours sustained overt friendliness and outwardly maintained good sociable relations (ibid.: 82, 85, 91).

The shift from bars and cafés to processes of relating in residential housing complexes illuminates the ephemeral, partial, ambiguous and often tense nature of sociable relations. Neighbour sociability takes time and effort; it involves mutual provision of minor services like watering plants or feeding pets. It is both instrumental and involuntary when living in close proximity with others who frown upon un-neighbourliness (ibid.: 87). Drawing on Simmel's idea that egalitarian relationality requires eschewing both self-promotion and personal revelation, Birenbaum-Carmeli contends that it is precisely the 'impersonal character of this presumed egalitarianism' that helps constitute a 'collective image of neighbourliness' as a generalized sociability in which all categories of residents may share (ibid.: 90). Rather than employing 'pure' sociability as a yardstick, she demonstrates how neighbours forge tenuous relations in an urban residential setting characterized by the impersonal egalitarianism of generalized sociability.

Birenbaum-Carmeli suggests that co-residents value 'neighbouring' because it anchors them in local worlds (ibid.: 90–91). Local anchorage involves carving fairly predictable, potentially useful and intentionally partial personal relations and roles out of a seemingly open relational field. It entails shifting investments of time and energy over time, as neighbours keep in and fall out of touch as they come and go. Such impersonalized sociability claims 'a heavy toll in personal terms' (ibid.: 91). Even when communication among co-residents proceeds smoothly across divisions of class and status, 'people, personal relations, and contexts [are] all eroded, stripped of subjectivity and intimacy' (ibid.; see also Bersani 2009). The study demonstrates that sociability matters, not just to politicians and social theorists, but also to individuals facing relational ambiguities in tight quarters of urban living. It is instructive of how sociability infused with ideologies of 'openness', a generalized exchange of all with all, may inadvertently become a substitute for more intimate relational forms.

Whereas Birenbaum-Carmeli demonstrates how Israeli women forge accessible, yet limited neighbour relationships, Amit-Talai's (1995) study of peer sociability in a Quebec high school examines how adolescent girls fashion intimate relationships in and against the constraints of school. Amit-Talai argues that friendship does not just take place, nor is it separate from, or outside specific social contexts. On the contrary, sociability between friends is heavily confined and restricted by quotidian contexts in which peer sociability is not voluntary. School organization compresses and intensifies peer interaction in age-specific groupings, making anonymity and social distance difficult to sustain; it is 'hard to avoid other adolescents if you are surrounded by them for six hours a day, five days a week' (ibid.: 153–154). The amount of time and kinds of spaces available to youth for freely chosen peer interaction are affected by hierarchical age-grades, tight schedules, adult monitoring, family restrictions and after-school work (ibid.: 150–151, 160). Moreover, Canadian school organization intentionally disrupts and dislocates relationships by reshuffling students each year into different classes and courses. Thus young Canadians learn to value friendship as a generalized relational form and process, even as they experience and come to expect that friends are replaceable (ibid.: 161).

While schools control time and space, students also utilize space and time – shared time, elapsed time, spent time – to forge, encompass and erase intimate relationships (ibid.: 150). 'Friends were supposed to spend time with each other, but which time, how much, when and where was a matter of ongoing, and often uneasy negotiation of expectations and limitations' (ibid.: 156). Marking spatial proximity and time spent together, students monitor the chosen sociability of free periods and free time for 'overtones of preference, attachment and rejection' in assessing the character and quality of friendship relations (ibid.: 160). Students continuously constitute friendship by extending or retracting opportunities for interaction, and by deftly see-sawing between intentional revelation and concealment, appropriate knowing and telling, spending and owing time, commitment and non-commitment (ibid.: 155–156). Amit-Talai's work draws attention to the ambiguous and unstable relationality connected with the daily maintenance of intimate relationships requiring clear signs of effort, investment, commitment, and domain extension while constrained by institutional projects of time and space control.

Amit-Talai cautions against relegating peer sociability to leisure domains because youth friendship works off domain distinctions and boundaries. The 'generative capacity of "making friends" derives from its blurring of boundaries between social roles and spheres', a blurring that creates critical ambiguities in definitions of the situation (ibid.: 155, 156).

> When a group of [students] gathered in the corridors, bathroom, or even in class, definitions of the situation could alternate between a private conversation between friends, a public gathering, a formal lesson, a display of comic talent, sometimes in the space of seconds, sometimes between simultaneous interpretations. (ibid.: 158)

As Amit-Talai demonstrates, youth friendship plays out through ongoing interactional framing, which is indexical, open to simultaneous, diverse interpretations, and thus always potentially something else. It involves a constant, creative play on tensions between roles and spheres of interaction, and acts of criss-crossing, bridging and blurring that both establish and destabilize particular desired working definitions.

Taken together, the work of Birenbaum-Carmeli and Amit-Talai adds a critical focus on temporality, contextual constraint, spontaneous framing and individual vulnerability to our understanding of sociability. The authors demonstrate that establishing or disrupting kinds of relations in and across settings of physical proximity involves particular ways of acting over time. They reveal the uncertainty, tension and effort adhering to acts of forging or erasing durable, personal relationships in domains of involuntary proximity, impersonal intimacy and generalized sociability (cf. Bersani 2009: 60). Both note the transient animation of valued relationships in settings where replaceable individuals draw together and fall away. Finally, both argue that, despite ambiguity, tension and transience, people value the abstracted relational forms that anchor them in quotidian worlds.

Studying sociability as a dynamic relational process of giving relationships form rather than as a sociological ideal type inserts critical dimensions of time, space, emotion and scale into our understanding of sociability. Sociability draws on and is generative of culturally specific prototypical forms – friend, neighbour – that both stir our informants and drive our analytical interests. However, neither Amit-Talai nor Birenbaum-Carmeli directly addresses this question of form. I return therefore to Simmel's understanding of sociability as a particular form of sociation in which the question of form is central. The point is not to reinstall sociability as 'pure' form, but rather to draw attention to the trouble with form facing all who participate in sociable occasions, moments and relations.

QUESTIONS OF FORM

I suggest that we view sociability not just as a form of sociation,[12] but as ultimately about form. Of particular interest for an investigation of sociability is Simmel's emphasis on good form and play-form. For Simmel, everyday forms of sociation are at the heart of the sociological enterprise: 'if society is conceived as interaction among individuals, the description of the forms of this interaction is the task of the science of society in its strictest and most essential sense' (Simmel 1950: 21–22). Cautioning against conceiving of society solely as permanent interactions 'crystallized as definable consistent structures' of state, family, organization and class, Simmel focuses on the 'less conspicuous forms of relationships and kinds of interaction' that comprise any society (ibid.: 9). He posits that for collectivity to happen there must be an ongoing interplay and syntheses of relatively variable content and relatively stable form (ibid.: xxxix, xlvi). Through mutual exchange, individuals transpose the micro-historical material (drives, interests, purposes, inclinations) of their lives into specific forms of being with and for (and against) each other (ibid.: 40–41). It follows that all sociation is infused with form.

Simmel was interested in how interaction inhering in particular forms of sociation might lead to more durable units of association, a common sociological and political concern. Anthropologists have focused more on processes of individual meaning-making (content) expressed and mediated through the joint usage of common symbolic forms (Cohen 1985: 20; Rapport 2007: 227). Rapport envisages 'shared worlds' not as durable units of association, but as collections of common socio-cultural artefacts, which individuals appropriate, personalize and deploy idiosyncratically. Coming together and exchanging common ways of acting, individuals maintain them in their usage (Rapport 2007). Focus here is not on any causal connection between process and form, but rather on the simultaneous interplay of content and form as process. Recognizable forms cohering, however fleetingly, in this interplay are crucial to individual attempts to distinguish a joint course of action, negotiate a modus vivendi and determine what just was in order to figure out what comes next (Levinson 2006).

As noted, anthropologists have embraced sociality for its promise to yield dynamic analyses of social life as contingent process rather than reified structure, society or culture (Toren 2012). Embracing sociability as our object of inquiry compels us to account for form for the simple reason that living together compels everyone to take form into account. Meaningful social interaction invariably involves conventions of conduct inhering in particular ways of behaving and kinds of relationship. Whether or not they invest or comply, people attend to conventions and the realization of social moments, which as we know may go well, middling or frightfully wrong. People take keen stock of good form, investing impressive amounts of time, worry and pleasure in evaluating their own and others' social adeptness, perhaps because it is through social adroitness and sensitivity that people touch each other's lives and tug on each other's life-worlds.

Graceful Conduct

The American Emily Post (1872–1969) is legendary for her book on etiquette. Over numerous editions, the first published in 1922, Post offers young women advice on social convention: how to write invitations, convey regrets, address those of higher or lower social standing, arrange formal dinners, conduct oneself in public, at balls and when travelling abroad with or without a chaperone. Post is surprisingly explicit on the contingency and relativity of the rules of etiquette.

> One cannot make rules for a subject as variable as the attitude of one person toward every other person ... It is obvious that the first rules of courtesy, which exact consideration for the rights and feelings of others, are as diverse as are the differences in human temperament, taste and point of view. (Post 1937: 621)

For Post, etiquette is attitude and aesthetics rather than social correctness. It involves concerted choreography, integrity, common sense and social grace. In a chapter entitled 'What We Contribute to the Beauty of Living', Post discusses the art of agreeability and its contribution to life's enjoyment (ibid.: 621). This art involves the poise to invoke pleasantness, and the discretion to mind the privacy and feelings of others (ibid.: 623). It also requires the cultivation of tact, without which there would be little friendship and little accord – among individuals and nations as well as in business (ibid.). Yet Post is keenly aware that tact is double edged; it can be sincere and motivated by kindness, or insincere and motivated by self-advantage (ibid.: 623). Thus in addition to adeptness in invoking pleasantness and ensuring the social comfort of others, affable social intercourse requires formidable skill in conveying sincerity, suppressing and concealing insincerity, while discerning and countering the sincerity and insincerity of others.

Post's work highlights significant themes for the study of sociability. Because good form is contingent and relative, it requires social acumen, integrity, and communicative skill. Gracing a chance meeting or planned occasion with good form involves fashioning a mutually improvised choreography of emotional and aesthetic balance. Post's emphasis on sensitivity to the feelings of others underlines the latent emotional discomfort of amiable moments, as the contingencies of grace and ambiguities of tact render conventions open to manipulation and interpretative uncertainty (cf. Amit-Talai 1995). In sum, Post's work reveals the import of social convention for the mutual creation and maintenance of well-formed relations. Social convention is not rigid rule. It is contingent acts of grace and balance, establishing the right distance between self and other, while foregrounding pleasantness, consideration and sincerity, and keeping unpleasantness, insincerity and inconsideration at bay. Tact, in all its equivocality, is indispensable in fashioning and sustaining such balance. With Post, we might conceive of sociability as highly stylized interaction in which participants act in subjunctive moods of conventional propriety and graceful conduct in efforts to stabilize the inherent lability of form.

Probing urban life, Simmel's seminal treatment of sociability, written in the same era of extensive urbanization and social change as Post's book of etiquette, invokes a similar theme of amiable social intercourse. Simmel renders sociability as a form of sociation in which 'everyone should guarantee to the other that maximum of social values (joy, relief, vivacity)', and 'the pleasure of the individual is always contingent upon the joy of others' (Simmel 1949: 257). The context for these claims is early-twentieth-century concern with anomie and other assumed dysfunctions of modernity (Lyon 2009). Lyon contends that Simmel's ideal type of sociability is: 'implicitly conceived ... as a corrective to the ungrounded pluralisation of the life-world associated with modernity. It provides palliation for the modern problems of alienation, of instrumental reason, of rationalist bureaucracy and specialization, of incommensurate experience across social strata' (ibid.: 688). Implicitly reflecting the emerging metropolis of Berlin, Simmel's work on sociability speaks to particular problems of urban sociation. Echoing Goethe and Eckermann Simmel's treatment of sociability addresses societal and personal apprehensions with burgeoning numbers of urban dwellers, that 'mere aggregation of isolated individuals' (Simmel 1950: 42), more or less willing to engage co-sociates not of the same 'nature'. Although coming at sociability from different angles, Post and Simmel draw attention to links between personal and societal concerns with proper conduct and co-presence.

Evoking Domains

Though insightful, Simmel's work is uncritically ethnocentric, implicitly positing 'Northern European, professional-class occasions [as] an adequate basis for generalization' (Henricks 2003: 27). Simmel's work is also atemporal, providing no description of how sociable gatherings begin, proceed and end, or any discussion of the relational consequences of sociable gatherings over the course of a season (ibid.). A third problem lies in Simmel's idea of sociability as inhabiting or comprising a particular social domain, complete with specific venues, occasions and adept social actors. To establish 'pure' sociability, Simmel posits two functionally differentiated conceptual domains, one encompassing all 'instrumental and goal-oriented life', practical achievement, need and 'reality of consequence', the other encompassing 'pure' relationship, the non-goal-oriented social exchange among reduced selves. The instrumental domain becomes a foil for the sociable domain replete with amiable, pleasurable and 'not quite for real' interaction (cf. Trías 1983). By attributing all sociability to a non-goal-oriented domain of salons, parties and social circles, Simmel deftly evicts any trace of sociability from goal-oriented domains of streets, factories and families.[13]

Conceiving sociability as a domain unto itself, fenced off from spaces of 'instrumental and goal-oriented life', and freed of practical purpose and 're-ality of consequence', corresponds poorly with ethnography. The real goal of fighting fires is not detached from, but rather generative of, fraternal social-izing among French volunteer firemen (Baker 1999). Time spent with work-mates in Parisian cafés is never free of 'real life' relationships, goal-oriented working-class politics or the exigencies of small apartments overflowing with children and wet laundry (Haine 1996). Canadian adolescent sociability is not detached from, but rather compressed, constrained and disrupted by goal-directed schools and families (Amit-Talai 1995). Ethnography shows that sociable relations may be rife with instrumentality and not necessarily voluntary, pleasurable or even satisfying (Birenbaum-Carmeli 1999).

Treating sociability narrowly as behaviour appropriate to and manifest in social occasions set apart in time and space from quotidian life, Simmel overestimates the voluntarism, joy and equality of his chosen settings (Hen-ricks 2003: 26). As Henricks notes, in Simmel's world, people sit at tables, where:

> they play with what spirit and skill they can muster; they avoid bad manners that would prevent their being invited back. At the conclusion, they say their good-byes to their host and leave. Again as any partygoer knows, real events feature a continual tension between staying and leaving, connecting with oth-ers and finding oneself isolated, feeling overstimulated or bored. (ibid.: 27–28)

Simmel's ideal type of 'pure' sociability remains thus awkwardly at odds with common knowledge of actual sociable moments and events.

Given such serious problems, Simmel's notion of 'pure' sociability taken in full is not a useful template for ethnographic inquiry. Rather than uncrit-ically mapping 'pure' sociability onto Wednesday-night bowling leagues or *Second Life*, we must explore how individuals work together to frame social interaction in ways that foreground or forestall particular definitions of the situation. Rather than inferring contrived, 'purified' domains, we must pay attention to ways of acting that evoke domains and lend them social and conceptual force.

Good Form, Play-Form

Simmel characterizes 'pure' sociability as a form of sociation in which all participants act in ways that focus on the success of the sociable moment. Allowing for different interpretations of success, this is true of all interaction;

participants generally act together in ways meaningful and relevant to the interactional genre at hand (grocery shopping, conversation, ritual). Simmel further characterizes 'pure' sociability as a play-form of sociation in which good form hinges on 'actual life conditions' appearing in reduced form and on the ability of participants to balance between upper and lower thresholds of self-enactment (Simmel 1950: 44). Yet as Jackson notes, all societies encompass a variety of contexts in which co-presence requires balanced self-enactment. 'Rather than some self-conscious standing out from the crowd or transcendence of one's egocentric standpoint, the issue is one of bringing personal proclivities and persuasions under control and so acquiring the ability to work and coexist with others in *practically* efficacious ways' (Jackson 1998: 12; original emphasis). According to Jackson, the practical relational work of co-presence – when greeting one another, sitting down together, working together or moving as a body – requires acts of self restraint and able performances of civility, etiquette and emotion (ibid.: 13).

The distinct contribution of Simmel's work on sociability lies in its focus on contexts that accentuate good form. How co-sociates play on and to relational form is heightened when the singular objective of interaction is to grant each other social equivalence and enjoyable company. Simmel characterizes this sociability as an abstracted play-form, akin to art and play, deriving from reality without evoking the frictions of reality (Simmel 1950: 43–45, 47). Similar to the playful nip that stands for, yet is not, a real bite (Bateson 1972),[14] sociable moments must be seamlessly enacted as both once removed from and permeated by (real) life, signalling neither empty artifice nor real aggression (Simmel 1950: 42). Simmel draws attention to the performative challenges posed by any artful play on form. Good form hinges on making actual life and selves appear in properly reduced forms.[15] Simmel reminds us that human beings find the sociable staging of abstracted, suspended interaction, rife with tension and ambiguity, both fascinating and compelling (ibid.: 43–44).

Hailing sociability as a democratic form of sociation in which participants act as if equal, Simmel lifts sociability beyond normative presumptions of 'empty idleness' (Frisby 1984: 125) and invites inquiry into interactional genres in which participants draw on abstracted form to grant each other commonality (cf. Hage 2002: 203). Ethnographic studies show that people value abstracted relational forms – friends and neighbours – even when animated by a transient series of individuals (Amit-Talai 1995; Birenbaum-Carmeli 1999). Simmel's argument that humans come to feel associated through extracted form (Simmel 1950: 43–44) concurs with Birenbaum-Carmeli's claim that people engage in 'neighbouring' for its potential to anchor them in local social worlds of generalized exchange (Birenbaum-Carmeli 1999:

90–91). Yet although working together to improvise abstracted relational forms may evoke a sense of similarity, fellow feeling or communality (Wardle 1995), this must not be taken for granted. In that collective behaviour is best understood as 'an aggregative and not an integrative phenomenon' (Rapport 2007: 226), the two small words 'as if' are important. Playing to the good form of sociable genres is perhaps best interpreted as acting as if associated, rather than as if equal or equivalent in any democratic, cultural or universal sense.

Ludic Licence

Simmel's notion of 'pure' sociability calls attention to how individuals play to and with distinctive social and cultural forms, working together to forge particular abstracted relations. Although all interaction is ludic, Simmel intuited that there are forms of sociation in which careful, tactful and iconic play on form is vital to the interaction. In Simmel's account, people act together, playing on form in ways that performed well bring forth an iconic version of 'real life'. As Post (1937) observes, there is licence in any play on form. People may act gracefully and tactfully in many appropriate ways as long as they do not derail the appropriate mood of an encounter or occasion. While both Simmel and Post acknowledge ludic licence; neither dwells on how an appropriate range of play is determined or what happens when ludic licence hits its limit.

Interactional genres that stress good form are inherently labile, though not always to the same degree. Lability inheres in the fact that individuals must work together to tactfully improvise a particular relational form and ambience. Individuals must collude – literally play together – to evoke desirable relationalities and preferred relationships, and avoid indexing bad form. The lability of sociable moments lies in their indexicality and openness to shifting interpretation (Amit-Talai 1995). We can interpret and act on them in many different ways, not all equally appropriate. The ambiguity of sociable moments appeals to moral judgements of good (and bad) action: good friends should find time; good neighbours should help; good mates should buy a round. It also speaks to aesthetic assessments of good (and bad) form, as in a 'pleasurable evening', 'a boring party' or a 'tense encounter'. Amit-Talai argues convincingly that incentives to comply with, or play to, collective senses of good form derive less from the 'onus toward conformity to a collective standard' of appropriateness than from the very 'indeterminacy of that standard' (Amit-Talai 1995: 158; cf. Rapport 1993: 168). Coupled with convictions that such standards exist, indeterminacy leads to the constant work of negotiating, establishing and sustaining appropriate definitions of the situation and thus the appropriateness of form. As such, any conceptual framing arrived at will be premised on the simultaneity of what particular actions should and should not denote (Bateson 1972). We might thus think of sociable ways of acting as the art of simultaneously drawing on, playing to and asserting prototypical referents of good form while banishing any referents of inappropriate form. Improvisatory skill at holding off or repairing acts that may be interpreted as inappropriate is at the heart of what we call tact, grace, discretion, consideration and diplomacy, to name a few.

Shadow Realms and Shadow Play

Simmel describes sociability as a 'shadow realm' of symbolic play, a form of sociation in which protagonists play with forms, 'enacting the mere silhouettes of their serious imports' (Simmel 1950: 51). 'Pure' sociability 'abstracts real forms' and 'gives them shadowy bodies'; it knows no friction 'because shadows, being what they are, cannot collide' (ibid.: 51, 54). A sociable quarrel is not a real quarrel in this amiable shadow play of 'real life' sociation (ibid.: 52). In positing frictionless silhouettes and setting them off from real forms in separate yet mutually constituting domains, Simmel offers a rather benign version of the shadow.

Amit-Talai's (1995) understanding of the uneasy indeterminacy of good standards along with the artful blurring and criss-crossing of interactional domains provides a more useful point of departure for understanding the shadow play of good sociable form. Here the shadow is not a frictionless silhouette, but a *Doppelgänger* that sustains a constant tension between what is visible and what is not (at the moment) visible (Corsín Jiménez and Willerslev 2007). In Simmel's iconic shadow play, appropriate acts pose as abstractions of real life. In Corsín Jiménez and Willerslev's understanding, constant tension between the visible and the invisible speaks to any working consensus of the situation. From their perspective, sociability is not a shadow realm unto itself, but a form of sociation rife with the shadows of its constituting subtractions and reductions. Rather than stabilizing neatly in any one domain, what stabilizes is the constantly posed question of which way of acting is momentarily most visible. Thus we may expect to find all the competition, hierarchy, conflict, goal orientation and social discomfort that Simmel relegates to a conceptual domain of 'real life' lurking in the good form of sociable moments and simultaneously constituting experiences, expectations, interpretations and engagement. And although good form is infused with ludic licence, the reversibility of abstracted form sets limits beyond which good form breaks down (cf. Corsín Jiménez and Willerslev 2007).

Embracing sociability as an object of enquiry moves us beyond ideal types threatening to reify as analytical wholes. Drawing on Trías's concept of limit, Corsín Jiménez and Willerslev argue that concepts have a double capacity to provide stable meaning and 'unsettle their own reificatory tendencies', in that 'things' are never just themselves, but always something else as well (ibid.: 528, 537). '[A] visible institution or practice is never simply identical with itself but always carries with it an invisible double or shadow, which can turn back upon it so that one crosses over and becomes the other' (ibid.: 528–529). Their theory of concepts concedes ludic licence, yet posits limits beyond which conceptual frames reverse, revealing the mutually constitutive negative referents carried by these frames.

Although Strathern (2011) cautions that not all concepts have shadows, I concur with Simmel that sociability does. Central to Corsín Jiménez and Willerslev's shadow theory is the tenet that within every conceptual description must be an 'ulterior space' for future description. This idea allows us to probe ludic licence and conceptual limits without gluing our examination to any reified concept of sociability (Corsín Jiménez and Willerslev 2007: 537). It raises questions of how good abstracted form is made to appear and disappear, both as spontaneous conceptual framing and a historically constituted category. It also drives the question of which 'future description' we want to pursue. Surely what concerns individuals, scholars and politicians about sociability is more than disciplined self-reduction and ludic shadow play.[16]

Living Together

Discussing Amazonian notions of conviviality, Overing and Passes focus attention on the social aesthetics and ethics of communal living to which relational qualities of affect, care, intimacy and social comfort are central (Overing and Passes 2000: 3–4, 8). They are critical of dominant conceptual frameworks that partition society into public and private, work and leisure, civil and domestic, because these lead us to overlook the intimate sociability of living together (ibid.: xiii; see also Kohn 2005: 839). Their work opens further questions about how both endosocial and exosocial relationships are enacted according to codes of sharing, trust and mutuality that serve to transform potential harm into harmony.

Although most agree that sociability 'brings people together', actual processes of transformation and conversion, incorporation and rejection are not well understood.[17] Employing conceptual frameworks that posit free-floating individuals interacting in exosocial domains, we forget to ask how interior and exterior agents are conceptualized, positioned and converted one into the other. And by fusing sociability with domains of democratic civil society, we mistakenly imagine a space in which everybody is welcome (cf. Candea and Da Col 2012: 4). We may thus fail to account for important questions of how common space is established, how entitlement to common social space is legitimated and how good conduct is constituted in common spaces where relations between insiders and outsiders, owners and newcomers, hosts and guests are made relevant.

LIVING TOGETHER IN A DANISH SCHOOL

Schools offer excellent vantage points for examining culturally preferred forms of sociation, conventions of good form and processes of relational conversion. The following example illustrates how relational pedagogies work to transform random involuntary sets of Danish children into intimates.

A central tenet of Danish educational policy is 'no child left alone'. Cultural policy should ideally contribute to all children viewing themselves as part of a larger whole (*fællesskab*) (Anderson 2008). In keeping with this, and in contrast to the constant reshuffling of children and youth in Canadian schools (Amit-Talai 1995), Danish schools organize children in family-like home classes in which they ideally live and grow up together during ten years of comprehensive schooling. Each class is assigned a class teacher responsible for 'parenting' the class, for knowing each child well and caring for their individual emotional, social and scholastic needs.[18] Permanent classes transform random sets of children into sibling-like intimates, and provide durable territories of indisputable belonging, in which children individually or as a group may receive or rebuff 'foreigners' – substitute teachers or children from a parallel class (Anderson 2004).

Permanent home classes are grounded in received dogma that children learn best when surrounded by 'those they know', familiars with whom they feel comfortable and free to speak up or make mistakes. Because it is good for children to 'be themselves', unfettered by adult direction, lessons are frequently conducted affably with much talking and working together. Classmates break into small groups, moving to the hall or library, where they fuse schoolwork with chatting, Facebook or online games, which often results in their meeting again privately to finish their work, or glibly announcing in class that they need more time.

Danish educators also view permanent classes as societal microcosms, 'playpens of democracy' where coming generations are trained in social competencies necessary for democratic citizenship (Korsgaard 2008). As members of a home class, children are continually prompted with aphorisms: 'we all have to be here' and 'there must be room for everybody'. They are encouraged to develop other regarding virtues, to care about each other's emotional well-being and feel mutual responsibility for the good social functioning and inclusive tone of the class. Drawing on an orthodox pedagogical stance that democracy is a way of life, and that democratic dispositions are best inculcated via quotidian practices of getting along with close consociates, teachers work to develop children's capacity for conflict solving through 'democratic dialogue' (ibid.).

Class teachers also work to create 'well-functioning' classes by bringing children and parents together, literally 'shaking them together' (*ryste dem sammen*) through an ongoing series of social events. At regular school camps, classes spend two or three days in the countryside, eating, bathing, sleeping, playing, working and singing together. Classes also arrange Christmas parties and summer picnics to which, in the younger grades, they invite parents and siblings. At parent–teacher meetings, class parents negotiate collective guidelines for privately held birthday parties, potentially harmful to a class's social functioning because they display and aggravate the 'loneness' of certain children. Parents may opt to hold collective birthday parties at school, or oblige each other to invite the entire class or all the boys or girls to parties held at home.

To ensure that no child is left alone, class teachers organize playgroups, which parents take turns hosting such that all classmate relations ideally extend, as if friends, into all private homes. Parents collectively decide on acceptable pocket money for class excursions, and as children grow older, parents lay down moral guidelines for class parties held in private homes. Finally, parents themselves are encouraged to spend time getting to know each other by sharing food and drink, because familiarity (*at kende hinanden*) is thought to generate connection and agreement, and thus lay the ground for amicable years together as class parents. Needless to say, there is a strong moral obligation to participate in class-based social events that both cross and blur boundaries between home and school.

In Danish schools, learning, self-development, democracy, legitimate belonging and insider authority are all made contingent on permanent home classes enacted as 'school families' replete with ideals of emotional mutuality, collective identity and a mutual obligation to shared life (Anderson 2000; Ford and Anderson 2008). The pedagogical work of converting strangers into intimates, and training children in the art of living well together in 'their own class', is a central feature of Danish schooling. Transforming random aggregations of children and parents into proper classes, at once both exosocial and endosocial, appears to require generous doses of intimacy-inducing sociability both within and beyond school.

This brief case highlights the importance of investigating forms of intimate sociability in societies long since partitioned into public and private domains, and rife with political rhetoric that assigns valued voluntary sociation to open domains of civil society. We would be mistaken to relegate all living together and sharing the same life, along with the emotional mutuality inherent in getting along, engendering trust and caring through which people construct themselves as moral beings, exclusively to kin-based domains of family and home, or even Amazonia (Overing and Passes 2000). As shown here, prescriptive pedagogies invoke moralities of participation and exosocial intimacy to fashion good classes that may temper and anchor the apparently uneasy (*utryg*) social openness of educational settings for children, parents and teachers alike.

CONCLUSION

Not idle pastime, sociability matters greatly to individuals and to those who feel responsible for society. Guiding this chapter's exploration of sociability was the question of the concept's heuristic potential. What might be gained by shifting focus from more generic sociality to more value-laden sociability? Neither neatly distinct from nor neatly nested within sociality, sociability poses tricky conceptual ground. Arguing against analytical conventions of tying sociability to particular social forms and emotional tonalities in particular venues and domains, this chapter opens up new questions. For example, how do people delineate, evoke and blur conceptual domains through particular ways of acting? How do they define in and out groups, and when and where do boundaries between them matter? Which relational moralities and valued aesthetics do they emphasize, and how have these gained legitimacy? What are the quotidian tensions and vulnerabilities of relating, and which permanent or fleeting affiliations are people attempting to create or circumvent? Finally, how do they think about personal preference and vulnerability with regard to the art of living well together?

Following Simmel, sociability points to questions of form, how social interaction takes and is given form, and how the subjunctive play of good form appears crucial to particular kinds of sociation and relationality. In uncovering what constitutes good form in any given society or situation, however, it is crucial to recognize that abstracted relational forms are labile to the core because they are full to the brim with what they must (also) not be. What then are the social implications of abstracted relational forms, whose constitution relies on the joint action of making disappear what must not be included? Reification here is not the problem; rather, it is our utter powerlessness to fix abstracted forms and relational concepts. In this instability lies the larger question of how people actually manage to act as if associated. What motivates participation, and how is the work of interacting as if associated practised, steadied and made relevant in particular times, settings and situations?

Installing sociability as an object of anthropological inquiry is productive only if we openly probe all forms – exosocial and endosocial, stilted and casual, generalized and intimate, common and segregated, hosted and guested, at home and 'out' – as conceived and practised by the people with whom we engage. We must pay attention to how they imagine commonality and collectivity, how they construct interior and exterior forces, spaces and agents, and the processes and forms through which they extend and convert relationships across domains. We must not neglect cases where participants do not act as if equal, but rather as solicitous kin or reluctant hosts and guests working through tensions of love and anger, suspicion and trust, calculation and spontaneity, in uneven exchanges that leave everyone something to talk about. If we try to capture sociability as a purified category, we will fail to grasp its full analytical potential for understanding the valued yet uneasy social forms and conventions through which people live together.

ACKNOWLEDGEMENTS

This chapter was developed through vigorous discussion in the good company of fellow contributors. Vered Amit deserves special kudos for unswerving direction and patience.

NOTES

1. Simmel's insights are contained in 'Die Geselligkeit', chapter three of his *Grundfragen der Soziologie* (1917), later translated into English as 'Sociability: An Example of Pure, or Formal, Sociology' (Simmel 1950: 40–57). This essay is widely credited as the first serious examination of sociability (Henricks 2003).
2. See, however, Bersani (2009).
3. Baker (1999) views voluntary associations as forms of sociability that provide opportunities for sociability, a typical example of fuzzy usage.

4. Hanks (2006) reminds us that both common and uncommon ground are produced and breached through joint action.

5. This definition is taken from a journal special issue on the subject of sociality (Long and Moore 2012). In their book based on this issue, Long and Moore (2013) separate this definition into two formulations. It makes sense here to keep them together.

6. Levinson (2006: 45) argues that fundamental social interaction operates independently of language.

7. Referring to nonviolent community activism, Pink defines sociality as 'different sets of concrete ... social relationships that develop around actual activities' (Pink 2008: 172). This definition, however, works equally well for less peaceable activity.

8. Although heavily criticized, Banfield's (1958) notion of amoral familism infuses many studies embracing the idea that non-kin-based exosociality is morally superior to familial endosociality.

9. See also Moorhead (1998: 59).

10. Civil sociality designates the exosocial (i.e. extra-domestic) relational space of organized voluntary associations, regarded in much Western social theory as the backbone of democratic society (Anderson 2008).

11. 'Home' and 'work' are not necessarily separate, sociability-free domains. Daily work relations among Piaroa are constituted through convivial 'bantering, slapstick, and ... bawdy humour' (Overing and Passes 2000: 16).

12. Simmel's *Vergesellschaftung* has been variously rendered in English as 'socialization', 'societalization, 'association' and 'sociality' (Wolff 1950: lxiii). I follow Wolff's gloss: 'sociation'.

13. That vital forms of sociability take place in domestic domains is illustrated by Meneley's (1996) work on the import of female socializing in Yemen, and Candea and da Col's (2012) work on hospitality highlighting ambiguous encounters between hosts and guests.

14. Play is a relational form based on the meta-message: 'These actions, in which we now are engaged, do not denote what would be denoted by those actions which these actions denote. The playful nip denotes the bite, but does not denote what would be denoted by the bite [e.g. the intention to harm]' (Bateson 1972: 180). Play-forms are thus locked into a relation with what they denote, yet do not denote in the same way. The indeterminacy and slippage between a play-form and its invisible, irreconcilable yet always present double affords ludic pleasure, uneasiness and licence.

15. Bersani (2009: 48, 60) sees this self-subtracted being, in which we are not quite ourselves, as a form of self-disciplining or ascetic conduct.

16. I thank Noel Dyck for the suggestion that there is more to sociability than mere play on form.

17. See, however, Howell (2003).

18. A class teacher heads a team of teachers ideally bound to a class over a span of several years.

REFERENCES

Agulhon, M. 1984. 'Working Class and Sociability in France before 1848', in P. Thane, G. Crossick, and R. Floud (eds), *The Power of the Past: Essays for Eric Hobsbawm*. Cambridge: Cambridge University Press, pp.37–66.

Amit, V., and N. Rapport. 2002. *The Trouble with Community. Anthropological Reflections on Movement, Identity, and Collectivity*. London: Pluto Press.

—— 2012. *Community, Cosmopolitanism and the Problem of Human Commonality*. London: Pluto Press.

Amit-Talai, V. 1995. 'The Waltz of Sociability: Intimacy, Dislocation and Friendship in a Quebec High School', in V. Amit-Talai and H. Wulff (eds), *Youth Cultures: A Cross-cultural Perspective*. London: Routledge, pp.144–165.

Anderson, S. 2000. *I en klasse for sig* [In a class of their own]. Copenhagen: Gyldendal.

—— 2004. 'Kunsten at drille en vikar' [The art of teasing a substitute], in U.A. Madsen (ed.), *Pædagogisk Antropologi: reflektioner over feltbaseret viden*. Copenhagen: Hans Reitzels Forlag, pp.100–121.

—— 2008. *Civil Sociality: Children, Sport, and Cultural Policy in Denmark*. Charlotte, NC: Information Age Press.

Baker, A.R.H. 1999. *Fraternity among the French Peasantry: Sociability and Voluntary Associations in the Loire Valley, 1815–1914*. New York: Cambridge University Press.

Banfield, E.C. 1958. *The Moral Basis of a Backward Society*. Glencoe, IL: Free Press.

Bateson, G. 1972. 'A Theory of Play and Fantasy', in *Steps to an Ecology of Mind*. New York: Ballantine Books, pp.177–193.

Bauman, R. 1972. 'The La Have Island General Store: Sociability and Verbal Art in a Nova Scotia Community', *Journal of the American Folklore Society* 85(338): 330–343.

Beaurepaire, P.Y. 2011. 'Sociability', in W. Doyle (ed.), *The Oxford Handbook of the Ancien Régime*. Oxford: Oxford University Press, pp.374–387.

Bersani, L. 2009. *Is the Rectum a Grave and Other Essays*. Chicago: University of Chicago Press.

Birenbaum-Carmeli, D. 1999. '"Love Thy Neighbour": Sociability and Instrumentality among Israeli Neighbours', *Human Organization* 58(1): 82–93.

Bomhoff, M. 2011. 'Long-lived Sociality: A Cultural Analysis of Middle-class Older Persons' Social Lives in Kerala, India', PhD thesis. Leiden: Leiden Institute for Area Studies, Leiden University.

Bourdieu, P. 1984. *Distinction: A Social Critique of the Judgment of Taste*, trans. R. Nice. London: Routledge and Kegan Paul.

Broadhead, P. 2001. 'Investigating Sociability and Cooperation in Four and Five Year Olds in Reception Class Settings', *International Journal of Early Years Education* 9(1): 23–35.

Brown, B., and M. Bell. 2006. 'Play and Sociability in There: Some Lessons from Online Games for Collaborative Virtual Environments', in R. Schroeder and A.-S. Axelsson (eds), *Avatars at Work and Play: Collaboration and Interaction in Shared Virtual Environments*. Dordrecht: Springer, pp.227–245.

Candea, M., and G. da Col. 2012. 'The Return to Hospitality: Strangers, Guests and Ambiguous Encounters', *Journal of the Royal Anthropological Institute*, special issue, 18, Issue Supplement.

Cohen, A.P. 1985. *The Symbolic Construction of Community*. London: Routledge.

Cohen, B.B. 2009. 'Networks of Sociability: Women's Clubs in Colonial and Postcolonial India. *Frontiers: A Journal of Women Studies* 30(3): 169–195.

Corsín Jiménez, A., and R. Willerslev. 2007. 'An Anthropological Concept of the Concept: Reversibility among Siberian Yukaghirs', *Journal of the Royal Anthropological Institute* 13: 527–544.

Cowan, B. 2005. *The Social Life of Coffee: The Emergence of the British Coffeehouse*. New Haven: Yale University Press.

Darieva, T., N. Glick Schiller and S. Gruner-Domic. 2012. *Cosmopolitan Sociability: Locating Transnational Religious and Diasporic Networks*. London: Routledge.

Dreissen, H. 1983. 'Male Sociability and Rituals of Masculinity in Rural Andalusia', *Anthropological Quarterly* 56(6): 125–133.

Ducheneaut, N., R.J. Moore and E. Nickell. 2007. 'Virtual "Third Places": A Case Study of Sociability in Massively Multiplayer Games', *Computer Supported Cooperative Work* 16(1/2): 129–166.

Dueck, B. 2007. 'Public and Intimate Sociability in First Nations and Métis Fiddling', *Ethnomusicology* 51(1): 30–63.

Dunbar, R. 1994. 'Sociality Among Human and Non-human Animals', in T. Ingold (ed.), *Companion Encyclopedia of Anthropology*. London: Routledge, pp.756–782.

Elias, N. 2000. *The Civilizing Process: Sociogenetic and Psychogenetic Investigations*. Oxford: Blackwell.

Enfield, N.J., and S.C. Levinson. 2006. *Roots of Human Sociality: Culture, Cognition and Interaction*. Oxford: Berg.

Ericsson, T. 1989. 'Kinship and Sociability: Urban Shopkeepers in Nineteenth-century Sweden', *Journal of Family History* 14(3): 229–239.

Flanagan, C. 1999. *Early Socialisation: Sociability and Attachment*. London: Routledge.

Ford, K., and S. Anderson. 2008. 'Klassens væsen' [The nature of the class], in J.B. Krejsler and L. Moos (eds), *Magtkampe i praksis, pædagogik og politik* [Power struggles in practice, pedagogy and politics. Frederikshavn: Dafolo, pp.41–60.

Friedman, J. 1997. 'Simplifying Complexity: Assimilating the Global in a Small Paradise', in K.F. Olwig and K. Hastrup (eds), *Siting Culture: The Shifting Anthropological Object*. London: Routledge. pp.268–291.

Frisby, D. 1984. *Georg Simmel*. London: Ellis Horword.

Glick Schiller, N., T. Darieva and S. Gruner-Domic. 2012. 'Defining Cosmopolitan Sociability in a Transnational Age: An Introduction', in T. Darieva, N. Glick Schiller and S. Gruner-Domic (eds), *Cosmopolitan Sociability: Locating Transnational Religious and Diasporic Networks*. London: Routledge, pp.1–20.

Habermas, J. 1991. *The Structural Transformation of the Public Sphere: An Inquiry into a Category of Bourgeois Society*, trans. T. Burger and F. Lawrence. Cambridge, MA: MIT Press.

Hage, G. 2002. 'The Differential Intensities of Social Reality: Migration, Participation and Guilt', in G. Hage (ed.), *Arab Australians Today: Citizenship and Belonging*. Melbourne: Melbourne University Press, pp.192–205.

Haine, W.S. 1996. *The World of the Paris Café: Sociability Among the French Working Class 1789–1914*. Baltimore: Johns Hopkins University Press.

Hanks, W.F. 2006. 'Joint Commitment and Common Ground in a Ritual Event', in N.J. Enfield and S.C. Levinson (eds), *Roots of Human Sociality: Culture, Cognition and Interaction*. Oxford: Berg, pp.299–328.

Henricks, T.S. 2003. 'Simmel: On Sociability as the Play-form of Human Association' in D.E. Lytle (ed.), *Play and Educational Theory and Practice*. Westport, CT: Praeger, pp.19–31.

Howell, S. 2003. 'Kinning: the Creation of Life Trajectories in Transnational Adoptive Families', *Journal of the Royal Anthropological Institute* 9(3): 465–484.

Ingold, T. 1993. 'The Temporality of the Landscape', *World Archaeology* 25(2): 152–174.

—— 2000. *The Perception of the Environment: Essays on Livelihood, Dwelling and Skill*. London: Routledge

—— (ed.). 1996. *Key Debates in Anthropology*. London: Routledge.

Jackson, M. 1998. *Minima Ethnographica: Intersubjectivity and the Anthropological Project*. Chicago: University of Chicago Press.

Kale, S.D. 2004. *French Salons: High Society and Political Sociability from the Old Regime to the Revolution of 1848*. Baltimore: Johns Hopkins University Press.

Kohn, E. 2005. 'Understanding the Intimacy of Amazonian Sociality', *Current Anthropology* 46(5): 839–840.

Korsgaard, O. 2008. 'Skolen som demokratiets kravlegård' [School as the playpen of democracy], *Sprog og Integration* 2: 4–7.

Kreijns, K., P.A. Kirschner and W. Jochems. 2002. 'The Sociability of Computer-supported Collaborative Learning Environments', *Educational Technology and Society* 5(1): 8–22.

Levinson, S.C. 2006. 'On the Human "Interaction Engine"', in N.J. Enfield and S.C. Levinson (eds), *Roots of Human Sociality: Culture, Cognition and Interaction*. Oxford: Berg, pp.39–69.

Lilti, A. 2009. 'The Kingdom of *Politesse*: Salons and the Republic of Letters in Eighteenth-century Paris', *Republics of Letters: A Journal for the Study of Knowledge, Politics, and the Arts* 1(1): 1–11.

Long, N.J., and H.L. Moore. 2012. 'Sociality Revisited: Setting a New Agenda', *Cambridge Anthropology*, special issue, 30(1): 40–46.

—— 2013 'Introduction: Sociality's New Directions', in N.J. Long and H.L. Moore (eds), *Sociality: New Directions*. Oxford: Berghahn, pp.1–24.

Lyon, J. 2009. 'Sociability in the Metropole: Modernism's Bohemian Salons', *English Literary History* 76(3): 687–711.

Meneley, A. 1996. *Tournaments of Value: Sociability and Hierarchy in a Yemeni Town*. Toronto: University of Toronto Press.

Moorhead, J.K. (ed.). 1998. *Conversations of Goethe with Johann Peter Eckermann*, trans. J. Oxenford. Cambridge, MA: Da Capo Press.

Nie, N.H. 2001. 'Sociability, Interpersonal Relations, and the Internet Reconciling Conflicting Findings', *American Behavioural Scientist* 45(3): 420–435.

Oldenburg, R. 1999. *The Great Good Place*. Cambridge, MA: Da Capo Press.

Overing, J., and A. Passes. 2000. 'Introduction: Conviviality and the Opening up of Amazonian Anthropology', in J. Overing and A. Passes (eds), *The Anthropology of Love and Anger: The Aesthetics of Conviviality in Native Amazonia*. London: Routledge, pp.1–30.

Pink, S. 2008. 'Re-thinking Contemporary Activism: From Community to Emplaced Sociality', *Ethnos* 73(2): 163–188.

Post, E. 1937. *Etiquette: The Blue Book of Social Usage*, rev. edn. New York: Funk and Wagnalls.

Postill, J. 2008. 'Localizing the Internet beyond Communities and Networks', *New Media and Society* 10(3): 413–431.

Putnam, R. 1995. 'Bowling Alone: America's Declining Social Capital', *Journal of Democracy* 6(1): 65–78.

Rapport, N. 1987. *Talking Violence: An Anthropological Interpretation of Conversation in the City*. St John's: Institute of Social and Economic Research, Memorial University of Newfoundland.

—— 1993. *Diverse World Views in an English Village*. Edinburgh: Edinburgh University Press.

—— 2007. 'Interaction', in N. Rapport and J. Overing (eds), *Social and Cultural Anthropology: The Key Concepts*. London: Routledge, pp.226–237.

Rheingold, H. 1993. *The Virtual Community: Homesteading on the Electronic Frontier*. Cambridge, MA: MIT Press.

Rudie, I. 1994. 'Making Sense of New Experience', in K. Hastrup and P. Hervik (eds), *Social Experience and Anthropological Knowledge*. London: Routledge, pp.21–33.

Schiffrin, D. 1984. 'Jewish Argument as Sociability', *Language in Society* 13(3): 311–335.

Seligman, A.B. 1992. *The Idea of Civil Society*. New York: Free Press.

Sibbald, A.M., D.A. Elston, D.J.F. Smith and H.W. Erhard. 2005. 'A Method for Assessing the Relative Sociability of Individuals within Groups: An Example with Grazing Sheep', *Applied Animal Behaviour Science* 91(1): 57–73.

Simmel, G. 1949. 'The Sociology of Sociability', *American Journal of Sociology* 55(3): 254–261.

—— 1950. *The Sociology of George Simmel*, trans. and ed. K.H. Wolff. Glencoe, IL: Free Press.

Smith-Hefner, N.J. 2007. 'Young Language, Gaul Sociability and the New Indonesian Middle Class', *Journal of Linguistic Anthropology* 17(2): 184–203.

Steinkeuler, C.A. 2005. 'The New Third Place: Massively Multiplayer Online Gaming in American Youth Culture', *Journal of Research in Teacher Education* 12(3): 17–32.

Strathern, M. 2011. 'Sharing, Stealing, and Borrowing Simultaneously', in V. Strang and M. Busse (eds), *Ownership and Appropriation*. London: Berg, pp.23–42.

Thompson, R.A., and M.E. Lamb. 1983. 'Security of Attachment and Stranger Sociability in Infancy', *Developmental Psychology* 19(2): 184–191.

Toren, C. 2012. 'Imagining the World that Warrants Our Imagination: The Revelation of Ontogeny', *Cambridge Anthropology* 30(1): 64–79.

Trías, E. 1983. *Philosophy and Its Shadow*, trans. K. Krabbenhoft. New York: Columbia University Press.

Varenne, H. 2009. 'The Powers of Ignorance: On Finding Out what to Do Next', *Critical Studies in Education* 50(3): 337–343.

Wardle, H. 1995. 'Kingston, Kant and Common Sense', *Cambridge Anthropology* 18(3): 40–55.

Weisner, T.S. 1976. 'The Structure of Sociability: Urban Migration and Urban–Rural Ties in Kenya', *Urban Anthropology* 5(2): 199–223.

Wolff, K.H. 1950. 'Introduction', in *The Sociology of George Simmel*, trans. and ed. K.H. Wolff. Glencoe, IL: Free Press, pp.xvii–lxiv.

5

Organizations
From Corporations to Ephemeral Associations

Gabriela Vargas-Cetina

Organizations seem to be present everywhere, representing a great diversity of interests and using an endless variety of methods to accomplish the tasks for which they were created. Although we could retrospectively conceptualize as organizations many types of structured groups, such as European guilds, the concept of organization was developed in the nineteenth century. The great transformations brought about by the process of consolidation of the nation-state, the emergence of the incorporated business company, the cooperative movement, the political parties and trade unions of the late nineteenth and early twentieth centuries, and the multiplication of clubs and charities, resulted in highly dynamic organizational environments in many regions of the world. The advent of real-time communications, which reached its current peak at the end of the twentieth century with the internet, has greatly changed how organizations function, how they establish ties with other organizations and to what extent they generally influence one another – or not. Over time, anthropologists have continuously adjusted their approaches in order to better understand these changing and varied organizational forms and configurations (Nash, Dandler and Hopkins 1976; Wright 1994; Baviskar et al. 1995; Partridge, Welker and Hardin 2011). It is important to point out, however, that the predominance of one or another type of organization, or of anthropologists' attention to it, does not mean that formerly existing types have disappeared or have been completely displaced. Furthermore, the same things may be looked at from conceptually new angles, and we might find that those 'new' things were already there before. Today we are studying issues of common-property resource management, but we can look back into the past and find that similar resource pools existed already, although we used to refer to them with different names. We continue to live in a world where kinship-centred and residence-based common-property resources, cooperatives and, certainly, business corporations, coexist with more ephemeral associations.

In this chapter I focus on several interrelated concepts – organization, corporation, cooperatives and ephemeral associations – in order to look at the ways in which anthropologists have approached organizations. As ways of organizing human life change in time, the forms in which we create and sustain social groups also change. These changes are effecting a shift from a focus on the perdurance of relatively stable groupings to a greater willingness in contemporary analysis to account for more fleeting forms of aggregation. Here I will argue that, even if temporary, these ephemeral forms of organization may still leave significant traces reshaping everyday life around the globe. Anthropology is well suited to map these changes and their implications, as the old ideas of corporate togetherness are increasingly supplemented, and often challenged, by non-self-perpetuating forms of organization. This chapter is therefore intended as a very short history of the conceptual voyage our discipline has traversed as it follows the changing paths of organizational formation and disbandment.

ORGANIZATIONS

The concept of organization in what became the social sciences emerged at a time when cities were growing, nation-states were becoming consolidated and bureaucracies were beginning to be tied to numerous aspects of social life that needed not only administration, but also actual problem-solving efficiency. During the eighteenth and the nineteenth centuries, during the period that Hobsbawm (1962) dubbed 'the age of revolution' (roughly 1789 to 1848), European philosophers started to write about organizations by applying to society some of the principles then emerging from the natural sciences and mathematics (Comte 1975, 1984; Saint Simon 1975). At this time, industrial capitalism was radically transforming the way humans related to land, property and other persons (Hobsbawm 1962; Bravo 1976). Two types of human aggregates became the privileged focus of philosophers' interest: 'society', and the different 'strata', 'segments' or 'classes' of individuals.

While some theorists, like Comte (and later Weber and Durkheim), were intent on using the emerging social sciences and concepts to understand humans better and further objective scientific analysis, others, like

Saint Simon and Owen (and later Marx and Gide), wanted to use the same disciplines and concepts to change the world in radical ways. It was during this time that the ideas behind what came to be called socialism, or the idea of creating the possibilities for a general redistribution of wealth, emerged and gained currency (Bravo 1976). The ideas surrounding organization as a quality (as in 'the organization of') and organization as a type of unit (as in trade union, or in the plural: organizations) became paramount in both academically-oriented and more action-oriented theories. We are still dealing with organizations in ways that would be recognizable to the theorists of those times: today we either try to understand organizations as they are, or try to understand them so as to put this knowledge to practical use.

Through the work of Rivers, Malinowski, Radcliffe-Brown, Boas and Lowie, anthropology became an academic discipline in the early twentieth century, and was influenced by the social philosophers and their theories. Because of their rootedness in long-term fieldwork, they tended to think of 'organizations' as fluid: in principle, any group of people could become an organization, in the sense of having common purposes. The tribe, the clan, the family, the club and the age group might at times become united in a single activity or purpose, and their grouping did not have to persist once these tasks were completed. At the same time, institutions such as a hospital or a school were not necessarily 'organizations' until people in them started working together. For example, the notion of school, Lowie (1948: 195–196) pointed out, could relate to a perceivable single organization, but not in all cases, since in some societies it could be a more diffuse function taken on by elders teaching individual children, or by society as a whole.

Social organization and organizations were key concepts in anthropology from the start, and the boundary between one concept and the other was seen as constantly changing, since the social organization of a human group might involve individuals belonging to one or more organization (Handelman 1977). However, what we understand today as the 'anthropology of organizations', the study of highly structured collectives, is considered to have begun with the Hawthorne studies, which between 1927 and 1932 involved anthropologists and other social scientists in the study of the social organization of the workplace (Wright 1994: 5–9; Schwartzman 1995: 1–26). Management staff at the Western Electric Hawthorne Plant, Illinois, invited Harvard specialists to test the principles of the new discipline of scientific management at their premises. Psychologist Elton Mayo joined in after the initial findings. Mayo was a friend of Malinowski and Radcliffe Brown, two famous British anthropologists. He called on their advice, as well as that of Lowie's student W. Lloyd Warner, who suggested considering the group under study as a small-scale society. This methodology resulted in the systematic description of the social organization of the group under study (Schwartzman 1995: 9). This could have been thought of as the beginning of the anthropology of corporations, but at that time in anthropology corporations meant something more than 'companies', as I shall now explain.

CORPORATIONS

It was probably Radcliffe-Brown who, inspired by Maine (1908), originally established the meaning of 'corporation' as it still tends to be used in anthropology: an estate that is held by a collective that perpetuates itself even if individual members leave or die (Radcliffe-Brown 1952: 34–37). In Maine's view, the question of membership and continuity of the corporation emerged when individuals from two different groups married. This type of situation immediately led to the establishment of rules of unilineal descent (ibid.: 46–48), since it was a way to determine access to corporately held resources. According to Schnepel (1990) and Whiteley (1985), Meyer Fortes and Jack Goody incorporated Maine's idea of corporations as self-perpetuating into the concept, thus establishing the most stable version of corporations. Anthropologists came to understand a corporation as a single entity made up of more than one individual that survives its particular members, holding resources as its common property, which succeeding members of the corporation inherit. Then, on the basis of this earlier composite definition, first M.G. Smith (1966) and later D.E. Brown (1974) tried to ascertain a set of 'characteristics' for the identification of corporations as basic units of social organization. Smith proposed that '[t]he decisive characteristics of all corporations, categorical and other, are their presumed perpetuity, closure, determinate identity, and membership' (Smith 1975: 209). However, according to Brown (1974), through the entire body of his work, Smith actually identified a wider set of characteristics that, in different combinations, generate diverging corporate forms: 'The characteristics of fully corporate forms are identity, presumptive perpetuity, closure, membership, exclusive common affairs, autonomy, procedures, and organization ... The principles which inform corporations include sex, age, ethnicity, locality, descent, common property interests, ritual or belief, occupations, rank, and voluntary association' (ibid.: 32).

The wide difference between the way in which 'corporation' is understood in Britain and its former colonies, where corporations are subjects of law, and in anthropology more generally, where corporations are not necessarily treated as legal entities, has not gone unnoticed. The terms of this debate have been clearly laid out by Glyn Cochrane:

Two traditions of usage exist with regard to the concept of 'corporateness' in relation to lineages or other kinds of organization; either, a loose construction has been placed on the term or, authors have claimed that they were using it in its Anglo-American legal sense. Neither, in fact, bears much relation to what the term now means, or has meant in the past, to lawyers. Because of this anthropologists using the concept have had only a choice between using 'corporateness' as a kind of anthropological colloquialism or of distorting ethnographic data. (Cochrane 1971: 1144)

Cochrane chose to base his understanding of the concept on the work of nineteenth-century law scholar F.W. Maitland, who outlined five essential characteristics of corporations: the right to perpetual succession; the power to sue and be sued as a whole body by the corporate name; the power to hold lands; the right to use a common seal; and the power of making by-laws (Maitland 1961: 54, cited in Cochrane 1971: 1145). Cochrane criticized Max Gluckman (1965) and Ward Goodenough (1951) for attempting to use the concept of 'corporation' as if it could have wide cross-cultural validity outside Anglo-Saxon law. Goodenough (1971) replied that restricting the term to those characteristics outlined by Cochrane would limit the utility of the concept to English jurisprudence.

James Dow (1973) joined the debate and proposed that the problem had to do with the fact that there were two different senses of 'corporation' that had been mixed into one. He singled out Meyer Fortes and Eric Wolf for putting together Maine's concept of corporation, derived from English law, with Weber's concept of *Verband*, which Parsons had translated as 'corporate group' but originally meant associations such as the state or a church (ibid.: 905–907). In Dow's view, Maine had used corporation as an abbreviated form of the concept's legal usage in Britain. However, Maine had put the emphasis mainly on 'a jural person who did not die and to whom certain legal rights and obligations were adhered', while Weber's concept 'stood for a group which was either closed, or which admitted outsiders by rules, and which was governed by an order enforced by a "chief" and administrators' (ibid.: 905). To avoid further confusion, Dow proposed developing a concept of 'corporate guardianship' that could be useful to anthropology, distinguishing 'the kinds of rights, and their patterns of distribution, which are "corporate" from the kinds of rights and patterns which are not "corporate"' (ibid.: 907). This way, the concept of 'corporation' would not be used by itself, and when speaking of 'corporate guardianship' the emphasis would be on resources and property forms, and not on imagined or real jural personhood.

In fact, M.G. Smith had already pointed out that the anthropological concept of corporation was based on definitions supplied by Maine and

Weber, a point he belaboured in his subsequent writings (Smith 1954, 1975). But he was not alone; some emic understandings of 'corporation' also spoke to these two definitions. Wolf would later explain, responding to Dow's challenge, that combining the two concepts of corporation into one 'is precisely what the Spaniards were trying to do' as they imposed their own laws in the New World, so jural persons and groups became fused as corporate entities, difficult to separate conceptually – or legally (Wolf 1986: 325). However, anthropologists had by then started paying attention to those entities labelled by Anglo-Saxon law as corporations, and some had already started using the more restrictive definitions of the corporation as current in other disciplines, including law and management, where corporations are specific types of legal entities, and political science, where corporatism and related concepts often refer to strategies for collective bargaining power among workers in Europe and in Latin America (Hansen 1976; Molina and Rhodes 2002; Vargas-Cetina 2011).

Given this historical debate, should anthropologists restrict the concept of corporation to only those organizations that are defined as business corporations by Anglo-Saxon law and stop using it in any other sense? Many of the issues conceptually inherent to the debate over self-perpetuating collectives relating to private and collective rights are now approached by anthropologists with the help of institutional economics (Wade 1989; Acheson 2003; Nonini 2007). Older definitions of 'corporation' and 'corporate' might not seem necessary in the analysis of collectively managed resources, since institutional economics puts the stress on types of resources, management, property, rules and arrangements. However, I think it would be unwise to keep the term 'corporation' solely as a reference to business enterprises, not-for-profit organizations, or multinational firms of the British and US type. Business and other corporations chartered under British, Australian, Canadian or US law are constantly evolving to adapt or react to the cultural environments of the localities where they are active, and to those where they are not necessarily so active but which they reach through the market. Other types of corporations or new configurations may emerge. After all, corporations are nothing more than consolidated structures that emerge from the coming together of individuals, and people continue to change the ways in which they come together: sociality in action is what determines the eventual forms of collectives, be they legal, political, recreational, religious or of any other possible type. People in different localities think and behave differently in, through and with corporate bodies of all sorts, including lineages, clans and common-property-holding groups.

Ethnographers have been documenting local lives for over a century now, and the results of the encounter between old corporate structures and newly formed corporate entities already amount to an extensive inventory. This ranges from the transformation of kin-based residential groups into administrative units with their own local bureaucracies (Fallers 1965; Biedelman 1971) to the transformation of corporate land tenure practices into common and private property holdings (Goodenough 1951, 1974; Vargas-Cetina 2000; Heatherington 2010) and the creation of collective resource-holding groups under socialism and in capitalist modernizing societies (Dunn and Dunn 1967; McClintock 1981), as well as the transformation of tribal and lineage-based groups into incorporated companies (Cattelino 2008; Comaroff and Comaroff 2009; Cook 2011). The concept of the corporation, as first developed in anthropology, puts the accent precisely on sociality as the basis of the construction of all human collectives, while institutional economics focuses more on the rules, resources being managed and rights of access. The older notion of corporation has heuristic advantages not yet superseded by the analysis of common-property management. Anthropologists have been among the very few scholars able to document the local transformations occurring between older corporations – including clans, lineages and collective management groups – and newer types, including the incorporated company. After all, the current form of business corporations is only one instance from the long history of the emergence, fusion and transformation of different types of collectives, including old and new-type corporations.

In the United States, for example, incorporated companies have changed over time. The current states of Massachusetts, Connecticut and Rhode Island were originally chartered as corporations, and after American independence the majority of private corporations chartered between 1780 and 1810 were 'churches, townships, schools, and voluntary organizations' (Kaufman 2008: 404). The way in which, for example, tribes in the US and Canada and ethnic groups around the world are employing the business-corporation model could introduce important changes into their ways of life and social organization. John and Jean Comaroff explain that in the US the Wheeler-Howard Act of 1934, also called the Indian Reorganization Act (IRA), made it possible for Native American tribes to become incorporated if all adult members of a tribe voted to ratify their incorporated status. If they did, the charter of incorporation, according to this law,

> may convey to the *incorporated tribe* the power to purchase, take by gift, or bequest, or otherwise, own, hold, manage, operate, and dispose of property of every description, real and personal, including the power to purchase restricted Indian lands and to issue in exchange therefore interests in *corporate property*; and such further powers as may be incidental to the *conduct of corporate business*. (Wheeler-Howard Act, cited in Comaroff and Comaroff 2009: 61)

Jessica Cattelino's work with the Seminole documents a case where a Native American tribe has become a player in the corporate business world, first through running casinos and then through the purchase and corporate management of the Hard Rock Café franchise (Cattelino 2008, 2011). In 1957, the Seminole chose to register two different legal personalities: the Seminole Tribe of Florida and the Seminole Tribe of Florida Inc. (Cattelino 2008: 132). It would be possible to characterize the complicated issues around sovereignty and business that Cattelino describes as the interplay between two types of corporate figures: on the one hand, the tribe as a body transcending its members, with its rules for admission and rejection of members, its corporate property, and the mechanisms to ensure its own endurance; and, on the other hand, the tribe as a business corporation, the rules and behaviour of which do not always coincide with its other corporate objectives. The tribe's aims as a kin- and residence-based corporation, in the sense that this concept has been understood since Radcliffe-Brown (which in this case is firmly grounded on notions of 'blood' and kinship), revolve around issues of sovereignty, collective access and internal control of common resources, while the tribe's aims as a business corporation (grounded on notions of legal personhood and asset management) revolve mainly around making money and succeeding in the market. The education, health and social services supported by the latter (the business corporation) on behalf of the former (the 'blood'-based corporation) are one of the key points of negotiation between the two (Cattelino 2011: 141) because these services relate directly to the situation, rights and everyday life of people and their understanding of these circumstances. Susan Cook's work among the Bafokeng also documents this tension (Cook 2011). Much would be lost if we stopped looking at both kinds of corporate models at play here, because each of them has the potential to change the shape and dynamics of the other.

Another reason to insist on a broader anthropological notion of corporation is that anthropology has always prided itself in recognizing diverse perceptions and local understandings. Outside the US, the UK, Canada and Australia, the concept of 'corporation' is used in very different applications from those in Anglo-Saxon law and in English-speaking countries' common usage (Vargas-Cetina 2011). In many parts of the world there are identifiable bodies that come very close to Maitland's characterization of a corporation: groups of people who have the right to perpetual succession, the power to sue and be sued as a whole body by the corporate name, the power to hold lands, the right to use a common seal, and the power of making by-laws (Maitland 1961: 54, cited in Cochrane 1971: 1145). The villages under the common-property land ownership regime in central Sardinia which I know from my own fieldwork can usefully illustrate this point.

In Italy, 'corporation' was historically used to refer to trade guilds, *corporazioni di mestiere* (Massa and Moioli 2005). In February 1934, Mussolini's fascists instituted a 'corporations' regime, under which all members of a distinct trade had to be members of a corporation (they fixed the number of corporations at twenty-two). Extending this meaning, the word is still often applied today to trade unions and common-interest groups, especially when perceived as blocking change (Vargas-Cetina 2011). Besides this common usage of *corporazione* and related terms, there are rural shareholding entities in central Sardinia that embody almost to the letter Maitland's definition of a corporation, even if they are not called that. These are the villages with common lands, which are called *comuni* like all other municipalities on Sardinia, but differ from those in that they administer a good part of their territory as communal lands. These *comuni* are mostly perched on mountain slopes, and have defended their rights to communal landholding since 1820, when the edict for the privatization of lands was issued. Since all proven residents of these villages have the right of access to communal lands, the village *consiglio* (government), to which members are democratically elected, is a very important institution of governance (the number of councillors is determined by a formula valid for each Sardinian province as a whole, based on the number of inhabitants as per the latest census).

The *consiglio comunale* meets twice every month, or more often if necessary, and its deliberations are open and can be attended by any member of the *comune*. The *consiglio* continuously issues regulations and by-laws, has a seal that makes its decisions and documents official, manages funds obtained through different sources, settles conflicts among villagers, changes the usage of communal land sections, and represents the village as a whole in the event of conflicts with other villages. Sardinian *comuni* are also able to establish for themselves, through legal procedures, local trademarks that single out cheeses, wines or other local specialties within the larger European Union. At the same time, the individual members of central Sardinia's *comuni* hold private property of different types, landed property included, since during the privatization process some communal land was allotted to families in the 1800s. Today's *comuni* have certainly outlived many of their former members, and those in central Sardinia each have their own dialect of Nuorese Sard, their own products and their own internal regulations pertaining to the management of their resources (Ayora-Diaz 1995; Vargas-Cetina 2000; Sorge 2009; Heatherington 2010). While central Sardinian *comuni* are not business corporations, they nonetheless share many of the traits described by Maitland.[1]

In short, I believe it is best to leave the concept of 'corporation' in anthropology as an outline of a few features, which can be adapted to the analysis of local circumstances, otherwise, the concept itself will lose its comparative usefulness. At the same time, I do think that we should always be careful to specify in each instance why we have decided to call any particular body acting as a single entity a 'corporation', in what way we are using the term, and how it relates to the everyday life of the groups it represents and of those it keeps outside its boundaries.

COOPERATIVES

Originally, the modern cooperative was a type of organization meant to alleviate the plight of the working class. Cooperatives and business corporations are two results of the same type of legal process: the constitution of legal persons that can be detached from their actual members and enter the market as single entities. While in a business corporation the capital can be provided by a small group of persons who own shares of the company and then profit according to the number of shares each of these investors holds, in a cooperative the shares are usually owned by all the members, and there is a maximum number of shares each member can own. While in a business corporation the company is usually run by those who have the largest numbers of shares, in a cooperative the general assembly is, in theory, the maximum decision-making organ, and it includes all the shareholders, regardless of their number of shares.

The birth of the international cooperative movement is most often associated with the Rochdale Society of Equitable Pioneers, formed by a group of workers in the city of Rochdale who, with the help of Robert Owen, a philosopher of utopian socialism, created the first retail cooperative in 1844 (Digby 1960). The cooperative principles as instituted by the Rochdale Society in 1937 were: open membership; democratic control; distribution of the surplus to the members in proportion to their transactions; limited interest on capital; political and religious neutrality; cash trading; and promotion of education (Fairbairn 1994: 24). Scholars and activists from around the world came to witness the Rochdale experiment, document it and then try to implement it at home. In Mexico, for example, scholars and urban workers adopted ideas about cooperatives emanating from utopian writers such as Charles Gide and Robert Owen (Rojas Coria 1984). But the period between the start of the First World War and the end of the Second World War was not a very auspicious one for cooperatives. In Europe and elsewhere, the cooperative movement lost force, partly because some of the members were engaged in fighting, but also partly because the authoritarian regimes of these periods perceived the cooperative movement as a

threat to nationalist ideologies (Vargas-Cetina 2011). Then, at the end of the
Second World War, the world became split between two major ideologies
– capitalism and socialism – and the governments espousing them shared
a strong drive towards 'progress'. Both capitalist and socialist governments
looked at cooperatives as tools to modernize society.

In the 1940s, many countries, across all continents, undertook large
projects of modernization based on the ideas that pooling resources and
bringing people together would result in efficient ways to produce, manage, process and market products. Cooperatives appeared to many planners
as one of the best ways to achieve these goals (Dore 1971; Worsley 1971a).
At first, anthropologists registered cooperatives as one more element in the
comprehensive landscape of local social organization (Lewis 1960; Friedl
1962; Wolf 1966; Langworthy 1968). However, given the obvious impact
of the changes being wrought on local populations, they soon joined other
social scientists in the study of cooperatives (Vincent 1971, 1982; Worsley
1971b; Nash, Dandler and Hopkins 1976; McClintock 1981; Krotz 1986;
Baviskar et al. 1995). Some governments, inspired by cooperatives, developed new forms of collectively controlled and managed resources. Here,
the cases of the Mexican *ejido* (Wilkie 1971), the *ujamaa* villages in Tanzania
(Rigby 1977), the *kolkhoz* and *sovkhos* in the Soviet Union (Dunn and Dunn
1967) and the kibbutz in Israel (Spiro 1956, 1958) were the most visible symbols of a new, emerging configuration of collectivized peasant modernity by
design, some enjoying more economic success than others.

With time, collectivization efforts subsided and began to fall apart,
but cooperatives became a model of what in Italy is called 'the social economy'; that is, a type of economy not centred on personal profit-making or
on a type of corporate profit-making that favours a few at the expense of
the many. In the 1980s a 'social solidarity market' developed, and the products of indigenous groups around the world began to be marketed through
these channels (Hernández Castillo and Nigh 1998). Many 'social solidarity'
businesses began to call themselves 'cooperatives', even when they did not
have the legal status of cooperatives in their countries (Vargas-Cetina 2002).
Then, in the 1990s, a new model for 'new generation cooperatives' developed, in which membership is closed and the shares each member holds
can vary in number. This has drawn many cooperatives closer to current
corporate business models than to the historical model of the cooperative
(Kotov 2001). Furthermore, at the end of the 1990s and the beginning of
the twentieth-first century, many large cooperatives, such as Amul in India,
Cruz Azul in Mexico and Mondragon in Spain, have become 'cooperative
corporations'.[2] Along with cooperative banks that have developed into international financial groups, such as Capital Desjardins Inc. and Raiffeisen

Bank International, these cooperatives are now competing on the international stock market along with larger business corporations in their respective economic sectors.[3] It is important to keep in mind that the fate of these entities in financial markets is far from the forms of sociality that originally bound them together, but smaller cooperatives are still sustained by the ways in which their members interact and envision their own lives and relations, not only among themselves but also with other people in their locality.

ASSOCIATIONS

The word 'association' continues to be used in ways not yet rigidly established by law or by custom. 'Association' in English and in many other languages is used to talk about any kind of gathering, whether or not it has a clear purpose, or whether or not the group having come together intends to regulate its membership. From this vantage point, then, all organizations are associations, but also other types of gatherings (or assemblages, in Lowie's language) are associations as well. However, association is often coupled with some other concept, as in 'voluntary association', 'professional association', 'religious association', 'recreational association', or, in the United States, registered lobby groups, such as the National Rifle Association. In the cooperative world, 'association' is very often used to designate a single cooperative, or a group of cooperatives or other organizations that have joined a larger group as corporate members. In Italy, cooperatives called 'associations' were for a long time considered part of the Catholic cooperative movement (Earle 1986), but in more recent times this specific meaning has been lost; 'association' now has a more generic ring in Italy, even when it names a cooperative or a consortium of cooperatives.

The concept of 'voluntary association' is very important in sociology and political science, but has not been too favourably accepted or widely used in anthropology, and neither has its anthropological counterpart, sodality. The latter concept, in its anthropological form, was coined by Lowie, who used it to differentiate between organized groups into which people are born (such as tribes, kinship and residence groups) and those associations one chooses to join at some point in life (Lowie 1948: 294–316). According to Lowie, '[s]ince the concept of sodalities is merely a convenient lumber room for a great variety of associations, we cannot link it with particular institutions or with any one psychological motive' (ibid.: 294). It is because of Lowie that 'sodality' and 'voluntary association' are often used interchangeably (Anderson 1971; Brown 1973). Elman Service later understood sodalities as groups within groups, which extended across other kinds of large units, for example clans cutting across bands. He reintroduced the element of kinship to write about kin-based and non-kin based sodalities, which would provide ways of integrating disparate larger social units. He defined pan-tribal sodalities as 'the means of solidarity that are specifically tribal additions to the persisting band-like means' (Service 1962: 113). While for Lowie the voluntary character of the sodality was key, for Service membership in a common recognizable group that often spanned several self-sufficient units was the primary element.

Following upon this early development of the concept, two main strands of it have been in use in anthropology, sometimes overlapping or at least touching one another: sodality as 'voluntary association' and sodality as 'ceremonial association'. In an article that generated considerable criticism (e.g. Dow 1973; Brown 1973; Hughes 1974), Robert Anderson proposed that 'voluntary associations' and 'sodalities' are two concepts that can be used interchangeably, and that they describe associations that can be placed 'in "the middle range" of societal evolution' and 'have important social and cultural functions' (Anderson 1971: 211–213). According to Anderson, these associations appeared before the emergence of strong states and tended to disappear with the strengthening of state power, such as in pre-industrial states (ibid.: 214–215), until they re-emerged with regained impetus in industrializing and industrial nations (ibid.: 214–216).[4] Brown (1973) however was critical of this interpretation, arguing first that Lowie's and then Anderson's treatment of the concept of sodality as a voluntary association was confusing because both scholars included among sodalities associations that were not voluntary. Hughes, in turn, accused Anderson of ignoring the historical record, which shows that voluntary associations were paramount in medieval European society, in what Anderson calls 'pre-industrial states' (Hughes 1974: 333).

Sodality is a well-established concept in the anthropology of ceremonial societies and other organizations among Native American populations, or when describing organizations elsewhere that are structured in ways similar to Native American ceremonial organizations (Weinberg 1976; Gelo 1999). Also, this concept continues to be important in religious practices, in religious studies and in the anthropology of religious organizations (Foster 1953; Crumrine 1970; Nosco 1993; Nishida 1998; Dinges 2001). This is because sodalities are particular kinds of organizations associated with Christianity, and recognized as such by the Catholic Church at least since the late Middle Ages (Hilgers 1912). The ethnography and historiography of Latin America, where many local religious-based sodalities are called *cofradías*, reflects this use of the concept (Crumrine 1970; Taylor 1987; Nishida 2003). Arjun Appadurai (1996: 8–9) has extended the concept of sodality to those forms of affiliation mediated by mass media and long-distance communication tools to form imagined communities around a common figure or interest. He offers the 'community of sentiment' generated by Salman Rushdie's *Satanic Verses* (1989) as an example of this new, global phenomenon.

In political science and sociology, 'voluntary associations' usually refer to civic associations pursuing diverse goals, and are considered to enhance public welfare and political participation (Banfield 1958; Putnam 2000). In anthropology, this concept has been used to describe clubs, secret societies, ceremonial societies and other associations, mainly in urban settings, that meet regularly for different purposes. Richard M. Bradfield (1973) embarked on the description of associations in kin-based societies, including several in Africa (Nuer, Yakö, Talense, Mende), Melanesia (the Trobriands, the Bank Islands), as well as a number of Native American groups (Hopi, Navajo, Great Basin Shoshoni). Through the work of fellow anthropologists and through his own fieldwork among the Hopi, Bradfield intended a comparison to show that in some of these cases – including the Yakö, the Mende, the Banks Islands and the Hopi – that there existed associations that could be conceived of as voluntary, which took on the functions of kin-based associations elsewhere. Bradfield defined voluntary associations in the following terms: '"voluntary" in the sense that a person's membership in any one of them is not implied by some prior event, as – for example – his membership of a particular kin-group is implied by birth' (ibid. Vol. I: 4).

Voluntary associations resembling those described in sociology and political science have most often featured in urban ethnographies. Kenneth Little argued that it was possible to group voluntary organizations in West Africa into three different types of 'cultural orientation': 'Traditional', 'Christian' and 'Modern Secular' (Little 1959: 285). He considered that these associations often took 'the place of the lineage and the extended family by providing their members with mutual aid and protection as well as companionship' (ibid.: 284), and helped rural migrants adapt to urban settings. P.D. Wheeldon (1969), describing what she called 'the operation of voluntary associations' in a small town in South Africa, found that there were several voluntary associations, in which members of the 'Coloured' community participated enthusiastically.[5] These associations, however, did not change the status quo, but rather helped maintain it. At their meetings, people were encouraged not to argue with one another, deliberations were long and no votes or clear decisions were taken, minutes were 'obscure or non-existent' and no clear consensus was ever reached (ibid.: 141). Wheeldon argued that, although other observers of similar associations decry the holding of meetings for the simple enjoyment of holding them, these associations did help members see themselves as a collective with shared interests, and gave them a common identity while helping keep their social ties strong. Similarly, Deborah Pellow found that in Accra, Ghana, a woman's voluntary association, the *zumunci*, brought women together 'not for economic advancement or primary financial welfare or political action but for the creation of a kin-like community in the stranger setting, analogous to male structures' (Pellow 1987: 489).

A concept that in the last three decades has gained great currency in the social sciences is social capital. In political science, social capital is often associated with voluntary associations, concerted civic action and democracy (Putnam 2000; Fukuyama 2001). In anthropology, social capital has often been perceived as one among several types of capital. Anthropologists tend to think of social capital as something that everyone has to some extent, in the form of relatives and friends. Usually, it is considered that social capital is regularly exchanged into other types of capital, so that, for example, personal networks can be translated into prestige (symbolic capital), votes (political capital) or exchange-related capital, some of which is money (Bourdieu 1973; Smith 2000). Paul Bohannan (1955) was perhaps the first anthropologist to explain different spheres of exchange in his work among the Tiv of Nigeria. Other anthropologists began to document the different types of exchange taking place in different societies, noticing that exchange itself was a means of cementing social relations, and thus creating other types of capital beyond monetary wealth (Smith 2000). In most societies, there has been at some point one or more areas of life excluded from monetary exchange, including land, people, some prestige tokens (such as the bracelets and necklaces in the Kula ring) and communication with non-human forces on behalf of the sick (usually performed by ritual specialists) (Raheja 1988; Parry 1989; Ayora-Diaz 2002). At the end of the twentieth century, the sphere of monetary exchange began to invade other spheres of capital and exchange in most societies, and where sociologists and political scientists now despair at what they see as the loss of social capital (Putnam 2000), anthropologists more often despair at the monetization of those realms of life where money used to not be the exchange medium but that are now quantified and valued in pecuniary terms, including land, people, body parts, religious and ceremonial objects, markers of achievement, along with social ties and social relations (Smith 2000; Scheper-Hughes and Wacquant 2002; Gudeman 2008).

Debates between political scientists and anthropologists over the importance of social capital and voluntary associations have periodically flared up. One of the most famous controversies within this debate involved Edward C. Banfield's *The Amoral Basis of a Backward Society* (Banfield 1958). Banfield, a political scientist, described an Italian town he called

Montegrano as 'backward', a condition that was to be explained 'largely (but not entirely) by the inability of the villagers to act together for their common good or, indeed, for any end transcending the immediate, material interest of the nuclear family', which he understood as an 'ethos' of 'amoral familism' (ibid.: 10). He contrasted this situation with the orientation he viewed as characterizing the US: the fact that people sought the advancement of 'community welfare' through an array of associations, and through engagement in public politics. But Banfield was criticized by several anthropologists because he had not looked at the ways in which Montegranesi cooperated to carry out 'successful group festive, ceremonial, [and] public works or other functions' (McCorkle 1959: 133). Cancian wrote that Banfield used faulty logic and projected his own ideas on to his subjects, as if they had to think the way some people did in the US. Banfield thought that peasants should aspire to change the world themselves, when from their point of view there was a whole class of Italian society whose job was precisely to engage in politics and change things constantly (Cancian 1961). Silverman (1968) argued that Banfield had put down as the cause something that was obviously the result of the peasants' material conditions; and Moss and Capanari (1960) pointed out that Banfield had ignored other binding bonds across families, such as co-parenthood and friendship. In short, anthropologists accused Banfield of overlooking bonds of sociality while insisting on the importance of forms of organization extraneous to the peasants' intentions and ideas.

At the end of the twentieth century we have seen the increased importance of new forms of association, which are non-corporate, in that they are not based on an ample platform of agreement among their members, do not result in self-perpetuating collective subjects and do not seek to acquire and maintain collective resources. I have called these 'ephemeral associations' (Vargas-Cetina 2004, 2005), and I find that they share the following general traits: they are ephemeral, in the sense that their members do not expect them to last indefinitely (in fact, they may be seen as highly contextual and in constant flux); their membership is completely voluntary, whether or not they are formally registered; their structure, membership, aims and purposes change continuously; their internal governance structure is weak, and their authority figures are contextual; and, finally, they are highly dependent on communications technology, from simple trails connecting hamlets to roads, long-distance travel means, phone lines, mobile phones and electronic media. Because of this, their collective life is often less dependent on actual meetings than it was with older types of associations, but they can also bring their members together at short notice.[6]

In the 1980s, highly motivated, idealistic young people with a university background wanted to help the poor, fill in holes in the social safety net created by the increased disappearance of social welfare programmes, and support the causes of indigenous peoples (Hirschman 1984; Fisher 1998; Cheema and Rondinelli 2007). I first came across these associations during my fieldwork in Chiapas. The activists were usually in their twenties and thirties, and had grown up in the cities of Chiapas, in other parts of Mexico or abroad. Many of them came to Chiapas and created, as others were doing around the world, 'civil society organizations' and 'non-governmental organizations'. In 1997, García Aguilar (1998b) had registered over 700 such associations operating in Chiapas, working in the areas of education, civil and human rights, violence against women, feminist and gender issues, indigenous rights, poverty alleviation, marketing crafts and agricultural products, art education collectives and religious organizations. Often, as in some organizations for the promotion of organic agriculture, religious organizations accompanied the establishment of cooperatives for the practice and promotion of productive activities (García Aguilar 1998a, 1998b; Vargas-Cetina 1999, 2002; Ayora-Diaz 2002; Hernández Castillo and Nigh 1998). Also, meditation groups, tour clubs and groups of tourists were enlisted as volunteers to work with one or more of existing association. Many of these organizations, especially in the aftermath of the Zapatista rebellion, managed to bring together, at very short notice, large groups of indigenous people and other Chiapans. These people included members of existing cooperatives, activists and non-activists, who came from all over Chiapas to gather in a single, pre-designated spot, such as a plaza in San Cristobal, Comitán or Tuxtla, or the premises of an organization. Some of these gatherings disbanded after a few hours, but at other times they carried on for several days. Some had responded to the call of the organizers in order to support requests before funding agencies; others had gathered to discuss more public issues, such as human or indigenous rights, or to protest against perceived injustices. The speed at which people came together, often in a matter of days or even hours, over such different interests and causes, from so many near and remote places, and the sheer numbers of people who came and went always amazed me. While the groups and crowds that came together and even many of the 'civic action associations' themselves disappeared very quickly, their lasting, mostly positive effects could be felt in all kinds of ways: increased respect for women, increased acceptance of gender diversity, a more vocal defence of indigenous languages and rights, new education programmes for children and adults. The groups had been diffuse and inchoate, but their effects, also diffuse, lingered sometimes for days, often for years.

In the twenty-first century we have seen these types of movements grow to have an important impact on local, regional and sometimes world politics, while relying increasingly on mass mobilizations supported by mobile technologies and social network digital applications. From the Arab Spring of 2010/2011 to the *indignados* movement in Spain in 2011/2012, to the Occupy movement in the United States and Canada and the #Yo Soy 132 movement in Mexico in 2012, young and old people are increasingly entering highly ephemeral associations. Anthropologists have been busy looking at these social movements (Postill 2008, 2012; Juris 2012; Kurnik 2012). For my part, I am very interested not only in the fact that people are organizing without having very clear and identifiable sets of goals or intentions, but also in the lasting effects that these non-corporate associations are having on the organizational environment, because even though ephemeral associations are not creating corporate structures, they are having an impact on more lasting collectives which they touch. A brief example from my current fieldwork will illustrate the way in which this is happening in Merida, Mexico.

In May of 2012, then presidential candidate Enrique Peña Nieto, supported by Mexico's Party of the Institutionalized Revolution (PRI), visited the campus of Universidad Iberoamericana, a private university in Mexico City. The students there accused him of having ordered the violent repression of flower vendors and their supporters in the municipality of Atenco when he was governor of Mexico state in 2006. Peña Nieto did not deny the accusations, but rather affirmed the right of the state government to use violence if need be. His answer enraged the students, who cornered him so that he had to be rescued by his security staff. Peña Nieto and his campaign staff later said that there had been 'planted agitators' among the students directing the protests against him. In response, a group of students at Universidad Iberoamericana made a video in which 131 students declared their names, showed their Universidad Iberoamericana ID cards and said that they had personally participated in the protest against Peña Nieto. They posted the video on YouTube on 14 May, and it was immediately shared across all of Mexico via social applications. According to Wikipedia (where there is a short description of the events surrounding this movement), six hours after the video had been posted it had been viewed by over 20,000 people. People began to post the video on their digital profiles with the hash tag #Yo Soy 132, implying that had they been there, they would have been part of the protesters and would have been on the video too. The following week, a #Yo Soy 132 social application for computers and mobile phones had been developed, and thousands of people were using it to exchange information about demonstrations and about political campaigns. Along with Facebook, Twitter and Google+, this application was used to coordinate a series of protests across the country and abroad.

In Merida, the Yucatan state capital, between May and July the demonstrations around #Yo Soy 132 engaged not only several hundred people who had learned about the issues through the internet, but also many of the established youth collectives that are regularly part of the music scene in the city. Young people, some of whom may be musicians, form these collectives. Each collective may be formed by, for example, a music band, a group of serigraphy artists, and a group in charge of promoting the collective's activities. Or else, the collective may be formed by hip-hop DJs and rappers, bebop dance groups and graffiti artists. Sometimes a single person may carry out two or three different activities within the collective. These collectives also acquire visibility in the city through their socially conscious economic activities (for example, doing serigraphy and batik on clothes and tee-shirts to express political or other types of ideas, creating products out of recycled materials, or providing low-cost recording services). In addition, they undertake projects to engage young people around the city and teach them to make their own music, or build their own skateboards, do serigraphy themselves, or create things out of rubbish. Several of these collectives immediately joined the #Yo Soy 132 movement and participated in the festivals and demonstrations that took place in protest against Peña Nieto. After the elections (which Peña Nieto won with just over a third of the votes), and then on the day that Peña Nieto became president of Mexico, the #Yo Soy 132 movement carried out new protests in Merida in which the collectives again participated. The movement did not accomplish the defeat of the PRI in Mexico or in Yucatan, but the collectives gained increased visibility, their members became familiar with other collectives, and acquired a renewed impetus to carry out their 'cultural' activities and projects. They are increasingly operating not as isolated groups but together in new configurations, sometimes joined or helped by civic societies and regional foundations.

In November and December of 2012, I attended two events in which several Merida collectives staged events in the neighbouring city of Progreso to try and reach the local youth there. In the first instance, they undertook a demonstration of hip-hop music, dance and graffiti; three weeks later other collectives held an impromptu festival in a public park where they distributed books, exhibited graffiti and art created with recycled products, demonstrated skateboard tricks or serigraphy on tee-shirts, and asked people to record comments on these activities. Out of the mass mobilizations for political demonstration, new forms of sociability have emerged, which validated the work of Merida's urban collectives and are now helping them connect and be active in new configurations of similar associations, with the approval of larger sectors of the Yucatecan population.

Most certainly, ephemeral associations have existed before today. The sociological and historical literature on 'social movements' chronicles many instances of impromptu gatherings and protests that later resulted in minor or even major social change (Keck and Sikkink 1998). Anthropologists, however, have only recently started to pay attention to this type of phenomenon, probably because it falls beyond established categories of kinship, social organization or the more regular aspects of local life. However, now the road is open and anthropologists are increasingly drawn to the close study of these 'crowds'.

CONCLUSION

Human sociality as the propensity of people to form groups has often resulted in the creation of lasting structures, which anthropologists have identified as organizations. From the beginning of their discipline, anthropologists have been recording and trying to understand principles of aggregation and the ways in which human aggregates justify and consolidate their collectivities. Here I have presented four interrelated concepts. The frontiers between them are often very thin. A group of people may decide to come together regularly, then to certify their association before the local authorities as a voluntary association, with specific goals and perhaps common property. This same association, with time, may be the basis of a cooperative or an incorporated business company, or it may dissolve as its members find other, more interesting pursuits. The ways in which each of these types of organization will behave, however, will be related to the other organizations around it, and also to the ways in which people interact with one another and find mechanisms for the expression of their collective will or the solution to internal (and perhaps also external) conflicts. In the twenty-first century, non-corporate forms of organization, such as those initiated through social-network computer and mobile technology applications, have already become very prominent forms of collective mobilization. It is still unclear whether they will become more important than the more perduring associations I described earlier in the chapter, but all evidence points at their increasing contemporary importance (Shirky 2008; Olson 2012).

Some types of organization enjoy a broader global acceptance. The incorporated company, the cooperative and now the ephemeral association seem to be examples of broadly accepted organizations. Recurrent debates over the nature of organizational mobilization can only sharpen our conceptual tools. Anthropology, however, should not surrender its traditional emphasis on collectivities associated with everyday forms of human sociality. Concepts of social organization, corporation, cooperative and voluntary association have had a somewhat different life in anthropology than these and similar concepts in other disciplines, precisely because of anthropologists' commitment to fieldwork and ethnography. Drawing on these traditions, anthropology can make a distinctive disciplinary contribution to an understanding of the multi-faceted ways in which people come together and the associations resulting from that sociality.

ACKNOWLEDGEMENTS

A chapter like this can only be possible thanks to many libraries and librarians. I especially thank the librarians at the Autonomous University of Yucatan, the University of California, Irvine, Brown University and San Diego State University, for their help in collecting information for this chapter. Thanks to Genny Negroe Sierra, George Marcus, Matthew Guttmann and Catherine Lutz, José Buscaglia and Ramona Perez for making it possible for me to take advantage of several universities' extensive libraries and collections. Also, thanks to all my fellow seminar participants of the sociality group through the years, including Sally Anderson, Igor Ayora-Diaz, Virginia Caputo, Noel Dyck, Christine Jourdan, Philip Moore, John Postill, Deborah Reed-Danahay, and especially our seminar's leader Vered Amit. They all contributed to this chapter with their comments and encouragement. Thanks to Philip Leis, Cristina Puga and Carmen Bueno Castellanos, who discussed with me many of the sources cited here, made comments on the chapter and led me to key references. A very special thanks to Steffan Igor Ayora-Diaz, my husband and fellow anthropologist, who has helped me think things through, has read and commented on several different drafts, and always shared my joys but also my angst and pain during all the complicated moments we had to face while I wrote this chapter. The research, though many years, and now the writing of this chapter have been funded by multiple agencies: McGill University, the Canadian International Development Agency, the Wenner-Gren Foundation, Centro de Investigaciones y Estudios Superiores en Antropología Social (CIESAS), Consejo Nacional de Ciencia y Tecnología (CONACYT) through Project Grant 156796, the Autonomous University of Yucatan (UADY) and the Programa Integral de Fortalecimiento Institucional (PIFI). All misrepresentations and errors, however, are my own.

NOTES

1. Institutional economics is one type of theory, but not the only one, that could apply to the study of Sardinian highland *comuni* or other such villages in Europe (Netting 1981; Viazzo 1989; Sheridan 1996).
2. On Amul, see www.amul.com/m/organisation, accessed 30 December 2012; on Cruz Azul, see CNNE (2010); and on Mondragon, see Cuevas Badallo (2004).
3. On Capital Desjardins Inc., see CDI (2012); on Raiffeisen Bank International, see http://investor.rbinternational.com/index.php?id=515andL=1, accessed 31 December 2012.
4. Anderson writes first about states and then about nations, and does not use the concept of nation-states.
5. The term 'Coloured' was a legal category in South Africa for people who were not considered either 'black' or 'white'.
6. Ephemeral associations have long been part of the political landscape of many social movements, as E.P. Thompson (1963) pointed out about England in the 1700s and 1800s. However, until recently they were not the object of sustained attention by anthropologists.

REFERENCES

Acheson, J.M. 2003. *Capturing the Commons: Devising Institutions to Manage the Maine Lobster Industry*. Lebanon, NH: University Press of New England.

Anderson, R. 1971. 'Voluntary Associations in History', *American Anthropologist* 73(1): 209–222.

Appadurai, A. 1996. *Modernity at Large: Cultural Dimensions of Globalization*. Minneapolis: University of Minnesota Press.

Ayora-Diaz, S.I. 1995. '(Pos)Modernización y la construcción de identidades en Cerdeña Central', *Nueva Anthropología* 47: 131–151.

—— 2002. *Globalización, conocimiento y poder: Médicos locales y sus luchas por el reconocimiento en Chiapas*. Mexico City/Merida: Plaza y Valdés/Autonomous University of Yucatan.

Banfield, E.C. 1958. *The Moral Basis of a Backward Society*. Glencoe, IL: Free Press.

Baviskar, B.S., D.W. Attwood, D. P. Apte, S. Bandyopadhayay, S.M. Batra, S.K. Bhowmik, R. Chopra, S. George, G.K. Karanth, A.S. Patel, N. Rajaram, J. Velacherry and D. Von Eschen. 1995. *Finding the Middle Path. The Political Economy of Cooperation in India*. Boulder, CO: Westview Press.

Biedelman, T.O. 1971. *The Kaguru: A Matrilineal People of East Africa*. New York: Holt, Rinehart and Winston.

Bradfield, R.M. 1973. *A Natural History of Associations: A Study in the Meaning of Community*. New York: International University Press, Vols. I and II.

Bohannan, P. 1955. 'Some Principles of Exchange and Investment among the Tiv', *American Anthropologist, New Series* 57(1) Part 1: 60–70.

Bourdieu, P. 1973. 'Cultural Reproduction and Social Reproduction', in R. Brown (ed.), *Papers in the Sociology of Education: Knowledge, Education and Cultural Change*. London: Tavistock, pp.71–112.

Bravo, G.M. 1976 [1972]. *Historia del Socialismo 1789–1848*. Barcelona: Seix Barral.

Brown, D.E. 1973. 'Voluntary Association: A Further Comment', *American Anthropologist* 75(1): 309–310.

—— 1974. 'Corporations and Social Classification', *Current Anthropology* 15(1): 29–52.

Cancian, F. 1961. 'The Southern Italian Peasant: World View and Political Behavior', *Anthropological Quaterly* 34(1): 1–18.

Cattelino, J.R. 2008. *Florida Seminole Gaming and Sovereignty*. Durham, NC: Duke University Press.

—— 2011. '"One Hamburger at a Time": Revisiting the State–Society Divide with the Seminole Tribe of Florida and Hard Rock International', *Current Anthropology* 52(S3): S137–S149.

CDI. 2012. 'Rapport Annuel 2012'. Montreal: Capital Desjardains Inc. Retrieved 30 December 2012 from: www.desjardins.com/fr/a_propos/investisseurs/rapports-annuels/pdf/rapport-annuel-cdi-2011.pdf.

Cheema, G.S., and D.A. Rondinelli (eds). 2007. *Decentralizing Governance: Emerging Concepts and Practices*. Washington: Brookings Institution Press.

CNNE. 2010. 'Cruz Azul hace empresas las cooperativas', CNN Expansión, 24 February. Retrieved 30 September 2012 from: www.cnnexpansion.com/expansion/2010/02/09/menos-cooperativa-y-mas-empresa.

Cochrane, G. 1971. 'Use of the Concept of Corporation: A Choice between Colloquialism or Distortion', *American Anthropologist* 73(5): 1144–1150.

Comaroff, J.L., and J. Comaroff. 2009. *Ethnicity Inc.* Chicago: University of Chicago Press.

Comte, A. 1975. *Auguste Comte and Positivism: The Essential Writings*, ed. G. Lenzer. New Brunswick, NJ: Transaction Publishers.

—— 1984 [1903]. *Discurso sobre el espíritu positivo*. Madrid: Planeta.

Cook, S. 2011. 'The Business of Being Bafokeng: The Corporatization of a Tribal Authority in South Africa', *Current Anthropology* 52(S3): S151–S159.

Crumrine, N.R. 1970. 'Ritual Drama and Culture Change', *Comparative Studies in Society and History* 12(4): 361–372.

Cuevas Badallo, A. 2004. 'La cultura tecnológica en la coporación cooperativa Mondragón (MCC)', *Revista Iberoamericana de Ciencia, Tecnología y Sociedad* 1(2): 47–66.

Digby, M. 1960. *The World Co-operative Movement*. New York: Hutchinson's University Library.

Dinges, W.D. 2001. '"An Army of Youth": The Sodality Movement and the Practice of Apostolic Mission', *US Catholic Historian* 19(3): 35–49.

Dore, R.F. 1971. 'Modern Cooperatives in Traditional Communities', in P. Worsley (ed.), *Two Blades of Grass: Rural Cooperatives in Agricultural Modernization*. Manchester: Manchester University Press, pp.43–65.

Dow, J. 1973. 'On the Muddled Concept of Corporation in Anthropology', *American Anthropologist* 75(3): 904–908.

Dunn, S.P., and E. Dunn. 1967. *The Peasants of Central Russia*. New York: Holt, Rinehart and Winston.

Earle, J. 1986. *The Italian Cooperative Movement: A Portrait of the Lega Nazionale Delle Cooperative*. Sydney: Allen and Unwin.

Fairbairn, B. 1994. *The Meaning of Rochdale: The Rochdale Pioneers and the Co-operative Principles*. Saskatoon: Centre for the Study of Co-operatives, University of Saskatchewan. Occasional Paper Series.

Fallers, L.A. 1965. *Bantu Bureaucracy: A Century of Political Evolution among the Basoga of Uganda*. Chicago: University of Chicago Press.

Fisher, J. 1998. *Nongovernments: NGOs and the Political Development of the Third World*. West Hartford, CT: Kumarian Press.

Foster, G.M. 1953. 'Cofradía and Compadrazgo in Spain and Spanish America', *Southwestern Journal of Anthropology* 9(1): 1–28.

Friedl, E. 1962. *Vasilika; A Village in Modern Greece*. New York: Holt, Rinehart and Winston.

Fukuyama, F. 2001. 'Social Capital, Civil Society and Development', *Third World Quarterly* 22(1): 7–20.

García Aguilar, M.C. 1998a. 'Las organizaciones no gubernamentales en los espacios rurales de Chiapas: reflexiones en torno a su actuación política', in M.E. Reyes Ramos, R. Moguel Viveros and G. van der Haar (eds), *Transformaciones Rurales en Chiapas*. Mexico City/San Cristóbal de las Casas: Universidad Autónoma de Metropolitana- Xochimilco/El Colegio de la Frontera Sur, pp.311–339.

—— 1998b. 'Las organizaciones no gubernamentales en Chiapas: algunas reflexiones en torno a su actuación política', *Anuario 1997 del Centro de Estudios Superiores de México y Centroamérica de la Universidad de Ciencias y Artes del Estado de Chiapas*, pp.37–80.

Gelo, D. 1999. 'Powwow Patter: Indian Emcee Discourse on Power and Identity', *Journal of American Folklore* 112(443): 40–57.

Gluckman, M. 1965. *The Ideas in Barotse Jurisprudence*. New Haven: Yale University Press.

Goodenough, W.H. 1951. *Property, Kin and Community on Truk*. New Haven: Yale University Press.

—— 1971. 'Corporations: Reply to Cochrane', *American Anthropologist* 73(5): 1150–1152.

—— 1974. 'Changing Social Organization in Romónum, Truk, 1947–1965' in R.J. Smith (ed), *Social Organization and the Applications of Anthropology*. Ithaca, NY: Cornell University Press, pp.62–93.

Gudeman, S. 2008. *Economy's Tension: The Dialectics of Community and Market*. New York: Berghahn Books.

Handelman, D. 1977. 'The Organization of Ethnicity', *Ethnic Groups* 1: 187–200.

Hansen, E.C. 1976. 'Transnational Corporations and Anthropology', *Reviews in Anthropology* 3(6): 601–608.

Heatherington, T. 2010. *Wild Sardinia: Indigeneity and the Global Dreamtimes of Environmentalism*. Seattle: University of Washington Press.

Hernández Castillo, R.A., and R. Nigh. 1998. 'Global Processes and Local Identity among Maya Coffee Growers in Chiapas, Mexico', *American Anthropologist* 100(1): 136–147.

Hilgers, J. 1912. 'Sodality', in C. G. Herbermann, E.A. Pace, C.B. Pallen, T.J. Shahan and J.J. Wynne (eds.), *The Catholic Encyclopedia*. New York: Robert Appleton. Retrieved 30 September 2011 from: www.newadvent.org/cathen/14120a. htm.

Hirschman, A.O. 1984. *Getting Ahead Collectively: Grassroots Experiences in Latin America*. New York: Pergamon Press; Washington D.C.: Inter-American Foundation.

Hobsbawm, E.J. 1962. *The Age of Revolution 1789–1848*. New York: Mentor Books.

Hughes, D.O. 1974. 'On Voluntary Associations in History: Medieval Europe', *American Anthropologist* 76(2): 333–334.

Juris, J.S. 2012. 'Reflections on #Occupy Everywhere: Social Media, Public Space, and Emerging Logics of Aggregation', *American Ethnologist* 39(2): 259–279.

Kaufman, J. 2008. 'Corporate Law and the Sovereignty of the States', *American Sociological Review* 73(3): 402–425.

Keck, M.E., and K. Sikkink. 1998. *Activists beyond Borders: Advocacy Networks in International Politics*. Ithaca, NY: Cornell University Press.

Kotov, I. 2001. *New Generation Cooperatives, a Case Study: A Short History of the Idea and the Enterprise*. Macomb: Illinois Institute for Rural Affairs.

Krotz, E. (ed.). 1986. *Cooperativas agrarias y conflictos políticos en el sur de Jalisco*. Mexico City: Universidad Autónoma Metropolitana.

Kurnik, M.R.A. 2012. 'The Occupy Movement in Zizek's Hometown: Direct Democracy and a Politics of Becoming', *American Ethnologist* 39(2): 238–252.

Langworthy, R. 1968. 'The Peasant World View in Italy and India', *Human Organization* 27(3): 212–219.

Lewis, O. 1960. *Tepoztlán: A Village in Mexico*. New York: Holt, Rinehart and Winston.

Little, K. 1959. 'The Organisation of Voluntary Associations in West Africa', *Civilisations* 9(3): 283–300.

Lowie, R. 1948. *Social Organization*. New York: Rinehart.

McClintock, C. 1981. *Peasant Cooperatives and Political Change in Peru*. Princeton: Princeton University Press.

McCorkle, T. 1959. 'Ethnology and Ethnography: The Moral Basis of a Backward Society', *American Anthropologist* 61(1): 133–134.

Maine, H.S. 1908 [1861]. *Ancient Law: Its Connection with the Early History of Society and its Relation to Modern Ideas*. London: John Murray.

Maitland, F.W. 1961. *The Constitutional History of England*. Cambridge: Cambridge University Press.

Massa, P., and A. Moioli. 2005. *Dalla corporazione al mutuo soccorso: organizzazione e tutela del lavoro tra XVI e XX secolo*. Milan: Franco Angeli.

Molina, O., and M. Rhodes. 2002. 'Corporatism: The Past, Present, and Future of a Concept', *Annual Review of Political Science* 2002 (5): 305–331.

Moss, L.W., and S.C. Capanari. 1960. 'Patterns of Kinship, *Comparaggio* and Community in a Southern Italian Village', *Anthropological Quarterly* 33: 24–32.

Nash, J., J. Dandler and N.S. Hopkins (eds). 1976. *Popular Participation in Social Change: Cooperatives, Collectives and Nationalized Industry.* Berlin: De Gruyter.

Netting, R.McC. 1981. *Balancing on an Alp: Ecological Change and Continuity in a Swiss Mountain Community.* Cambridge: Cambridge University Press.

Nishida, M. 1998. 'From Ethnicity to Race and Gender: Transformations of Black Lay Sodalities in Salvador, Brazil', *Journal of Social History* 32(2): 329–348.

—— 2003. *Slavery and Identity: Ethnicity, Gender, and Race in Salvador, Brazil, 1808–1888.* Bloomington: Indiana University Press.

Nonini, D.M. (ed.). 2007. *The Global Idea of 'the Commons'.* New York: Berghahn.

Nosco, P. 1993. 'Secrecy and the Transmission of Tradition: Issues in the Study of the "Underground" Christians', *Japanese Journal of Religious Studies* 20(1): 3–29.

Olson, P. 2012. *We Are Anonymous: Inside the Hacker World of LulzSec, Anonymous, and the Global Cyber Insurgency.* New York: Little, Brown.

Parry, J. 1989. 'On the Moral Perils of Exchange', in J. Parry and M. Bloch (eds), *Money and the Morality of Exchange.* Cambridge: Cambridge University Press, pp.49–93.

Partridge, D., M. Welker and R. Hardin (eds). 2011. 'Corporate Lives: New Perspectives on the Social Life of the Corporate Form', *Current Anthropology*, supplement, 52(S3).

Pellow, D. 1987. 'Solidarity among Muslim Women in Accra, Ghana', *Anthropos* 82(4–6): 489–506.

Postill, J. 2008. 'Localizing the Internet beyond Communities and Networks', *New Media and Society* 10(3): 413–431.

—— 2012. 'Democracy in the Age of Viral Reality: A Media Epidemiography of Spain's *Indignados* Movement', unpublished paper.

Putnam, R.D. 2000. *Bowling Alone: The Collapse and Revival of American Community.* New York: Simon and Shuster.

Radcliffe-Brown, A.R. 1952. *Structure and Function in Primitive Society.* Glencoe, IL: Free Press.

Raheja, G.G. 1988. *The Poison in the Gift: Ritual, Prestation, and the Dominant Caste in a North Indian Village.* Chicago: University of Chicago Press.

Rigby, P. 1977. 'Local Participation in National Politics: Ugogo, Tanzania', *Africa* 47(1): 89–107.

Rojas Coria, R. 1984 [1952]. *Tratado de cooperativismo mexicano.* Mexico City: Fondo de Cultura Económica.

Saint Simon, H. 1975. *Henri Saint Simon, 1760–1825: Selected Writings on Science, Industry and Social Organization*, trans. K. Taylor. London: Taylor and Francis.

Scheper-Hughes, N., and L. Wacquant (eds). 2002. *Commodifying Bodies.* London: Sage.

Service, E.R. 1962. *Primitive Social Organization: An Evolutionary Perspective.* New York: Random House.

Schnepel, B. 1990. 'Corporations, Personhood, and Ritual in Tribal Society: Three Interconnected Topics in the Anthropology of Meyer Fortes', *Journal of the Anthropological Society of Oxford* 21(1): 1–31.

Schwartzman, H.B. 1995. *Ethnography in Organizations*. London: Sage.

Sheridan, T.E. 1996. *Where the Dove Calls: The Politics of a Peasant Corporate Community in Northwestern Mexico*. Tucson: University of Arizona Press.

Shirky, C. 2008. *Here Comes Everybody. The Power of Organizing without Organizations*. London: Penguin.

Silverman, S.F. 1968. 'Agricultural Organization, Social Structure, and Values in Italy: Amoral Familism Reconsidered', *American Anthropologist* 70(1): 1–20.

Smith, M.E. 2000. *Trades and Trade-offs: Using Resources, Making Choices and Taking Risks*. Prospect Heights, IL: Waveland Press.

Smith, M.G. 1954. 'On Segmentary Lineage Systems', *Journal of the Royal Anthropological Institute* 86(2): 39–80.

—— 1966. 'A Structural Approach to Comparative Politics', in D. Easton (ed.), *Varieties of Political Theory*. Englewood Cliffs, NJ: Prentice Hall, pp.113–128.

—— 1975. *Corporations and Society: The Social Anthropology of Collective Action*. Chicago: Aldine.

Sorge, A. 2009. 'Hospitality, Friendship, and the Outsider in Highland Sardinia', *Journal of the Society for the Anthropology of Europe* 9(1): 4–12.

Spiro, M.E. 1956. *Kibbutz: Venture in Utopia*. Cambridge, MA: Harvard University Press.

—— 1958. *Children of the Kibbutz*. Cambridge, MA: Harvard University Press.

Taylor, W.B. 1987. 'The Virgin of Guadalupe in New Spain: An Inquiry into the Social History of Marian Devotion', *American Ethnologist* 14(1): 9–33.

Thompson, E.P. 1963. *The Making of the English Working Class*. New York: Pantheon Books.

Vargas-Cetina, G. 1999. 'Flexible Looms: Weavers' Organizations in Chiapas, Mexico', *Urban Anthropology and Studies of Cultural Systems and World Economic Development* 28(3/4): 299–325.

—— 2000. 'From Handicraft to Monocrop: The Production of Pecorino Cheese in Highland Sardinia', in A. Haugerud, M.P. Stone and P. Little (eds), *Commodities and Globalization*. Lanham, MD: Rowman and Littlefield. pp.219–238.

—— 2002. 'Globalización y artesanías: Organizaciones artesanales en Chiapas', in G. Vargas-Cetina (ed.), *De lo privado a lo público: Organizaciones en Chiapas*. Mexico City: Miguel Angel Porrúa/Centro de Investigaciones y Estudios en Antropología Social, pp.111–190.

—— 2004. 'La Asociación efímera: Repensando el concepto de comunidad desde la literatura cyberpunk'. Retrieved 31 December 2012 from: www.academia.edu/170543/La_Asociacion_Efimera_Repensando_el_concepto_de_comunidad_desde_la_literatura_cyberpunk.

—— 2005. 'Anthropology and Cooperatives: From the Community Paradigm to the Ephemeral Association in Chiapas, Mexico', *Critique of Anthropology* 25(3): 229–251.

—— 2011. 'Corporations, Cooperatives, and the State: Examples from Italy', *Current Anthropology* 52(S3): S127–S136.

Viazzo, P.P. 1989. *Upland Communities: Environment, Population and Social Structure in the Alps since the Sixteenth Century.* Cambridge: Cambridge University Press.

Vincent, J. 1971. *African Elite: The Big Men of a Small Town.* New York: Columbia University Press.

—— 1981. *Teso in Transformation: The Political Economy of Peasant and Class in Eastern Africa.* Berkeley: University of California Press.

Wade, R. 1989. *Village Republics: Economic Conditions for Collective Action in South India.* Cambridge: Cambridge University Press.

Weinberg, D. 1976. 'Bands and Clans: Political Functions of Voluntary Associations in the Swiss Alps', *American Ethnologist* 3(1): 175–189.

Wheeldon, P.D. 1969. 'The Operation of Voluntary Associations and Personal Newtworks in the Political Processes of an Inter-ethnic Community', in J.C. Mitchell (ed.), *Social Networks in Urban Relations: Analyses of Personal Relations in Central African Towns.* Manchester: Manchester University Press, pp.128–180.

Whiteley, P.M. 1985. 'Unpacking Hopi "Clans": Another Vintage Model out of Africa?' *Journal of Anthropological Research* 41(4): 359–374.

Wilkie, R. 1971. *Life in a Mexican Collective Ejido.* Stanford: Stanford University Press.

Wolf, E. 1966. *Peasants.* New York: Prentice Hall.

—— 1986. 'The Vicissitudes of the Closed Corporate Peasant Community', *American Ethnologist* 13(2): 325–329.

Worsley, P. 1971a. 'Introduction', in P. Worsley (ed.), *Two Blades of Grass: Rural Cooperatives in Agricultural Modernization.* Cambridge: Cambridge University Press, pp.1–40.

—— (ed.). 1971b. *Two Blades of Grass: Rural Cooperatives in Agricultural Modernization.* Cambridge: Cambridge University Press.

Wright, S. 1994. 'Culture in Anthropology and Organizational Studies', in S. Wright (ed.), *Anthropology of Organizations.* London: Routledge, pp.1–31.

6

Network
The Possibilities and Mobilizations of Connections

Vered Amit and Virginia Caputo

'Network research is "hot" today', declares a recent review article in the journal *Science* (Borgatti et al. 2009: 892). According to Borgatti et al., there has been 'an explosion of interest' in the concept of network across the physical and social sciences (ibid.). This very popularity however conveys its own problems. Thus, just a year earlier, John Postill (2008: 417) was complaining that the paradigmatic dominance of community and network as theoretical concepts had blinkered rather than opened up the study of local internet technologies.

The concept of network has a long history across a variety of social sciences, but that standing can obscure some important differences in its usage between different disciplines (Knox, Savage and Harvey 2006). Within anthropology, the concept of network has had a chequered history. At the start of the 1980s, Ulf Hannerz's observation that a 'great deal has been claimed for network analysis during its years as an anthropological growth industry' (Hannerz 1980: 186) turned out to be the tolling bell for the near demise of this form of analysis within anthropology over the remainder of the twentieth century. The concept of the network has become popular again within anthropology during the twenty-first century, not least through its prominence as part of actor-network theory (ANT) within science and technology studies, but Postill is not alone in his unease with it. Hannah Knox, Mike Savage and Penny Harvey have noted that even many actor-network theorists have abandoned the eponymous concept of 'network', and that this 'turn away from networks has earlier progenitors' (Knox, Savage and Harvey 2006: 133).

While there are important differences between the particular applications of network within its earlier efflorescence during the twentieth and now in the twenty-first century, there are also some significant convergences between the dissatisfaction of anthropologists with the growing popularity of the concept then and now. In both periods, the concept became, or threatened to become, in effect 'hollowed out'. As we shall see, the earlier incarnation of network analysis within anthropology was overtaken by demands for morphological rigour that effectively narrowed the range of situations in which it could be successfully applied. In its current ubiquitous but often-unquestioned status both within and outside the academy, the concept seems to be well on its way towards serving as a 'truism' (ibid.: 133) of connectedness.

But Knox, Savage and Harvey have also argued that the concept of network can still be a useful medium for posing questions within social research, even while it is important 'to recognize the limitations of networks as an explanatory tool' (ibid.: 134). In this chapter, we wish to take up this examination of the potential utility of the network concept for anthropological analysis, while also raising some concerns about the enthusiasm expressed by Knox, Savage and Harvey and other authors for a focus on network as a cultural category. Their focus points to one of two quite distinct general conceptualizations of network – as a system or cultural form on the one hand, and as a personal compilation of relationships on the other – that point to rather different sets of questions. Caution therefore needs to be exercised to ensure that one of these potentially productive lines of inquiry is not eliminated in the rush to pursue the other.

THE MANCHESTER SCHOOL

As J. Clyde Mitchell noted in a preface to the 1969 collection *Social Networks in Urban Situations*, most of the researchers who pioneered the use of network as a concept within anthropology – including John Barnes (1954), who first broached it – had at one point or another spent some time in the Department of Social Anthropology and Sociology at the University of Manchester (Mitchell 1969a). In his introduction to this volume, Mitchell traces the growing enthusiasm for network analysis to a growing dissatisfaction, among anthropologists, with structural-functionalist analyses. Within 'small-scale localized societies', structural-functionalist analysis had seemed to offer a 'marked step forward in sociological analysis' (Mitchell 1969b: 9).

Yet when anthropologists began to move towards conducting research in a wider range of situations, the 'inadequacy of this approach became apparent' (ibid.).

> Thus Van Velsen who studied a 'stateless' society whose social relationships were marked by a lack of predictability and certainty, found the 'structural' approach inadequate. He notes that structuralist [i.e. structural-functionalist] interpretations involve generalizations about the behaviour of people in terms of the positions they occupy in the social system but that these generalizations based as they are on abstractions ignore individual deviations from the pattern. These deviations, however, van Velsen argues are essential elements of social action and must be subsumed by the analysis. In his study he does this through situational analysis ... : in the studies presented in this book the notion of the social network is used instead. (ibid.)

While *Social Networks in Urban Situations* was published over forty years ago, there are several key arguments made by Mitchell that still speak tellingly to debates over the status of network today. First and foremost, Mitchell was clear that as a general metaphor for social relations, network was hardly novel; indeed, it had a long history in social research. But to move from metaphor to an analytical concept required a specification of those characteristics or properties of networks that were heuristically useful or, put another way, this required expanding a network into an analogy (ibid.: 2). Network was not, however, being offered by Mitchell and his colleagues as a new master concept or framework for analysis. It was viewed as only one among a number of different ways of abstracting from actual behaviour, and as such it was intended to complement not replace other frameworks of sociological or anthropological analysis. Hence Mitchell argued that the concept of network was best suited to the investigation of the 'personal order by means of which the behaviour of people in either structured or unstructured situations may be interpreted in terms of the personal links individuals have with a set of people and the links these people in turn have among themselves and with others' (ibid.: 10). If studies of structural or categorical orders of social relationships were not sufficient to explain the 'details of social behaviour' (ibid.), by implication, neither was network analysis sufficient to account for other kinds of situations or social relationships.

Mitchell and his colleagues were thus very aware of, and even insistent regarding, the limitations of the concept. It was a heuristic device that was helpful in posing certain kinds of questions that could not be accounted for by other forms of anthropological analysis, but it was not meant to and could not account for any and all forms of social relationships, situations or behaviour. As a heuristic device, the concept of network allowed the analyst to take into account the possibility that an individual might be affected not only by people with whom they are directly in contact, but also by more indirect links. For example, the way my friend or colleague interacts with me might well be influenced by their relationships with other people – spouse, offspring, parents, workmates, friends – with whom I may or may not be acquainted. So to understand the context influencing their interaction with me, I would need to know something as well about their relationships with some or all of these other persons. This means that the critical factors shaping any one situation might well extend beyond what can be observed in that one venue.

> The person to whom the actor is orienting his behaviour may not be physically present though he would almost certainly be in the individual's personal network. The behaviour of a child towards another in a classroom, for example, will probably be conditioned by its knowledge that its mother knows the mother of the other. The network links in this case would need to extend beyond the classroom to the parents of the children. (ibid.: 13)

It is not difficult to understand why a group of ethnographers who were beginning to regularly conduct fieldwork in rapidly expanding urban settings would feel the need to take account of the partiality of their direct encounters and observations. One of Mitchell's Manchester colleagues, A.L. Epstein (1969: 78–79), noted that the majority of Africans resident in the Copperbelt town of Ndola were recent newcomers. This was an ethnically, culturally and linguistically diverse and mobile population among which people were constantly coming and going. People moved from one section of town to another, in part because their housing was frequently tied to their employment – change or lose the job and you also lost the housing – but also because people were regularly moving back and forth between their home villages and the city. 'The fact is that each individual African is involved in a network of social ties ... which ramify throughout the urban community and extend to other towns and to the tribal areas' (ibid.: 80).[1]

To demonstrate this, Epstein asked Chanda, one of his interlocutors, to record his movements around the town of Ndola, and to list the contacts that he made with various people over the course of several days (ibid.). Epstein observed that, while the contacts that Chanda recorded included face-to-face contacts with a wide range of people, this was still only a partial assortment of all of his social links in the town, let alone beyond it (ibid.: 109). The contacts ranged across people Chanda knew from various different locales, including his home village, the nearby town of Luanshya, as well as people he had met in Ndola. They included Chanda's wife, his visiting affines, a sibling, classificatory brothers and sisters, friends, friends' spouses, workmates, neighbours, officials, merchants, as well as people that Chanda did not know but with whom his contacts stopped to talk. Among these were people of a variety of ethnic backgrounds, languages, ages and political, occupational and organizational affiliations, and who resided in different parts of the town and for different periods of time and so on. Hence these people did not constitute a group or even a collectivity:

> they have no corporate existence whatsoever: all they may be said to possess in common is the social tie which links each of them individually to a central fig-ure, Chanda. Chanda, that is to say, is in touch with a number of people, some of whom may be in touch with each other, and some of whom may not. (ibid.: 109)

So urban ethnographers like A.L. Epstein had to account for situations, which could not be analysed simply in terms of one overriding organiza-tional structure or clearly defined and bounded groups. The contacts of Chanda pointed to the need to take account of social links of varying in-tensities that crossed a number of sectors, institutional frameworks, social classes, ethnicities, origins and histories. Particular encounters could be shaped as much by people who were not there, as well as by those who were. Hence the first person Chanda met in the course of his movement through the town was a woman who had just arrived in Ndola from Fort Roseberry.

> She was of his own tribe, a Lunda of Kazembe, and he greeted her. At first she did not recognize him, for it was a long time since they had last met when Chanda was on a short visit to his rural home. He introduced himself as ShiChomba, father of Chomba, and said that he was the former husband of Agnes K of Mulundu. At length the woman realized who he was and apolo-gized for having forgotten him. 'Now I remember you well', she said, 'because your daughter resembles you so much'. (ibid.: 81)

As an analytical concept, network therefore had the potential to trace influential absences as much as presences in any one situation. As such, it could be approached without an a priori definition of social and physical boundaries, or assumptions of institutional integration (Mitchell 1969b: 47). It is this capacity to take account of what is not there as well as what is, and to trace contacts that cut across different situations and institutions, that has imparted to the concept of network its open-ended quality.

But for Mitchell and his Manchester colleagues, this did not mean that social networks should be viewed as inherently infinite or 'endless' (Strathern 1996). Rather, it meant that one's analytical starting point did not need to be premised on 'presuppositions of closure and equilibrium' (Mitchell 1969b: 47). How far a network could or should be traced by the researcher was a question of fieldwork pragmatism rather than ontology. It depended, Mitchell argued, on what social situation and problem the analyst was attempting to account for, and which links were useful in explaining a particular form of behaviour. Fieldwork thus necessarily and usefully dealt with a finite rather than infinite set of linkages. Similarly, the issue of how the network would be anchored – that is, what would be the initial starting point from which the network would be traced – was also a matter of practicality and effectiveness.

Mitchell noted that, in John Barnes's seminal article on a rural parish in Norway (Barnes 1954), when Barnes 'originally wrote about social networks he had in mind the general ever-ramifying, ever-reticulating set of linkages that stretches within and beyond the confines of any community or organization', the 'total network' in other words (Mitchell 1969b: 12).[2] But, '[t]he idea of the total network is essentially a general heuristic concept: as with similar general concepts such as Gemeinschaft and Gesellschaft, when it comes to actual fieldwork it is always necessary to specify the context' (ibid.: 12–13), and the most effective way of doing that, in the view of Mitchell, was to use an individual as the anchor for the network being investigated (ibid.). So in the ongoing debate about analyses based on 'whole networks' as opposed to 'ego-networks' (Knox, Savage and Harvey 2006: 118), Mitchell and his colleagues came down solidly in favour of the effectiveness of the latter, although Mitchell expressed a preference for the term 'personal network' (Mitchell 1969b: 13).

The Manchester School thus viewed networks as facilitating an examination of cross-cutting relationships, a form of analysis precluded by the presuppositions entailed in other analytical frameworks (ibid.: 49). But whatever form of analysis they might employ, as social anthropologists, the members of the Manchester School were first and foremost concerned to account for behaviour. Networks were not being marked out, in and for themselves. Rather, investigating the reach, intensity, durability, content, direction and meanings of social relationships was intended as a means of tracing influences on people's behaviour. Tracing people's social links in order to understand their behaviour involved two key suppositions. First, it involved an assumption that the range of people to whom and from whom there might be certain expectations of rights and obligations were not fixed in space or time but were constantly changing (ibid.: 26–27). Second, it also included the premise that the extent of identifiable people with whom these kinds of expectations were associated was not coterminous either in duration or reach with the more limited set of links that at various times might be mobilized to achieve a particular action, or to communicate particular information or ideas (ibid.). That is to say, the interaction and discrepancy between the potentiality and the actualization of links was a key part of what was being investigated in utilizing the concept of network analytically.

NETWORK DRIFT

We noted above the ambivalent endorsement of Knox, Savage and Harvey (2006) regarding the utility of network analysis, at the same time as they cautioned about the limitations of network as an explanatory tool. This kind of ambivalence had also been voiced by the researchers who had earlier pioneered the use of network as a concept in anthropological analysis. In his introduction to *Social Networks in Urban Situations*, as well as in a later review article (see Mitchell 1969b, 1974), Mitchell drew attention to the gap between the morphological and interactional criteria that were developed in connection with social networks and the kind of data that most fieldworkers would be able to marshal. He also noted that, 'Since the notion of "social networks" was first introduced by Barnes in 1954 ... perhaps its most striking characteristic has been that it has stimulated much more development and elaboration of the idea itself than empirical field work based upon the idea ... This has led to a proliferation of concepts and terms' (Mitchell 1974: 279). John Barnes himself observed that a 'terminological confusion' had become associated with the concept of network as it had become more popular (quoted in ibid.: 279). Barnes was also dismissive of any attempt to claim social network as a theory: this was a 'basic idea and nothing more' (cited in ibid.: 282).

In a 1980 overview of urban anthropology, Ulf Hannerz noted the persistence of these issues. On the one hand, the criteria associated with the conceptualization of network suggested an 'admirable' rigour (Hannerz 1980: 181). 'It is a rigor, however, which is accompanied by practical limitations. It is extremely difficult and time-consuming to realize this potential of exactness in other than fairly small network units' (ibid.). Hannerz nonetheless still regarded the concept of network as a useful one with which to think about urban life if it was employed with flexibility rather than with an obfuscating insistence on methodological precision (ibid.: 186).

But over the two decades that followed Hannerz's call for a 'normalization of network thinking' (ibid.: 186), the use of network waned in anthropological analysis, even as it continued within sister disciplines such as sociology and geography. In 1969, Mitchell had already noted the lack of interaction between 'sociological graph theorists on the one hand and fieldworkers on the other' (Mitchell 1969b: 35), and five years later he noted that this gap still persisted (Mitchell 1974: 296). Far from being reconciled, this gap continued to grow further. Knox, Savage and Harvey have noted that social network analysis became ever more specialized and concentrated on mathematical concepts and techniques associated with graph theory, and writers in this tradition are 'often keen to announce themselves as "true keepers of the flame"' (Knox, Savage and Harvey 2006: 117).

But anthropologists have not been alone in noting the limitations of this approach. For example, in a volume considering the relationship of networks to mobility, Jonas Larsen, John Urry and Kay Axhausen (2006) – whose expertise traverses geography, sociology and transport planning – argued that approaches emphasizing the networked nature of social life, such as social network and 'small world' analyses, have not paid sufficient attention to the efforts people undertake to sustain their social relations through face-to-face even if intermittent interaction. They argued that far more important than enumerating the number of links that people might be said to possess was to take account of the various ways in which people contrive to meet, as well as the embodied and performative nature of networks and practices of networking (ibid.: 19–20).

In so doing, Larsen, Urry and Axhausen reasserted the importance of grounding attention to personal networks in social interaction rather than relying on overly abstracted maps of potential social links. Their critique of contemporary approaches to social networks is therefore reminiscent of some of Mitchell's observations regarding the gap between sociological graph theory and fieldwork approaches to the concept of network; similarly, their emphasis on the interaction between mobility and personal links resonates with A.L. Epstein's charting of Chanda's social and spatial pathways through Ndola. But other recent conceptualizations of network both within anthropology as well as in other social sciences have often tended to privilege more structural or cultural conceptions of network.

As Knox, Savage and Harvey have observed, the concept of network has increasingly escaped the academy. In more recent years, invocations of network (or networking) have become popular vehicles with which to represent new forms of information and communication technology, as well as various forms of globalization (Knox, Savage and Harvey 2006: 125). These forms of popular discourse in turn have influenced representations within scholarly analysis, including the renewal of anthropological interest in the concept of network.

NETWORK AND STRUCTURE

As we noted at the start of this chapter, network analysis has become a commonly encountered approach within the study of internet technologies (Postill 2008). But it is Manuel Castells who has been most explicitly associated with the conceptualization of network as a form of social structure characteristic of a 'new' information age (Castells 2000: 5). In spite of its title, what is 'new' about the contemporary period is not the role of knowledge and information – which is important in any society – but a new set of information technologies, which are revolutionary in their implications, not least for the emergence of a 'new' economy (ibid.: 10). Castells argued that three key features characterize this new economy: it is informational; it is global; and it is networked (ibid.). It is networked because: 'At the heart of the connectivity of the global economy and of the flexibility of informational production, there is a new form of economic organization, the network enterprise. This is not a network of enterprises. It is a network made from either firms or segments of firms, and/or from internal segmentation of firms' (ibid.: 11). Network, reborn through technology as a new form of social structure, has, according to Castells, wide-ranging transformative implications for relations of production and consumption, politics (particularly in terms of the status of the nation-state), cultural expression, performance and decision-making.

This then is a very different notion of network than that offered by the Manchester School. If, for Mitchell and his colleagues, conceptions of network provided an opportunity to explore issues precluded by structural analysis, for Castells, network *is* structure. Castells's vision of network is not directed at tracing the ramification of personal links. Rather, it is the vehicle for identifying a historically revolutionary form of social architecture that subsumes and transforms domains of politics, economics and culture.

Apart from the importance of technology as a catalyst for both Castells's notion of the 'network society' as well as for actor-network theory (ANT), which arose through science, technology and society (STS) studies, these conceptions otherwise have very different conceptions of network. For Castells, information networks are 'automatons' that are programmed by social actors, but that once programmed assume an inexorable logic that imposes itself on its members (ibid.: 16). 'Actors will have to play their strategies within the rules of the network' (ibid.). As social structures, therefore, networks eventually assume an inertia that inhibits social change, at least within their own internal frame of reference.

In contrast, actor-network theory, according to Bruno Latour (2005), is a 'sociology of associations' that does not rely on a priori assumptions of, or about, society or the social. This kind of approach does not proceed from a list of pre-existing aggregates that are presumed to establish a context for action. Rather: 'actors are always engaged in the business of mapping the "social context" in which they are placed, thus offering the analyst a full-blooded theory of what sort of sociology they should be treated with. This is why it is so important *not* to define in advance what sort of social aggregates could provide the context for all of these maps' (ibid.: 32; original emphasis). Nor is stability or inertia a singular historical achievement because groupings constantly have to be made. Hence perdurance or stability cannot ever be assumed by the analyst as a backdrop for what they are examining but must be explained (ibid.: 34–35). What the sociologist of association is tracing are all the means by which aggregates are made and remade. Each association is utterly specific (ibid.: 36). So, if for Castells network is a social structure that has already come into existence and serves as a context for a wide variety of institutions, for Latour, ANT is 'not about a *thing* called a network' (Oppenheimer 2007: 485). In the ANT focus on tracing associations, 'every choice of a departure point will lead to the drawing of a completely different animal, fully incommensurable with the others' (Latour 2005: 36). Social links are not simply there, they 'have to be traced *by the circulation* of different vehicles which cannot be substituted by one another' (ibid.; original emphasis).

Yet however labile and particular, the associations that Latour is attempting to trace are not simply or even primarily networks of sociality – in the sense of social relationships and interactions – so much as formations in formation. These are systems that can encompass more durable power relations and differentiation, not primarily through social ties or local interactions but through the capacity to extend beyond these kinds of linkages (ibid.: 66). 'When power is exerted for good, it is because it is not made of social ties; when it has to rely only on social ties, it is not exerted for long' (ibid.). And the means that are mobilized to extend beyond the weak capacities of social skills in and of themselves are non-human: an artefact, a space, a schedule and so on.

> For sociologists of associations, what is new is not the multiplicity of objects any course of action mobilizes along its trail – no one ever denied they were there by the thousands; what is new is that objects are suddenly highlighted not only as being full-blown actors, but also as what explains the contrasted landscape we started with, the overarching powers of society, the huge asymmetries, the crushing exercise of power. (ibid.: 72)

So, if for Castells network is already a fully developed formation that subsumes other domains, and for Latour network is a performative formation perpetually in formation, effectively both are still describing systems rather than social ties.

Hence, in spite of the differences between these respective conceptions of the 'network society' and the 'actor network', ANT is similarly distinct from the conception of network that was offered by the Manchester School.

While both the Manchester School and ANT treat network/association as a form of abstraction that eschews premature closure in the presuppositions brought to the analysis, these are nonetheless conceptualizations that seek to operate at very different levels of abstraction. For Mitchell, the concept of network was most effective if it stayed very close to the pragmatic ground of fieldwork. ANT, on the other hand, is offered as a new 'ontology of association' (Oppenheimer 2007: 472), a comprehensive 'recasting of the central hope of social science' (Latour 2005: 40). The former is offered as one approach within a larger inventory of abstractions about sociality; the latter is after a far more extended notion of association that can include any kind of entity or material (Strathern 1996: 522–523).

Robert Oppenheimer (2007: 485) has urged anthropologists to engage with ANT beyond the domain of science and technology studies. Specifically, Oppenheimer argues for a reading of ANT through spatiality that can speak to anthropologists' own efforts to rethink their categories of space and place. But in this chapter, our concern is in the way in which anthropological engagements with ANT have tended to be linked with a reinterpretation of network as cultural systems, and the implications of this shift.

CUTTING THE NETWORK

In an early and influential example of anthropological engagement with ANT, Marilyn Strathern argued that the strength of ANT's conception of network is its 'auto-limitlessness; that is[,] a concept which works indigenously as a metaphor for the endless extension and intermeshing of phenomena' (Strathern 1996: 522). For Strathern, network provides a relatively neutral way to refer to interconnectedness because it can be used to link 'disparate entities without making assumptions about level or hierarchy' (ibid.: 522). But the very strength of this conception of network, its limitlessness, also poses analytical problems.

> If *diverse* elements make up a description, they seem as extensible or involuted as the analysis is extensible or involuted. Analysis appears able to take into account, and thus create, any number of new forms. And one can always discover networks within networks; this is the fractal logic that renders any length a multiple of other lengths, or a link in a chain of further links. Yet analysis, like interpretation, must have a point; it must be enacted as a stopping place. (ibid.: 523)

How then, Strathern asked, can this be done? How can the network be 'cut', 'stopped' (ibid.)? In response, she provided several different illustrations of ways in which respectively the network is cut or flows can be stopped and

restarted, examples she notes that are drawn from more conventional notions of social-network analysis and kinship theory, as well as from ANT
(ibid.: 531). For example, the discovery of the hepatitis C virus led to the
invention of a blood test, which was subsequently patented. Given the
length of time in which hepatitis C was being investigated before the virus
was isolated, and the broader field of scientific knowledge which nurtures
any one invention, Strathern argues that the 'social networks here are long;
patenting truncates them. So it matters very much over which segment or
fragment of a network rights of ownership can be exercised' (ibid.: 524). In
another example, this time of 'stopping flow', Strathern drew on Daniel de
Coppet's account of the 'Are'are of the Solomon Islands, who distinguish
three types of living creatures: body, breath and ancestral image (de Coppet
1994). On death, people are decomposed into these different elements, each
of which is commemorated; body through the consumption of taro and veg-
etables; breath through the slaughter of pigs; and ancestral image through
the circulation of shell money from one funeral feast to another.

> Marking an event in monetary terms gives it an official seal. It also builds up
> the person as a composite of past transactions with diverse others. There is a
> further dimension to money. This stimulator of flows can stop flow ... Now, at
> death there is a finalizing sequence of exchanges in which the living being's
> two other components become money; in one sequence taro is converted into
> money, in another pigs ... The ancestor-image encompasses both, and the se-
> quences stop at that point. (Strathern 1996: 526)

It is noteworthy that the 'Are'are are themselves explicit in referring to
this finalizing sequence as a 'stop' or 'break' (ibid.: 527).

In a further illustration, Strathern observed that the notorious open-end-
edness of bilateral kinship systems led to considerable anthropological debate during the 1950s and 1960s about the seeming absence of internal
boundaries in these modes of kinship calculation (ibid.: 529). But Strathern
argued that modes of reckoning never operate alone:

> Social relations depend on multitudinous factors that truncate the potential of
> forever-ramifying biological relations. Biological relatedness – 'blood ties' – can
> thus be cut by failure to accord social recognition (someone is forgotten), just
> as social relationships can be cut by appeal to biological principles (dividing
> 'real' kin from others). So in practice one does not trace connexions for ever.
> (ibid.: 530)

For quite different reasons, both J. Clyde Mitchell and Bruno Latour did
not attach the same importance to the question of how networks are cut or

stopped. For Mitchell, as we described earlier in this chapter, the question of how far the calculation of network links is extended was a pragmatic matter of analytical utility and fieldwork resources. How far the analyst went in their tracing of network links depended on how far they had to go to usefully answer a particular research question. In other words, he tended to treat this issue as methodological rather than substantive. For Latour, the cutting of networks is not a subject for specific examination because associations are viewed as so inherently fragile that they could stop at any time. Latour starts off with dislocation and disjuncture as the starting point and foreground for analysis. In this reading, the cutting or stopping point for the network is therefore always imminent: 'For ANT, if you stop making and remaking groups, you stop having groups' (Latour 2005: 35). So it is stability, the capacity to extend the association a little further and to make it stand a little longer that requires explanation, not its stopping point (ibid.). As Caroline Humphrey has remarked, Latour's interest is focused on the 'building up' and not the 'cutting down' of networks (Humphrey 2008: 365).

But Strathern's argument is important for reminding us that the mobilization of social links is shaped by the interchange between, on the one hand, the recognition or affirmation of associational claims and, on the other hand, both explicit and more oblique means of refusing, limiting, ignoring or simply misunderstanding such claims. And it is the uncertain direction and outcome of this interchange – that is, it is never simply automatic – that impels the kind of efforts required for assembling associations that Latour emphasizes. While ANT has trained our attention on the means that are enlisted to build associations, Strathern has reminded us that a variety of means are also enlisted to stop or cut off these associations. To understand how associations are made and mapped, we need to understand both sets of means.

But if this process is never automatic or axiomatic, then don't we need to acknowledge the purposefulness and self-consciousness involved in the work of assembling associations? Yet as Humphrey observes, neither Strathern nor Latour appear to reference intentionality in considering respectively processes of cutting or assembling: 'cutting the network in Strathern is an effect of cultural systems like "kinship", and in Latour a subject is produced by external actants, "plug-ins" such as official and legal papers, and intention is replaced by supplementary tools ("supplementary souls") that equip people to choose and calculate (for a consuming subject these would be labels, trade-marks, prices)' (Humphrey 2008: 365).

According to Latour, the actor is 'not the source of an action but the moving target of a vast array of entities swarming towards it' (Latour 2005: 213), and 'Being a fully competent actor now comes in discrete pellets, or, to borrow from cyberspace, patches and applets, whose precise origin can be Googled before they are down-loaded and saved one by one' (Latour 2005: 207). But who, Humphrey wonders, 'does the composing, Googling and saving, and why?' (Humphrey 2008: 365).

Humphrey's interest in noting the elision of intentionality in both these accounts is in their respective renderings of subjecthood, a field of concern we do not have the space to take up in this chapter. But in respect to our more specific interest in the conceptualization of network, we do want to suggest that the capacity to sidestep intentionality in both Strathern's and Latour's accounts is at least partly also a factor of how far they have moved away from a notion of network as a personal assembly of relationships. In the process, network has becomes less a personal accomplishment, albeit an insecure one, fashioned by particular people at particular moments in space and time than a function of more general cultural or ontological systems. Oddly enough, while Strathern and Latour respectively offer up very different visions of networks to the 'automaton' of Castells, in all three accounts, people appear to be not so much authoring as inhabiting networks. If anthropologists were first attracted to the concept of network because structural-functionalist accounts seemed to leave out the particularity of individual behaviour, half a century later, contemporary readings of network seem to be on the verge of producing similar gaps. The more that networks become imagined as general forms or representations, the further the role of individuals as agents of sociality threatens to recede from the analytical viewfinder.

NETWORK AS FORM

The recasting of network as an institutional form is an explicit focus of Annelise Riles's monograph, *The Network Inside Out* (Riles 2000). Riles's study concerned the activities of governmental and non-governmental organizations based in Suva, the capital of Fiji, that were preparing for the United Nations Fourth World Conference on Women. The UN conference took place in Beijing in 1995, but it was preceded by a number of preparatory meetings that took place in New York and Suva. Riles approaches the set of activities that she observed as part of a larger class of phenomena that involve a 'set of institutions, knowledge practices and artifacts thereof that internally generate the effects of their own reality by reflecting on themselves'; hence the notion of the network as a form that is 'inside out' (ibid.: 3).

The people involved in these Suva organizations were a disparate collection of people, distinguished in terms of country or region of origin, ethnicity, religion, educational background, profession, political stance and activism.

Like the set of people that Chanda met over the course of several days in Ndola, these people seemed to have little in common with each other. But unlike Chanda's network, these people were not connected through their personal linkage to a particular individual, but through 'their involvement in local, regional, or global networks – institutionalized associations devoted to information sharing' (ibid.: 59). Indeed, for the people involved in the Suva organizations, Chanda's contacts would probably not be viewed as a network because they are not formal relationships (ibid.: 66). 'For networkers in Suva, a network was an entity of a particular form' (ibid.). Yet at the same time, these networkers also recognized that personal relationships underpinned many of their organizational activities. Participants' accounts of this Network[3] thus oscillated between a notion of it as an 'artifact of preexisting personal relationships', and its representation as a radically different and formalized type of social organization (ibid.: 68–69).

This representation of Network as a new kind of institution is by no means specific or original to the organizations Riles was observing in Suva. It is, Riles argues, one of the forms of the global, celebrated rhetorically as emancipating, but enacted through prosaic activities and artefacts such as meetings, documents, panels and conferences (ibid.: 172). Yet its effectiveness is associated with its recursivity:

> We have here a simple illustration of the central insight of this book: that the effectiveness of the Network is generated by the Network's self-description. As we have seen, the naming of a Network is the existence of a Network and the existence of a Network is synonymous with Action on its behalf. The Network is analysis (the missing 'link'), and it supersedes reality; in other words one does not show a link once one pronounces the existence of a network. (ibid.: 172)

But this representation of the Network also, Riles acknowledges, leaves certain things out (ibid.: 174). And what it seems to leave out are the variety of organizational difficulties that may be entailed in actually mobilizing a particular – in this instance regional – network. In the example Riles provides of the Omomo Melen Pacific (Women Lifeblood of the Pacific) Network, these organizational difficulties included shortfalls in which prospective members could actually attend meetings; problems in securing stable funding; weak communication links; getting members to actually produce the documents that the organization was supposed to 'take to Beijing'; and eventually also the logistical problems and disappointments entailed in attending the Beijing Conference.

Riles is very clear that what she is describing is a very different matter compared to the kind of social networks analysed by the Manchester School. This is network conceptualized as an institutionalized form that is standardized. And it is a version of network that is not 'latent' and awaiting discovery by outside analysts (ibid.: 66). It comes with its own full-blown recognition and representation, in terms that are likely to be familiar to anthropologists but which have not been generated by them. The momentum for this kind of reading of network thus draws scholars in, but it is not being driven by the academy. Indeed, it is the increasing ubiquity of this and other versions of network as a global form that has rekindled anthropological interest in the concept of network over the last fifteen years.

But while it is not difficult to understand why anthropologists should want to investigate this kind of representation, it is not clear to us why we should either take this kind of depiction at face value, nor why it should restrict the ways in which we might choose to employ the concept of network as a heuristic device. Different representations of community have also exerted various pulls on the popular imagination well beyond the academy, and these have been the subject of scholarly examinations that may proceed along quite different lines (see Amit and Rapport 2002). That is to say, our examinations of different popular representations of community do not necessarily pursue only one set of phenomena, nor are we necessarily asking only one set of questions under the rubric of that conception. So we can take account of the way in which a particular conception of Network is being marshalled, but also leave ourselves open to pursue other conceptions of network, whether from a different vantage point brought to bear on the same situation or in respect to entirely different circumstances. Network imagined as a new form of bureaucratic arrangements does not serve and should not be taken as a replacement for a more open-ended investigation of other forms of sociality. Investigating network as a new institutional form on the one hand, and network as a range of personal relationships that cut across different situations and frames on the other, can take us in different but equally valid directions of inquiry.

Thus, without taking away from the richness and innovativeness of Riles's account of the Suva organizations, one can also conceive that another researcher might have reasonably pursued a different set of research questions with the same or overlapping set of actors. It is not difficult to imagine that a Manchester School style of network analysis could have been applied to this terrain, which would have sought to trace the social links of organizers and activists beyond the Network. Did their personal relationships beyond these organizations shape their involvement or reading of these institutions, and if so in what ways?

It is also worthwhile noting that Riles herself closes with a cautionary note about the celebratory rhetoric surrounding the Network. In noting the challenges faced by a set of organizers in convening a new Network, and their consequent disappointment with the Beijing conference, Riles herself is surely going beyond a literal treatment of Network as entirely recursive towards a consideration of the dialectic between the imagination and actualization of organizational relationships.

CLOSING REMARKS

Twice over the course of the last third of the twentieth and the first decade of the twenty-first century, the concept of network in the sense in which it was initially conceived by members of the Manchester School, as 'a means of bringing the individual and his or her actions back in' (Riles 2000: 64), has been overtaken. During the 1970s, it was overtaken by the increasing prevalence and restrictiveness of mathematical representations, which eventually rendered the complexity and particularity of individual actions and relationships more and not less elusive. More recently, it has been overtaken by a tendency to represent network in structural and/or cultural terms, rather than as a matter of personal links. This notion of network as system or cultural form has come from distinct if sometimes complementary developments: one, a broader rethinking of sociological ontology, which has involved reformulations of the status of the social as well as of the person; the other, the interrogation of new forms of the global, whether in terms of new forms of technology or institutional arrangements. The former positions network as a new theoretical framework with which to ask questions about the social, and the other positions network as a new set of social arrangements altogether. In other words, one appropriates the term network for a reformulation of how theorists ask questions, and the other as an icon of or idiom for new structures 'out there'. Both of these kinds of reformulations have helped rekindle anthropological interest in the concept of the network.

Both approaches can make important contributions to anthropological conceptions of network – for example, attention to the means employed to extend, stabilize and cut networks or new cultural readings of network – but if they displace rather than complement the earlier interest in investigations of sociality that do not rely on premature forms of closure, we may lose as much as we gain from this orientation. At its most banal yet nonetheless influential level, if network becomes reduced to a popular (or populist) metaphor for connectedness, it is at risk of being dismissed as a hackneyed stereotype for the global 'now'. There are indications that this is beginning to happen, particularly in respect to the study of new forms of media and communication. This brings with it the attendant danger that a potentially useful concept will be treated reductively and set aside before we have had a chance to fully think through its more productive aspects.

Even if network does not fade away from our conceptual repertoire but is primarily conceptualized as an institution or system at the expense of considering more ephemeral and particular personal relationships, we are still faced with the possibility that several productive lines of inquiry will be eclipsed. First, as we noted earlier, we could diminish or lose altogether consideration of individual agency and intention; that is, an interrogation of how particular persons claim, assemble, mobilize or are influenced by a set of social links that cut across a variety of situations, statuses and moments, situated at particular points in space and time. Second, we face the possibility of understating or even ignoring the dialectic between the imagination of particular forms of association and the complex efforts invested – including failures – in mobilizing these links. Even in the case described by Riles, in which the 'naming of a network is synonymous with the existence of a network', beyond the realm of political rhetoric, it is clear that naming or imagining is not homologous with the actualization of these associations.

This gap is well illustrated in Green, Harvey and Knox's study of the imagination and implementation of the European Union's (EU) policy on information and communications technology:

> the metaphor of connection that was being used to describe interactions mediated by these technologies, networked connection, seemed ideal for the EU's 'subsidiarity' policy – that differences between regions and peoples should be maintained (and even celebrated in 'cultural heritage' terms) but that this should form no hindrance to ever-increasing flexible, open-ended, and transparent connections between regions and peoples. (Green, Harvey and Knox 2005: 809)

But when several Manchester organizations were given funding to try and develop these kinds of mediated connections, their idealization hit the shoals of the entanglements, shortfalls and logistical difficulties involved in the efforts to mobilize these desired networks (ibid.: 817). Naming the network might have been an important part of 'bringing it into existence', but so too were the difficulties in actualizing it (ibid.). 'This points to the complication of imagining new kinds of connections that are potentially independent of the preexisting and always already entangled places and peoples they are supposed to link together' (ibid.).

What can be mobilized is no more significant than what can be imagined and claimed, but neither is it the same. Conceptual recognition of and attention to the dialectic and gaps between the potentialities and actualities of networks, both personal and systemic, offers fruitful possibilities for investigating the workings of associations – old and new – without over determining these links. With all of its limitations and stymied promise, these are possibilities that were recognized in pioneering anthropological conceptions of network, and it is worthwhile to retain them in investigations of contemporary connections.

As an illustration of this dialectic, we close with a brief ethnographic account to illustrate the potentialities and actualities of network in young children's lives. The premise here is that children, like adults, experience a range of personal associations, both ephemeral and sustained, that cut across and exceed the boundaries of situations. These experiences comprise intention and investment in mobilizing these links. While childhood scholars have not taken up network analysis as vigorously as in some of the other scholarly areas noted above, since the early 1990s they have nonetheless called for attention to the complexity of social linkages in children's lives. By codifying children as agents in proposing a 'new paradigm' for the social study of childhood (James and Prout 1990), these scholars focus on the ways children may be understood as social actors 'shaping as well as [being] shaped by their circumstances' (James, Jenks and Prout 1998: 6). This move away from socialization models to one that views children as agents who both inhabit and author acts of sociality opens up possibilities for employing the concept of network. Although often criticized, the view that children are 'on their way to becoming' full members of society when they reach adulthood, rather than fully present members of society, still appears in some scholarly treatments of childhood (James 2007; Montgomery 2009). In some ways, this 'in process' configuration pre-empts discussions of children's intentionality and agency on the basis that children's subjectivity is partial. Conversely, childhood scholars argue that beginning analyses of children's lives in contemporary situations from the premise that they act with intentionality allows a full range of possible social situations to emerge, along with displays of competence and understanding on the part of children of their social worlds. Thus, employing a social network concept is useful if it allows both imagined and actual networks to emerge fully, encompassing the possibilities of both connection and disconnection.

The following ethnographic account demonstrates some of the richness that may emerge by using the concept of network to attend to children's social relations. The example is drawn from fieldwork with children in an after-school children's programme run at a downtown urban Canadian community centre (here called the Centre).[4] The Centre serves children who attend elementary schools from both within the neighbourhood's boundaries as well as from outside this local catchment area. The children travel to the Centre after school each day by bus to spend supervised time there until they can return home. Eight-year-old Katie and her 'best friend' Nadine are two of the girls who went to the Centre on a regular basis after school each day. The Centre was a place for them to interact informally, as well as to participate in planned activities organized by adult supervisors that included preparing food and participating in dancing, drama and music-based activities.

In one sense, the community centre, with its pre-given boundaries and quasi-institutional setting, presents an opportunity for exploring children's social relationships. However, beginning an analysis from a presupposition of closure precludes a consideration of other exogenous factors that can also influence the relationships playing out at the Centre. The example below of Katie's 'hate list' illustrates this point, and it supports the view that using the concept of network for understanding social relations requires that it remain open to the possibilities of partial and ephemeral social links and instances of connection and disconnection that cut across different social situations. In this regard, the excerpt includes social linkages occurring both at the Centre and beyond.

On this occasion, Katie and Nadine described how they used lists and notes to determine who would be included in their group of 'friends'. Katie explained the basis upon which she included particular names on her list. Her reasons had much to do with acceptable performances of the identities 'girl' and 'child'. For instance, the names of those girls transgressing conventional expectations held by members of the group of girlhood, femininity or of childhood, were added to the list. Far from innocuous or trivial, Katie called hers a 'hate list'.

Carefully tucked into her pocket, Katie produced her list during an informal conversation about friendships. The list included names of girls with whom she had once been friends, or who were or had been someone else's friend, but whose connection to the group of girls was stopped, or at least temporarily suspended. Far from static, a girl's name, Katie explained, could appear on one list, only to disappear in another version of the list. List membership thus appeared as part of a negotiated process among girls. This dynamic feature points out how someone with whom a girl had once interacted, or in some cases with whom she continued to interact, might or might not have appeared on the list. Katie explained, however, that particular girls' names consistently made her list. Amanda, a girl who attended both Katie's school and the after-school programme, is one example of this kind of treatment. Katie and Nadine explained that Amanda's appearance and lack of proper hygiene were the main reasons for her permanent placement on the list: 'Fat Amanda'. Katie pointed to her name on the list. 'Fat Amanda', Nadine chanted. 'Oh she's smelly too. She stunk up the whole laundry room. When my mother went down there, she had to plug her nose'. Katie continued to comment on Amanda's appearance and body image: 'Yeah, her hair is always messy and her clothes are dirty'. Nadine, nodding in agreement, added: 'She doesn't even match'.

Not only did the girls express their objections to Amanda's appearance, they mocked the keen interest she showed in Mark, a student at their school and one of the boys who attended the after-school programme. They continued by criticizing her apparent lack of material possessions. As Katie said: 'I hate it 'cause she's always talking about Mark. She thinks he likes her'. The girls agreed that Amanda was always trying to get Mark's attention during free playtime at the Centre or during activities. Katie added: 'Yeah, she doesn't even have anything to play with at her house'.

As Katie and Nadine explained, Amanda did not have the toys, games and other possessions they had in their homes. How they knew what Amanda had in her home, or whether or not it was true that she had 'nothing' to play with, Katie and Nadine nonetheless used this information to include Amanda's name on the hate list. And yet, despite these markers to exclude Amanda, Katie and Nadine continued to interact with her in some of the organized activities at the Centre. Thus, this example demonstrates that girls' interactions at the Centre were shaped by what happened in this context as well as relationships and other factors extending beyond it and across a number of social situations. The hate list became a mechanism that Katie and Nadine used to include and exclude, and, in Amanda's case, to stigmatize, particular girls.

Moreover, as Katie explained, list-making was a common practice among girls she knew. When asked about list-making, Katie responded, 'My grandfather is stupid'. She continued, 'He doesn't know what he's saying'. Katie went on to describe his physical appearance. He had a 'balding head with hair that sticks up'. She added, 'I hate my grandmother and my stupid cousin too'. When asked if she and other people she knew usually carried a hate list of names, Katie replied: 'Of course ... yeah, lots of my friends do. We put names of boys we hate on it'.

Katie explained that her list also included names of boys she hated, as well as the name of her cousin. The common use of hate lists amongst Katie's friends brings attention to the multi-layered meanings embedded in girls' social interactions. It also points to girls' agency in shaping their social circumstances. Yet without an understanding of the partiality of encounters, and how social links may exceed contextual boundaries, one might miss this complexity.

Agency in this example is interwoven with questions of how dominant notions of girlhood and femininity shape and are shaped by girls' experiences. One sees that, for Katie, not only is establishing friendships a highly contested and negotiated process, it is also a gendered one that is far from static or something that can be assumed. That the girls themselves assembled and used the lists and recognized them as an important way to imagine associations with others, as well as to negotiate the contours of their social networks in their lives, is important. In the hate list example, social links are imagined and set in motion with intentionality across situations having varying results and with far-reaching effects. Importantly, the list itself did not encompass everyone with whom the girls interacted, and therefore could not be understood without taking account of when, how and which factors influenced the ways relationships unfolded in specific situations. For example, a feature of Katie's list is that it included girls who did attend the after-school programme (Amanda) as well as others who did not attend but who were discussed with some of the other girls at the Centre. In the following excerpt, Nadine pointed to the name of a girl on Katie's list who attended their school but who did not go to the Centre. Katie asked, 'You like her?' Nadine responded by describing how she had played with 'Jacqui' the week before at school: 'Yeah, she's fun'. Nadine went on to describe the craft that they had made together with glitter glue.

In their absence, the girls who did not attend the after-school programme continued to inform Katie's encounters with those girls who did. In the act of comparing names on each other's lists, this activity not only influenced how and whether Katie and Nadine would associate with some children attending the programme, but affected who they might be inclined to associate with outside the programme as well. The list also raises questions about the gap between the way Katie, for instance, imagined her social links, and which relationships she actually mobilized. Thus despite stigmatizing Amanda by including her as a persistent notation on the list, Katie still acknowledged playing with her at the Centre.

As this example illustrates, the ephemeral and dynamic nature of social relations in children's lives here precludes an understanding of these relationships as a network fully formed and already 'out there'. Indeed, relying solely on the list as a description of sullied network links would have missed much of the complexity of the social relations in this situation. Using the concept of network in a processual way problematizes this view by raising questions about stability and connection in children's relationships. Through these lists, girls such as Katie and Nadine asserted aspects of their identities and illustrated the ways social connections are imagined, sustained and mobilized beyond the confines of a particular locale. But vis-à-vis those targeted by it, the list also involved a representation of potential disruptions or ruptures in social connections. This final point draws on Strathern's questioning of the seeming limitlessness of networks and her concern to interrogate how to 'cut' a network. The hate list appears to be one way that some girls attempted to 'cut' and/or extend their networks. It involved a process of exclusion, inclusion and boundary-making that was dynamic and that involved the exercise of purposeful agency. This point illuminates the view that the associations of children, like those of adults, are not automatic or guaranteed; they can thus be informed by possibilities of both connection and disjuncture. The resulting contingence and fragility of social relationships reminds us of the considerable effort that is required to mobilize social links in different contexts.

Finally, for anthropologists seeking to find ways to account for a full range of children's social linkages in contemporary circumstances, the network concept offers one possibility for addressing how children assemble, play with, resist and refuse some social links, and how they mobilize and extend others within and across different situations. As childhood scholars Allison James and Alan Prout argue:

> childhood is a shifting social and historical construction and the corollary of this position is that all accounts of childhood must be carefully placed in their proper temporal and spatial context. As such what we do advocate is a theoretical perspective which can grasp childhood as a continually experienced and created social phenomenon which has significance for its present, as well as the past and future. (James and Prout 1990: 231)

As a productive line of enquiry for understanding children's relations, therefore, network provides an approach for attending to the ways children make sense of the worlds they create, where imagined and mobilized networks emerge along with possibilities for both connection and disconnection. An understanding of network that privileges its status as a metaphor without considering questions of interaction and mobilization would therefore miss this complexity and account only for a very partial telling of the nature of social connection.

NOTES

1. In this quote, Epstein refers to both Barnes (1954) and Bott (1957).
2. John Barnes's and Elizabeth Bott's early studies influentially developed a framework of social network analysis. From Barnes's (1954) study of a close-knit network in Bremnes, a fishing and farming community in northern Norway, to Bott's analysis of a large loose-knit network of spouses and their social linkages in an urban location, these writers extended the analysis of connectedness. In Barnes's account, class inequalities emerged in his analysis where the notion of

social equality underscored social relations. His conceptual work to understand a 'total network' of relations demonstrated that self-perception within a network impacted on one's actions and that of other persons involved in the network. In Bott's exploration of how the division of domestic tasks between spouses developed in relation to the social linkages sustained by each spouse, she noted the influence of indirect patterns of contacts on behaviour. Bott's work drew further anthropological interest in employing the concept of network.

3. Riles uses the capitalized 'Network' when she is referring to this particular institutionalized form. We therefore follow her in this usage, using Network (capitalized) to refer to this institution, and network (non-capitalized) to refer to networks in the more general sense.

4. While conducting fieldwork at the community centre, the children understood that Virginia Caputo (who carried out the research; see Caputo 1996) was not a paid employee of the Centre, nor did she organize the activities there. Her interactions with the children took the form of 'hanging out' with them over a long and consistent period of time. Informal conversations frequently arose. At times, these conversations moved in unexpected directions, ranging from sensitive topics such as sexual harassment and violence to conversations regarding fashion and music. In the case of the hate list example, this conversation took place after Caputo had been at the centre for a number of months. Her discussion with Katie and Nadine began informally about friends, and the girls initiated it.

REFERENCES

Amit, V., and N. Rapport. 2002. *The Trouble with Community: Anthropological Reflections on Movement, Identity and Collectivity.* London: Pluto Press.

Barnes, J.A. 1954. 'Class and Committees in a Norwegian Island Parish', *Human Relations* 7: 39–58.

Borgatti, S.P., A. Mehra, D.J. Bass and G. Labianca. 2009. 'Network Analysis in the Social Sciences', *Science* 323: 892–895.

Bott, E. 1955. 'Urban Families: Conjugal Roles and Social Network', *Human Relations* 8(4): 345–384.

Caputo, V. 1996. 'Musical Matters: Performativity, Gender and Culture in an Anthropology of Urban Canadian Childhoods', Ph.D. diss. Toronto: Department of Anthropology, York University.

Castells, M. 2000. 'Materials for an Exploratory Theory of the Network Society', *British Journal of Sociology* 51(1): 5–24.

Coppet, D. de 1994. ''Are'are', in C. Barraud, D. de Coppet, A. Iteanu and R. Jamous (eds), S. Suffern (trans), *Of Relations and the Dead: Four Societies Viewed from the Angle of their Exchanges.* Oxford: Berg, pp.40–65.

Epstein, A.L. 1969. 'The Network and Urban Social Organization', in J. Clyde Mitchell (ed.), *Social Networks in Urban Situations: Analyses of Personal Relationships in Central African Towns.* Manchester: Manchester University Press, pp.77–116.

Green, S., P. Harvey and H. Knox. 2005. 'Scales of Place and Networks: An Ethnography of the Imperative to Connect through Information and Communication Technologies', *Current Anthropology* 46(5): 805–826.

Hannerz, U. 1980. *Exploring the City: Inquiries Toward an Urban Anthropology.* New York: Columbia University Press.

Humphrey, C. 2008. 'Reassembling Individual Subjects: Events and Decisions in Troubled Times', *Anthropological Theory* 8: 357–380.

James, A. 2007. 'Giving Voice to Children's Voices: Practices and Problems, Pitfalls and Potentials', *American Anthropologist* 109(2): 261–272.

James, A., C. Jenks, and A. Prout. 1998. *Theorizing Childhood.* Cambridge: Polity Press.

James, A., and A. Prout (eds). 1990. *Constructing and Reconstructing Childhood: Contemporary Issues in the Sociological Study of Childhood.* London: Falmer Press.

Knox, H., M. Savage and P. Harvey. 2006. 'Social Networks and the Study of Relations: Networks as Method, Metaphor and Form', *Economy and Society* 35(1): 113–140.

Larsen, J., J. Urry and K. Axhausen. 2006. *Mobilities, Networks, Geographies.* Aldershot: Ashgate.

Latour, B. 2005. *Reassembling the Social: An Introduction to Actor-network Theory.* Oxford: Oxford University Press.

Mitchell, J.C. 1969a. 'Preface', in J. Clyde Mitchell (ed.), *Social Networks in Urban Situations: Analyses of Personal Relationships in Central African Towns.* Manchester: Manchester University Press, pp.v–vi.

—— 1969b. 'The Concept and Use of Social Networks', J. Clyde Mitchell (ed.), *Social Networks in Urban Situations: Analyses of Personal Relationships in Central African Towns.* Manchester: Manchester University Press, pp.1–50.

—— 1974. 'Social Networks', *Annual Review of Anthropology* 3: 279–299.

Montgomery, H. 2009. *An Introduction to Childhood: An Anthropological Perspective of Children's Lives.* Chichester: John Wiley.

Oppenheimer, R. 2007. 'Actor-network Theory and Anthropology after Science, Technology and Society', *Anthropological Theory* 7: 471–493.

Postill, J. 2008. 'Localizing the Internet beyond Communities and Networks', *New Media and Society* 10: 413–431.

Riles, A. 2000. *The Network Inside Out.* Ann Arbor: University of Michigan Press.

Strathern, M. 1996. 'Cutting the Network', *Journal of the Royal Anthropological Institute* 2(3): 517–535.

Epilogue

Sociality and Uncertainty
Between Avowing and Disavowing Concepts in Anthropology

Nigel Rapport

> We set up a word at the point at which ignorance begins, at which we can see no further, e.g., the word 'I', the word 'do', the word 'suffer':– these are perhaps the horizon of our knowledge, but not 'truths'.
> —Friedrich Nietzsche, *The Will to Power*

This slim volume has the ambition to interrogate some of the fundamental aspects of anthropological practice, even to challenge them. How should sociality be studied by anthropologists and what concepts should be deployed in its elucidation?

In the Introduction, Vered Amit explains that the intent is not to reinvent the wheel, gratuitously negating what has gone before in the discipline. Indeed, she decries a 'theoretical faddishness' that sees concepts come and go in a merry-go-round of unreasonable intellectual expectations and inevitable dissatisfactions. The sober practice is to recognize how all our concepts are enmeshed in a history of debates and reflections, however uneven, and not to try to make any concept do too much work. Sociality has long been conceptualized in anthropology: What conceptual inventory best serves contemporary purpose? What best engages with issues and circumstances in ethnography today? What best addresses a repertoire of analytical questions anthropology would today pose?

Four key insights underlie Amit's vision for the volume and its work. The first, as intimated above, is that contemporary circumstances may necessitate a refocusing of anthropology's conceptual toolbox. For our concepts – our analyses and our theorizations – are grounded in our experiences of data gathering. Anthropology is an empirical, data-driven discipline. We allow each ethnographer to be their own analyst and theorist; we expect this, indeed. The act of ethnography – of data-gathering more generally – warrants its individual licence, for the experience vouchsafes its own truths. But, second, this does not merely deliver an endless catalogue of individual case studies, as though monads, Amit is assured. Because an individual case study of human social life, undertaken by an individual researcher, if described and analysed and theorized with sufficient truthfulness or authenticity, gives rise to insights that extend beyond the particular case study, ultimately to a human scale. Each case study is ultimately, potentially, a human document, the individual instantiating the whole. In short, anthropological conceptualization is grounded in but not restricted to particular ethnographic contexts. Third, however, is a recognition by Amit of an intrinsic pragmatism in the discipline. Steeped in the niceties of particular intimacies, anthropologists give short shrift to generalities that do not bear the stamp of lived experience. The journey from the individual to the human whole is a complex one. How to navigate it without reducing or otherwise corrupting the detail of individual truth? Hence, Amit's claim that anthropology is more likely to be effective if it focuses its conceptual efforts on 'mid-level' rather than meta-level articulations, neither too narrowly defined nor too sweeping. Indeed, this represents a range of conceptualization that the discipline can claim to have been very good at. Finally, however, Amit concludes that any conceptual application will likely only be partially successful, given the nature of sociality (its complexity, its shifting forms, its diversity). This calls for self-conscious acknowledgement on the part of practitioners. Indeed, anthropology might look to this lack of comprehensiveness as a virtue, the very partiality of concepts, their ambiguity vis-à-vis particular cases, being intrinsic to their viability. To be good to think with is also to be good to think against.

These four tenets – concerning the groundedness of anthropological conceptualization; the human universality of individual truths; the ubiquitous complexity of individual details that cannot be sacrificed to general abstraction; and the intrinsic partiality of any attempt at conceptualization – are taken forward in the six chapters that follow the Introduction. Each chapter offers a particular conceptualization of sociality, as well as reviewing the history of debates around that concept (or its family terms), providing ethnographic vignettes that illustrate the concept in use, and suggesting a critical way of taking the concept forward in the future.

Disjuncture

For Vered Amit, sociality is as much a matter of disjuncture as of engagement and association. The course of human lives – both temporal and spatial – entails repeated acts of engaging and disengaging, comings and goings that are as much a part of everyday relationships and routines as are commitment and engagement. To begin one activity is to break with another; each different activity may involve interactions with different others; we may assume very distinct roles and statuses during the life course and through shifts in location; and so on. Spatial and temporal mobility is necessarily about both moving from and moving to, about departure as well as arrival, and the necessary gap between them. These gaps, in turn, call for a host of smaller and larger works of mediation that carry with them the capacity to smooth over but also to magnify the disjunctures.

It might even be argued that our various social involvements and interactions are not only routinely punctuated but enabled by the intervals between them. Disjuncture may feature as an object of desire in personal projects – as much to be pursued, and as difficult to achieve, as fixity. Disjuncture expresses an aspiration for new modes of activity, association and fulfilment. Far from being reluctantly accepted or even feared, people may actively and self-consciously seek out disjuncture.

And yet, until recently at least, disjuncture has come to figure in our theorizations of sociality only when it has involved major cleavages or transformations – revolutions and fissions – and as derogations from previous states of aggregation and stability. Disjuncture has been conceptualized as supervening upon situations involving already existing collectivities, structures, relations, daily routines and practices, rather than as a process in its own right, and worthy of its own attention. By interpreting disjuncture as a process working upon existing forms of sociality, onus is placed on explaining the rupture, dissociation or disengagement rather than explicating the seeming routine or fixity. Is it not the case today, however, that the assumptions underpinning this kind of conceptual ordering – disjunctures as 'coming after' – may hamper our appreciation of the nature of social reproduction and change? What if we turned this conceptual order on its head and viewed disjuncture as the starting point rather than the end point of analysis?

Fields

John Postill understands social fields to be 'dynamic clusters of practices, games and socialities'. A field is an organized, heterogeneous domain of practice and action in which unequally positioned social agents can be seen to compete and cooperate over the same public rewards. In Crossley's summation: '[fields are] sui generis social spaces ... organized around the common participation of ... "players" in a historically and culturally specific social "game"' (Crossley 2002: 674). Postill's particular approach is inspired by the work of Pierre Bourdieu and the Manchester tradition of Max Gluckman and Victor Turner. In this work, the metaphor of a game is used to refer to social exchange that goes beyond rational-actor models of human agency. It is also recognized how important is a diachronic appreciation, and a resisting of structural-functionalist notions of social contexts as self-regulating entities. Conflict comes to assume centre stage, both group-driven conflicts that spill over established fields (Turner), and the conflict-driven trajectories of individual agents within a given field (Bourdieu).

It is patent that social exchange is not a 'game' comparable to tennis, chess or Monopoly. For unlike these, 'players' in a social field will also struggle over the definition of what counts as the rules and the stakes at play. Yet the analogy is instructive nevertheless: a social field is a space of competition, as in a game where players enter and position themselves according to the powers and moves available to them. We might further distinguish between 'fields of practice' (such as anthropology, art or rock climbing) and 'fields of action' (such as protests, war or disaster relief).

Equally patent is how far such conceptualization is removed from the received wisdom of 'field theory' as a formulation that stresses social reproduction and that does not account for dynamism or change. To repeat: fields are dynamic clusters of practices, games and socialities, not conservative domains of habitual practice. The concept has the further advantage of being a neutral term, lacking the normative idealism of such others as 'public sphere' and 'community'. Finally, social field has an appropriate sense of scale for anthropology, as being generally smaller than states while still allowing for internally diverse configurations of people, practices and technologies.

Social Space

Deborah Reed-Danahay is interested in exploring the concept of social space as means to encompass a social setting, a set of social parameters and a number of social boundaries (some fluid and some more fixed). In particular, emic notions of affinity, mobility and inclusion-cum-exclusion are appropriately illustrated as aspects of social space, as well as allowing us etically to reflect on the related issues of social distance and nearness, and the visibility of groups in social exchange. Imagining sociality in spatial terms possesses both emic and etic currency.

Social space proves to be a subtle concept. It is increasingly evident in contemporary social life that people may be close to others socially but distant physically; or close in physical terms but distant socially. As Hilda Kuper tellingly advised, we must beware of 'equat[ing] space, as a feature of the physical (tangible) world, with "social space"' (Kuper 1972: 411). Nor is social space fixed in other ways. Both domicile-making and group-making may be said to be emic projects aimed at creating social fixities, but we are also always etically aware of movement in the positions and positioning of individuals in and across such symbolic classifications. It is perhaps the case that social spaces are imagined as more concrete at the local level than the regional or global: the social space of an urban market or a physical-education class assumes an abstractness when applied to an ethnic identity, and more again when applied to, say, postmodernism as an ethos. Finally, social space allows for a move away from 'container' notions of sociality; social space is a looser and more fuzzy concept that encourages thinking about the politics, metaphors and practical ambiguities of space as it is everyday conjured up by individuals and groups. Social space, one might conclude, is a condition of social relations, something that people act not through but with.

Sociability

Sally Anderson would develop an emic notion of being 'sociable' into a flexible analytical tool. Sociability can be understood in a common-sense way as the tendency to seek the company of others, to be friendly, especially with non-kin and semi-intimate others (friends, acquaintances, workmates), and extending to civil encounters with less familiar people beyond personal and professional circles (in voluntary associations and societies, lodges and clubs). These peaceable acts of relating, ludically unfettered by more structured conventions, are often deemed to be forms of social exchange distinctly beneficial to people. Georg Simmel was drawn to sociability as a form of sociation, remarking on its democratic qualities: people engaging with each other in the style of equals, and seemingly with no instrumental purpose other than the success of the moment. In a development of this, Anderson encourages an appreciation of sociability as a heuristic device (rather than an ideal, normative blueprint) that throws significant light upon the tenuous and dynamic processes through which all relations – the apparently structured and the seemingly ludic, the endosocial and the exosocial, the stilted and the informal, the intimate and the distant – are effected. The concept would draw attention to the 'trouble' with form facing all who participate in sociable occasions, moments and relations.

Though often used interchangeably with sociality, sociability clearly rests on different conceptual ground, indexing forms, moments and venues of open interaction and relationality across social differences, and among individuals stripped for the occasion to 'just themselves'. Attending to reciprocity and the etiquette of 'good form' are also essential aspects of sociability, and they index the need to stabilize an immanent lability in social exchange: good form helps transform the potential harm of individuals in interaction into harmony. But do not, as Simmel did, mistake sociability for a form in itself – an ideal type with particular structural properties. For this fails to grasp sociability's full analytical potential and the questions it raises: How do people work the shadows of good form and bad form? What are the generative capacities of a 'play-form' for constituting relationships both within and across social domains? To what extent is it the case today that a generalized sociability of all with all substitutes for more intimate relational forms?

Organizations

Gabriela Vargas-Cetina begins by observing that human sociality, understood as the propensity of people to form groups, has often resulted in the creation of lasting structures, which anthropologists have identified as 'organizations'.

With the advent of real-time communications, however, and the rise to dominance of the internet, there has been a great change in how organizations must function, how they establish ties with other organizations, how they might reciprocally influence one another. This calls for a shift in conceptual emphases from a focus on the perdurance of relatively stable groupings to a greater willingness to entertain in analysis more fleeting forms of aggregation. Moreover, even if temporary, these ephemeral forms may still leave significant organizational traces, reshaping everyday life globally.

Vargas-Cetina's work is to suggest a conceptual arc from the perduring to the momentary: from 'organization' through 'corporation' to 'cooperative' and 'ephemeral' association. The contemporary project in anthropology should be to gauge and chart how these interrelated forms influence and merge and challenge one another. This will provide an understanding of the multi-faceted ways in which people come together, and the varied agglomerations resulting from their sociality.

In particular, Vargas-Cetina would give due weight to the increased importance of new forms of association which are non-corporate, in that they are not based on a broad platform of agreement among their members, do not result in self-perpetuating collective subjects, and do not seek to acquire or maintain collective resources. Such associations are ephemeral in the sense that their members regard them as contextual and fluxional, and do not expect them to last indefinitely. Their membership, furthermore, is voluntary; whether or not members are formally registered, their internal governance is weak (their figurations of authority contingent), and their structure, memberships, aims and purposes change continuously. Married to new communication technologies, one might expect the significance of such ephemeral organization to increase further.

Networks

Vered Amit and Virginia Caputo recall how anthropologists have long been attracted to the concept of network because structuralist accounts have a tendency to obviate the particularity of individual behaviour. 'Network' points up the personal, the partial, the temporal and the practical in social relationality.

For its early Manchester School advocates, the network was suited to elucidate how behaviour had a personal order deriving from how individuals were personally linked with a particular set of other people, and the links these others had in their turn. These links may cut across a variety of situations, statuses and moments, thus drawing attention to individual agency and intention: to an interrogation of how particular persons claim, assemble, mobilize or are influenced by a set of social connexions. Equally, network lent itself to an encompassment of the partiality of an encounter, and the way in which critical factors shaping one situation might well extend beyond what is observable in that one setting. Networks had the potential to trace influential absences as much as presences, and to trace contacts that cut across different situations and institutions in an open-ended fashion. Moreover, the range of people to whom and from whom an individual might hold certain expectations of rights and obligations were no more fixed in time than in space, and might be always changing. (The total extent of identifiable people with whom expectations were associated was not necessarily coterminous with the more limited set of links that an individual might mobilize at particular times for the achievement of particular actions.) Finally, network recognized the dialectic between the imagination of particular forms of association and the complex efforts that had to be invested in potentially mobilizing these links; the individual's idea of their network and the considerations involved in putting the network into action might only partially overlap.

Ironically, in recent decades, anthropology has imagined network to be some kind of general emic structural and cultural form: a systemic assemblage rather than a matter of subjective personal links. In actor-network theory, for instance, as in the 'New Melanesian Ethnography', people appear to be not so much authoring as inhabiting networks willy-nilly. The role of individuals as agents of sociality threatens to recede from analytical view, as do the partial, temporal and practical aspects of making, mobilizing, affirming, denying, unmaking and refusing social links.

The continuing worth of the network is in encompassing the ephemeral and dynamic nature of social relations in some lives, problematizing the tension between connection and disconnection, between stability and flux.

CONCLUSIONS AND IMPLICATIONS

Before joining this volume I found myself considering a conceptual framework that might identify anthropological disciplinarity, its breadth and complexity, and the necessary tension between its terms. I imagined six nodes, all linked to one another:

humankind :: individuality :: society :: culture :: environment :: history

I further imagined how I might gloss the above terms, at a lower level of abstraction, as involving:

capacity :: substance :: relation :: medium :: material :: occasion

This six-noded framework encouraged me to see the following. First, as human beings we possess in common certain universal bodily capacities. Second, these are, nonetheless, individually substantiated in unique lives. Third, it is then manifesting these uniquenesses, expressing them, seeking to fulfil them and share them and not share them and hide them, that give rise to society and its complex of interactions and relations. Fourth, these interactions take place by way of certain symbolic media, certain languages of exchange, or cultures. Fifth, moreover, these interactions take place within certain environmental spaces, material and temporal, domiciliary and transient. And sixth, these interactions take place at certain moments; between moments there is entropic regress – things falling apart – but also attempts to have moments bear consequences – a routinization of things.

What are the special affordances offered by the six nodes put forward in this volume? They could be characterized as:

disjuncture :: field :: social space :: sociability :: organization :: network

Firstly, there is the flexibility of their potential interrelations. To set, for instance, disjuncture against sociability, social space against field, network against organization is to be provided with a series of scales all of which, in interestingly different ways, might be said to turn on the distinction between openness and closure. How, in a particular social setting does the openness of disjuncture give way or give rise to the relative closures of sociability? How do the open extensions of network marry with the apparent anxieties of closure of organization? How does a social space come to assume the institutional closures of a field, and why on some occasions and not on others?

But then each of the terms can be recognized as being internally complex ('polythetic') as such. Organization thus spans an arc from the more routinized to the more ephemeral; disjuncture is seen not only to cut a social tie but also to provide opportunities for new ones to close. An appreciation of openness and closure, in short, and how these might imbue different kinds, occasions and scales of social relations, would seem one of the key affordances of this volume's terms, both severally and in conjunction.

If open versus closed already has a famous provenance in human science – a key heuristic in the social, historical and moral analyses of Karl Popper, for instance, and among his anthropological readership (see Rapport 2005) – then the particular use of movement in this volume is something more striking. One is led to consider people moving towards and away from sociality in particular ways. Will one organize? Or will others endeavered to organize you? If so, will the outcome be an institution, a corporation, a cooperative or a more ephemeral association? Will one be sociable? If so, in what cultural medium will this take place? With politeness? After work? Among non-kin? And what effects will this sociability have on existing relations to which one might be committed or tied? Will there be a cost of disjuncture to be paid, or a prize of disjuncture to be sought? As one endeavours to move across one's social space, will there be physical hindrances – national borders and mountain ranges – and will space coalesce into a social field in which the moves open to one are apparently narrow or rule-bound, and the resources available to fund one's movement are competed after? In short, the volume recognizes that sociality is not to be taken for granted. It is variable in nature, colouration and scale. It depends on personal perspectives and on moments. It is not an abiding condition. At least, it is so varied in expression and so internally diverse as a concept that it behoves the anthropologist more to examine its precise form in particular interactions than to assume it as a background. Sociality must be foregrounded as a necessary object of description and analysis whose shape and form is constantly in process, continually being worked.

Key to this version of movement, it seems, is doubt, or uncertainty. The movement towards and away from sociality is uncertain in outcome. Will sociality result? At the very least, what shape and form will sociality take? Will, emically, the outcome be satisfying, felt appropriate? Will, etically, the outcome be something that the anthropologist can sufficiently comprehend as sociality, and appropriately represent?

This recognition of movement and uncertainty is surely a key finding of the volume and a tantalizing conceptual question, as is the way it ties together the emic and the etic. Our research subjects move in their lives along uncertain trajectories towards and away from social relations. Do they fulfil their intentions? We anthropologists endeavour to describe, analyse, theorize upon and compare these uncertain movements. Do we do them justice?

In 1992, Anthony Cohen published an article entitled 'Post-fieldwork Fieldwork' in which he reflected on the provisional nature of anthropological knowledge. Did he understand his research subjects on the Shetland island of Whalsay aright, Anthony Cohen asked himself? Had he captured the moment in his analysis? And was it not the case that the ethnographic moment seemed different to him each time he reflected upon it? Moreover, that moment had now been possibly superseded by so many more in his informants' lives. What was it to say he had 'completed' a description or an analysis? Surely every such claim in human science had to be provisional. Any understanding and any description-cum-analysis was momentary (see Cohen 1992; cf. Rapport 2012a).

The epigram from Nietzsche with which I began this chapter would seem to take Cohen's sentiment to its radical conclusion: any words we use about human life – whether of those who live that life or observe it – are markers of hope rather than claims to certitude. They more display our ignorance, perhaps, than our knowledge. They more register our uncertainty and our anxiety than our confidence – or should be deemed to. They mark our life journeys, the words we put to frequent use being a kind of horizon, speaking to the issues we are currently having to deal with and hoping to get beyond.

I do not believe that the contributors to this volume would be disconcerted by Nietzsche's conclusion. The concepts of disjuncture, field, social space, sociability, organization and network, are, in the editor's words, attempts conceptually to come to terms with contemporary issues and circumstances. They are words for today (cf. Rabinow et al. 2009; Rapport 2013). Do they serve the pragmatic end of allowing for a rethinking of anthropology, a provisional thinking?

But then how is this to be judged? What is a satisfactory (provisional) conceptualization? For Nietzsche, setting up words as bulwarks against ignorance could nevertheless be seen to serve a definite pragmatic end. There was a purpose to human life, albeit that truth was elusive. In Nietzsche's view, the purpose of concepts (and other forms of art) was personal confidence and fulfilment (cf. Rapport 2003). It was within the capacity of each human being to overcome the givens of the situations in which they found themselves and to live a life according to their own lights, by virtue of their own authorship, as 'Master' not 'Slave'. At least, this thought contained the fictional claim and conceptual apparatus ('Overman', 'Master', 'Slave') that Nietzsche found did him good. 'I willed it thus'.

What is the anthropological purpose, if conceptualization and writing is ever a matter of provisional judgements? 'Justice' would seem a key contemporary term. Both doing justice in one's writing in an aesthetic sense to what one has experienced among one's research subjects – writing-up in the 'best' way one can – and doing justice morally: 'This is honestly what I experienced', and, 'This is honestly what I feel my research subjects are due'.

'Justice' I see as a concept of a different order of magnitude to the 'mid-level' ones that Vered Amit has mooted as being anthropology's forte. Nevertheless, it is on a 'meta-level' beyond the comfort zone of the middle that I want, finally, to take my comments. Amit herself recognizes the possibility and the legitimacy of this kind of intellectual movement in her account of the way in which ethnographic descriptions might find themselves 'illustrated' by concepts, and her suggestion that mid-level conceptualization, while grounded in particular ethnographic occasions, need not be 'restricted' by these. In other words, one travels intellectually from ethnography to conceptualization and back. But mid-level concepts are, by definition, not the furthest possible reaches of this journey.

It would be a meta-level of conceptualization in human science that I would understand as containing not only 'justice' but also the six-noded framework that I introduced previously:

humankind :: individuality :: society:: environment :: culture:: history

The significance of this conceptual level is that I believe it takes anthropology beyond the provisional, beyond Nietzsche's merely pragmatic notions of truth. These meta-level terms describe ontologies of the human condition.

In a brief case study I consider how the mid-level concepts of sociality show-cased in this volume might give on to meta-level truths.

A CASE STUDY

Michel Eyquem de Montaigne (1533–1592) – more usually known today simply as Montaigne – is celebrated for the *Essays* he published between 1572 and 1588 (Montaigne 1993). The third son of a country nobleman, Montaigne spent the first part of his adult life as a counsellor and member of the *parlement* in the city of Bordeaux, also as a courtier to King Charles IX in Paris. However, in 1572, his elder brothers having died and having himself had a near-death experience after falling off a horse, Montaigne left public life and 'retired' to the country estate he had inherited at Chateau de Montaigne. The disjuncture did not herald a hermetic existence exactly, for he lived the sociable life of a country gentleman, with neighbours, friends and family, together with occasional trips to Paris and a tour to Germany, Switzerland and Italy. It was the case, however, that the games of politics and religion into which he had been drawn at the royal court he found de-bilitating. And cruelty, whether in the context of religious persecution, legal justice or even hunting, was hateful to him. In particular, the holy zeal and unreasoning violence of religious fanaticism – France was then in the throes of the warring between Catholics and Protestants – was, Montaigne reck-oned, 'putting a very high price on one's conjectures': it seemed there was 'no hostility that exceed[ed] Christian hostility' (cited in Bakewell 2010: 209, 214). Hence, for the remaining twenty years of his life, Montaigne opted for a very different social space; his chief chosen habitus was now to remove himself to the chateau tower that contained his library of Classical authors, and whose beams he had carved with philosophical slogans from the Sto-ics, Epicureans and Cynics in particular. Apart in his library, Montaigne followed advice from Pliny: 'Each man is a good education to himself, pro-vided he has the capacity to spy on himself from close up'. 'I turn my gaze inward', Montaigne himself wrote: 'I fix it there and keep it busy. Everyone looks in front of him; as for me, I look inside of me; I have no business but with myself; I continually observe myself, I take stock of myself, I taste my-self ... I roll about in myself' (cited in ibid.: 224). This habitus was not born out of hubris: 'I set forth a humble and inglorious life; that does not matter. You can tie up all moral philosophy with a common and private life just as well as with a life of richer stuff' (cited in ibid.: 317–318). By writing about himself, may he not grind a lens through which others might espy their own humanity? In particular, might not such a habitus enable him and others to begin to come to terms with the truthful texture of a human life, its universal mixture of the grand and the petty, the wise and the inane, the wild and the gentle, the comic and the tragic, the consistent and the inconstant? 'Our life is part folly, part wisdom', Montaigne wrote. 'Whoever writes about it only reverently and according to the rules leave out more than half of it' (cited in ibid.: 155).

A key part of such a 'truthful texture' would include the perpetual movement of human life. 'I do not portray being, I portray passing', Montaigne wrote, and not so much 'the passing from one age to another' as the passing 'from day to day, from minute to minute' (cited in ibid.: 36). The essays that he wrote about himself, about his perceptions and his conclusions, were therefore precisely that: 'essays', 'assays', provisional attempts. He would revisit his writings and reconfigure them (even after publication) until his final days.

And yet, authorship remained his, and his alone. These were *his* perceptions and *his* attempts at conclusions. Life remained individual, notwithstanding the vicissitudes affecting all physical things, including the meandering human mind. There was an 'I' upon which the vicissitudes fell, abidingly and continuingly; an 'I' that lived the journey through life, continuously and uniquely and in one direction, an 'I' that perceived and imagined and interpreted, constantly, however provisionally. One consequence of this insight, for Montaigne, concerned institutionalism, or the nature of the social fields in which human beings placed themselves and others. Each human being ought to find their own way according to their own lights, Montaigne concluded. From childhood on, nothing should be taken on mere authority or trust. For the world was more varied and complex, and more evolving, than could be incorporated in any system of knowledge that human beings might hope to hand down. Furthermore, each life contained its own nature, its own particular way of being consistent and inconstant, ongoing and diverse: 'There is no one who, if he listens to himself, does not discover in himself a pattern all his own, a ruling pattern which struggles against education' (Montaigne, cited in ibid.: 58).

Another consequence of the individuality of life concerned social space. In Rouen, Montaigne came into contact with a group of Tupinamba Indians from Brazil; on his tour of Italy, he visited synagogues and attended a home circumcision; reading in his library, he shared the time and the space with other living creatures, wild and domestic; around his estate, he was confronted with trees and plants that also represented living beings. In all these cases, Montaigne realized, an element was shared: 'one and the same nature' runs its course throughout all, he concluded (cited in ibid.: 179). To recognize this was to follow a kind of inclusive sociability that was both moral and ludic. If a pet cat or dog wished to play when he, Montaigne, wished to write, then was there not a symmetry of rights to be respected? Why was he any more than a mere pastime to his cat? In the nature of things there was no hierarchy of being. When a human being looked at a cat in a mood for play, even more when that human looked at a kitten or a puppy that was to be drowned in a bucket of water, one looked at a creature who looked back: a life looked at a life. Were not all living things owed justice or mercy and the space to be? No abstractions, no conceptualization, need to interfere here at all. Human being confronts cat and dog, kitten and puppy, Frenchman confronts Tupinamba and Italian Jew, and always 'there are only two individuals, face to face, hoping for the best from one another' (ibid.: 327). Individual lives abut against one another: the sheer, physical, concrete truth of this strangeness-cum-banality Montaigne saw as providing the moral principles behind an everyday sociability that outweighed any fantasy of political or religious or other ideological rectitude.

On 3 January 1889, Nietzsche collapsed on a street in Turin, precipitating a final eleven years of life in a state of seeming physical and mental decline. His last act before collapsing was to embrace a cart horse that was being beaten by its driver, and to weep. Nietzsche had previously written of his admiration for Montaigne, the 'freest and mightiest of souls' whose writing 'truly augmented the joy of living on this earth' (Nietzsche 1997: 135). If Montaigne had construed an intellectual network that took him back, by virtue of a series of links of personal appreciation, to the likes of Pliny, Plutarch, Tacitus, Marcus Aurelius, Seneca and Epictetus, then after his death commensurate intellectual and literary networks were to be elicited by those who looked to him for inspiration. Shakespeare was merely one of the first of many readers of English translations of Montaigne's work. Alexander Pope claimed that '[Montaigne] says nothing but what everyone feels at the heart' (cited in Bakewell 2010: 282). For Ralph Waldo Emerson, the sentiment was to be put even more personally: 'It seemed to me as if I had myself written the book, in some former life' (Emerson 1889: 181), a claim precisely echoed by André Gide, Stefan Zweig and Leonard Woolf. The imagery favoured by Virginia Woolf was of minds 'threaded together' in a chain across time, hers and Montaigne's: 'any live mind', she wrote, 'is of the very same stuff as Plato's and Euripides' [and] it is this common mind that binds the whole world together' (Woolf 1990: 178).

What kind of phenomenon is the network that Virginia Woolf (and these others) elicited? The links she claimed with Montaigne, and back before him to Plato, are as much an insistence on disjuncture or decontextualization from her present – England in the early 1900s – as they are an insistence of conjuncture with other writers. Yet it was not a scholarly tradition or set of scriptural conventions to which she attended so much as a series of individuals puzzling over the same human questions of condition: what is my life? In the words of another nineteenth-century English admirer, the poet and critic Matthew Arnold, Montaigne engaged in a 'dialogue of the mind with itself' (Arnold 1965: 591), and this is the nature of the network Virginia Woolf and others have construed. She and Arnold and Pope and Emerson and Nietzsche recognized in Montaigne – as he recognized in Pliny and Plutarch et al. – the individuality of a human being in discourse with itself. When I wrote, above, that one of the critical departures of this present volume of anthropological essays was the querying of whether sociality would result at all in the uncertain coming together of individual actors – whether they would be sociable and meet others in a social space, form a kind of organization perhaps, partake in a social field of common interests, extend themselves across networks of links – it was this kind of 'transcendent' possibility that I was adverting to. In finding oneself 'in conversation' with Plutarch, Tacitus, Marcus Aurelius, Seneca and Epictetus (Montaigne), and in finding oneself 'in conversation' with Montaigne (Shakespeare, Pope, Emerson, Nietzsche, Gide, Zweig and the Woolfs), what is being effected in the way of sociality? It is surely very different to what anthropologists have commonly taken to be sociality's grounds and form. Yet it is a sociality which the conceptual framework of this volume allows us to address: an imaginative disjuncture and conjuncture that exists in the mind alone; a social field that involves the 'game' of setting down in words on paper the often ephemeral sensations of a flowing consciousness; an association of self-conscious individuals who never need to or can meet to draw up an organizing credo; and a universal social space that breaches time and space, and that is possibly invisible and unrecognized by all others; a sociability by way of personal judgements of others' authentic voices. Here is a human conversation consisting of individual acts of introspection (Rapport 2007, 2014). The uncertainty of sociality in a face-to-face coming together of individuals is balanced by the possibility of a meeting of minds that transcends time and space.

I find it necessary to think in terms of the meta-concepts humankind, individuality, society, environment, culture and history in order to comprehend what Montaigne and his admirers are doing here in their particular usages of disjuncture, network, sociability, social space, social field and organization. To cite Montaigne one final time, one of his key claims was that, 'Every human being bears the whole stamp of the human condition' (cited in Bakewell 2010: 193). In other words, humanity manifests itself in individuality: between humanity and individuality there exists an ontological homology. Every individual is a paradigmatic instantiation of the human, each equally human, each wholly human, each only human. This is something that Montaigne recognized, Nietzsche too, and Virginia and Leonard Woolf. According to the literary critic Philip Furbank (1999), the insight has played a major role in the history of literature. He calls it, appropriately enough, the 'monadic hypothesis', drawing attention to its asocial potential. There is, Furbank (ibid.: 29) elaborates, nothing in the assertions by Durkheim and sociology concerning so-called 'collective consciousness' and 'collective representations' – the imaginaries and metaphors said to link individuals to communities and states – that is half so real (or so mysterious and under-conceptualized) as that which universally links individuals to one another as exemplars of the human species.

According to the present volume, a monadic hypothesis also has significant pertinence for a human science such as anthropology. One recognizes how individual human beings call out to one another – even through their introspective writings – within a species space and across gulfs of history, environment, culture and society.

ENVOI: THE UNIVERSAL, THE INDIVIDUAL AND THE MOMENTARY

Montaigne distinguished his essays in self-writing from the writing of 'scholars': those who operated with analytical systems and presented their ideas with evidential proofs, as if definitive. His principal aim, contrastively, was to record personal experience in a way that seemed truthful to him (however non-systemic and non-evidential and provisional the result). Where does anthropology locate itself in this classification? It is, I would say, both a scholarly pursuit and one in self-writing.

Ethnography as a methodology presents a natural affinity to Montaigne's efforts. The fieldworking anthropologist aspires to experiences that consist of sensory moments with particular others. Furthermore, the fieldworker insists on the possibility and the propriety of conducting research relations with any and all human beings who might be encountered. Irrespective of symbolic classifications that might define an individual as having an essential nature, status or character by virtue of their nationality, religiosity, ethnicity, profession, age or gender, the ethnographer deems any informant to be equally and paradigmatically human. The informant is a human Anyone and at the same time a human Everyone.

But what is the anthropological propriety after fieldwork? The ethos of this volume has been to make a virtue out of uncertainty: any conceptual apparatus is tentative, ambiguous and provisional, a pragmatic attempt to reflect circumstance and to join up individual cases. One must be loath to pawn the details of fieldwork for generalities and abstractions in which momentary identities and identifications are lost. In this essay, nevertheless, I have wished to consider how one might marry a 'mid-level' uncertainty to a 'meta-level' conceptual stability, warranted by a science of human ontology. My final argument is that the individual case and the momentary construal, such as Montaigne and the ethnographer alike would deem to possess intrinsic value, also speak intrinsically to the universal: the individual case and the momentariness of its apperception can be conceived of as universal aspects of the human condition. The anthropologist who endeavours, in their writing-up, to preserve the substance of individual lives – in all their complexity, diversity, contrariety and momentariness – and to preserve the moments of their being known, is thereby acceding to aspects of human universality. For in doing justice to the individual substance of lives, the anthropologist also bears witness to species-wide human capacities; and to norms of social-relationality; and to traditions of culturo-symbolic expression; and to habits of environmental dwelling; and to the occasions of their practice and exchange.

Furthermore, in doing justice first and foremost to the individual substance of lives, the anthropologist encounters other transcendent conceptual realities – humanity, society, culture, environment, history – in their true concrete forms and not as abstractions. For all culturo-symbolic expression must be mediated and animated by individual intentionalities; all norms of social relationality must be experienced through individual interpretations; all the materiality of dwelling must be practised by individual bodies; and all the occasions of the above mediation, experience and practice must be acknowledged by way of momentary individual sensibilities. Given the unique contingencies of individual human embodiment, precisely how cultural media, social relations and environmental dwellings will manifest themselves on any one occasion is inevitably a matter of uncertainty. It is such uncertainty that this volume has rightly, and innovatively, placed centre stage. The anthropologist of uncertainty – let me rather call them the 'cosmopolitan anthropologist' – continues to privilege the momentariness, complexity, diversity and contrariety of individual lives, and aims to preserve the integrity of individual detail beyond the level of description, even to the level of meta-conceptualization.[1] The ethnographic encounter is never to be reduced to concepts, categories or classes that would corrupt either its uniqueness or its universality.

Michel Eyquem de Montaigne, I learn, died on 13 September 1592, at the age of 59, of a quinsy that caused him to be unable to breathe. He was propped up in bed at the time, with family and servants in attendance, as well as a doctor, and a priest who performed a Mass. I preserve these details;

I remember that they belong to Montaigne, and that they describe a human death from suffocation; also that how precisely he lived this death – how he animated the formal style of being a dying 'Frenchman', a *'seigneur'*, a 'Catholic', a 'household head', in the 'sixteenth century' – is something I might imagine and hope intuitively to grasp but cannot definitively know.

NOTES

1. Regarding the cosmopolitan anthropologist, I understand 'cosmopolitan' here, after Kant, to be the attempt to write an anthropology that always bears in mind the necessary relation between *cosmos* or human whole, and *polis* or individual instantiation (hence 'cosmo-politan'). For Kant, this was both a scientific and a moral project. The 'cosmopolitan anthropologist' sought to deliver conceptual insight into the universal mediation of forms, relations, materials and occasions by Anyone, in any individually lived human life. By doing so, the cosmopolitan anthropologist hoped to pave the way both to objective knowledge of human capacities and to just procedures for their global acknowledgement (Amit and Rapport 2012; Rapport 2012b).

REFERENCES

Amit, V., and N. Rapport. 2012. *Community, Cosmopolitanism and the Problem of Human Commonality*. London: Pluto.

Arnold, M. 1965. *The Poems of Matthew Arnold*, ed. K. Allott. London: Longmans, Green.

Bakewell, S. 2010. *How to Live: A Life of Montaigne in One Question and Twenty Attempts at an Answer*. London: Chatto and Windus.

Cohen, A.P. 1992. 'Post-fieldwork fieldwork', *Journal of Anthropological Research* 48: 339–354.

Crossley, N. 2002. 'Global Anti-corporate Struggle: A Preliminary Analysis', *British Journal of Sociology* 53(4): 667–691.

Emerson, R.W. 1889. *Works*. London: Routledge.

Furbank, P. 1999. *Behalf*. Lincoln: University of Nebraska Press.

Kuper, H. 1972. 'The Language of Sites in the Politics of Space', *American Anthropologist* 74: 411–425.

Montaigne, M. de. 1993. *The Complete Essays*, trans. and ed. M.A. Screech. Harmondsworth: Penguin.

Nietzsche, F. 1968. *The Will to Power*, ed. W. Kaufmann. New York: Random House.

—— 1997. *Untimely Meditations*. Cambridge: Cambridge University Press.

Rabinow, P., G. Marcus, J. Faubion and J. Rees. 2009. *Designs for an Anthropology of the Contemporary*. Durham, NC: Duke University Press.

Rapport, N. 2003. *I am Dynamite: An Alternative Anthropology of Power*. London: Routledge.

—— 2007. 'An Outline for Cosmopolitan Study, for Reclaiming the Human through Introspection', *Current Anthropology* 48(2): 257–283.

—— 2012a. 'Shy and Ticklish Truths as Species of Scientific and Artistic Perception', *Indo-Pacific Journal of Phenomenology* 12 (July), 1–9.

—— 2012b. *Anyone: The Cosmopolitan Subject of Anthropology*. Oxford: Berghahn.

—— 2013. 'A Quantum Anthropology of Contemporary Moments of Being: Seven Observations', *Social Analysis* 57(2): 117–128.

—— 2014. 'Voice, History, and Vertigo: Doing Justice to the Dead through Imaginative Conversation', in C. Smart, A. James and J. Hockey (eds), *The Craft of Knowledge: Experiences of Living with Data*. London: Palgrave, pp.112–127.

—— (ed.) 2005. 'Democracy, Science and the Open Society: A European Legacy?' *Anthropological Journal of European Cultures* 13.

Woolf, V. 1990. *A Passionate Apprentice: The Early Journals, 1897–1909*, ed. M. Leaska. London: Hogarth Press.

Notes on Contributors

Vered Amit is Professor of Anthropology at Concordia University, Montreal. Her research has focused on a diverse range of circumstances including ethnic boundaries among Armenians in London, youth cultures, ethnic lobbying, expatriates in the Cayman Islands, transnational consultants, international student travel and inherited dual citizenship. Running through all of these projects has been an ongoing interest in the workings of and intersections between different forms of transnational mobility. She is the author or editor of twelve books, including the recently co-authored *Community, Cosmopolitanism and the Problem of Human Commonality* (2012) and the co-edited *Young Men in Uncertain Times* (2012).

Sally Anderson is Associate Professor in Educational Anthropology at the Department of Education, Aarhus University, Denmark. She has done extensive fieldwork in Denmark, in various sites of childhood – sport associations, integration projects and public and faith-based private schools. Her work examines how state policies and pedagogical projects actively engage in organizing and shaping quotidian social relations and social knowledge in public spheres. She is the author of *I en klasse for sig* [In a class of their own] (2000) and *Civil Sociality: Children, Sport, and Cultural Policy in Denmark* (2008).

Virginia Caputo is Associate Professor and Director of the Landon Pearson Research Centre for the Study of Childhood and Children's Rights at Carleton University, Ottawa. Her interdisciplinary work focuses on girlhoods, gendered childhoods and the changing contours of young people's lives in an era of globalization. She has published articles on such topics as theoretical and conceptual approaches in childhood studies, children's rights, gender and schooling, children and violence, and music and gender in young people's lives. Her current research interests include children and food justice, and early and forced marriages in girls' lives.

John Postill is Vice-Chancellor's Senior Research Fellow at RMIT University, Melbourne, and Digital Anthropology Fellow at University College London. Currently he is conducting anthropological research on new forms of digital activism and civic engagement in Indonesia, Spain and globally. He is also currently working on a book concerning digital activism and popular protest in the twenty-first century. His publications include *Media and Nation Building* (2006), *Localizing the Internet* (2011), and the co-edited volumes *Theorising Media and Practice* (2010) and *Theorising Media and Change* (forthcoming).

Nigel Rapport is Professor of Anthropological and Philosophical Studies in the Department of Social Anthropology at the University of St Andrews, and Founding Director of the St Andrews Centre for Cosmopolitan Studies. He has also held a Canada Research Chair in Globalization, Citizenship and Justice at Concordia University, Montreal. His research interests include social theory, phenomenology, individuality, literary anthropology, symbolic interactionism, human rights, globalization and liberalism. His recent publications include *Of Orderlies and Men: Hospital Porters Achieving Wellness at Work* (2008), the co-authored volume *Community, Cosmopolitanism, and the Problem of Human Commonality* (2012), *Anyone, the Cosmopolitan Subject of Anthropology* (2012) and the edited volume *Human Nature as Capacity: Transcending Discourse and Classification* (2010).

Deborah Reed-Danahay is Professor of Anthropology at the State University of New York at Buffalo, where she has taught since 2008. She has conducted research in France and in the United States. Her interests include political anthropology, anthropology and education, migration, autoethnography and social theory. She is currently working on a book concerning Pierre Bourdieu and the idea of social space. She is the author of *Education and Identity in Rural France: The Politics of Schooling* (1996) and *Locating Bourdieu* (2005), and the co-author of *Civic Engagements: The Citizenship Practices of Vietnamese and Indian Immigrants* (2012). She has also edited the collection *Auto/Ethnography: Rewriting the Self and the Social* (1997) and co-edited *Citizenship, Political Engagement and Belonging: Immigrants in Europe and the United States* (2008). She is past president of the Society for the Anthropology of Europe (2010–2012) and has been a Fellow at Magdalene College, University of Cambridge, since 2012.

Gabriela Vargas-Cetina is Professor of Anthropology in the Anthropological Sciences Faculty of the Autonomous University of Yucatan, Merida, Mexico. Over the years, her research has focused on organizations of many types, including tribal committees for the organization of powwows in Alberta, Canada; shepherds' cooperatives in highland Sardinia; sisal-grower land collectives in Yucatan, Mexico; weaver cooperatives and teachers' organizations in Chiapas, Mexico; and musicians and music-related organizations in Yucatan, Mexico. Her current research is focused on technology, music and organizations in the state of Yucatan, Mexico. Her recent publications include the edited collection *Anthropology and the Politics of Representation* (2013).

Index

Lightning Source UK Ltd.
Milton Keynes UK
UKOW07n2001240215

246819UK00005B/54/P